OPERATION *RYPE*

OPERATION *RYPE*

A World War II OSS Railway Sabotage Mission in Norway

FRODE LINDGJERDET

CASEMATE
Philadelphia & Oxford

Published in the United States of America and Great Britain in 2023 by
CASEMATE PUBLISHERS
1950 Lawrence Road, Havertown, PA 19083, USA
and
The Old Music Hall, 106–108 Cowley Road, Oxford OX4 1JE, UK

Hardcover Edition: ISBN 978-1-63624-134-0
Digital Edition: ISBN 978-1-63624-135-7

A CIP record for this book is available from the British Library

Printed and bound in the United Kingdom by CPI Group (UK) Ltd, Croydon, CR0 4YY
Typeset in India by DiTech Publishing Services

For a complete list of Casemate titles, please contact:

CASEMATE PUBLISHERS (US)
Telephone (610) 853-9131
Fax (610) 853-9146
Email: casemate@casematepublishers.com
www.casematepublishers.com

CASEMATE PUBLISHERS (UK)
Telephone (0)1226 734350
Email: casemate-uk@casematepublishers.co.uk
www.casematepublishers.co.uk

Contents

Foreword

This book began as a translation of a Norwegian one, published in 2016 under the title *Kampen om Nordlandsbanen* (*The Battle of the Nordland Railway*), but soon escalated into a completely new project. The subject of the Norwegian book was the sabotage attacks on the Nordland Railway to prevent German troops being redeployed from Norway to take part in the final battles of the Third Reich, with an emphasis on the American Operation *Rype*. Captain (retired) Erik Brun, President of the 99th Battalion Educational Foundation, proposed the translation of the book into English. However, new primary sources became available and had to be included in the project. In addition, rewriting it allowed for a higher academic standard—including footnotes, extensive historiography, and accounting for the source material as well as some consideration of methods to be included in the text.

This book also investigates several problems, such as British–American rivalry and cooperation, an angle of the story that continues into the weeks following the German surrender and which is given full attention instead of being treated as an afterthought. Another issue that is addressed is the technology used in World War II special operations under sub-Arctic conditions, as well as the cultural aspects of bringing together people of very different backgrounds into close cooperation. A more academic perspective on Operation *Rype* allows for a broader international context through a closer examination of the general literature on the Office of Strategic Services (OSS). A large part of this book deals with planning, deployment, and logistics. Together with social and technological aspects, this is not only part of the current trend within academic military history, which sets it apart from the traditional "operational history" and "commander's perspectives," but it may also be said to reflect the nature of special operations—that for each man in the field and for each demolition, there was a much larger support apparatus at work, as compared to the operations of regular units.

I want to thank Captain Brun for initiating the writing of an English book on the topic. Thanks also to Trond Ramsøy for providing much of the archival material. A big thank you goes to Hanne Rollag and the rest of my colleagues at the Norwegian Resistance Museum in Oslo for digging into their archival collection. I would also like to thank the family of Herbert Helgesen for providing me with invaluable insights into his life and the efforts he made as a main character in this book, both through conversations as well as unique written material left in his personal files. Geir Høiland, in addition to archival material, has provided valuable insights into World War II radio communications. Other individuals who have been helpful in providing various sources are Bob Pearson of Norwich, England, and Per Helge Martinsen of Norway. Also, thanks to the library at the University of Nebraska for sending copies of the OSS archive in their depository. I would also like to thank Felicity Goldsack, Isobel Fulton, Ruth Sheppard and the rest of the staff at Casemate Publishers for their cooperation and meticulous reading of my manuscript.

For an author to have the chance to write another edition of a book is like a chance of redemption for past mistakes and errors. Whether that chance has been honored is up to the individual reader to judge.

Introduction

Operation *Rype* was carried out by a unit of the OSS called the Norwegian Special Operations Group—NORSO—and its men were mostly of Norwegian descent. It was led by Major William E. Colby, who later became head of the Central Intelligence Agency (CIA). The unit was dropped over the Snåsa Mountains in Norway at the end of March 1945. Given its operational significance and the number of men involved, compared to the combined activities of the service's members, it is quite understandable that it has not claimed more space in the annals of the OSS. However, on a strategic level and as a historical case study, its importance seems larger. Firstly, Operation *Rype* was the only American ground operation on Norwegian soil during World War II. Secondly, it sheds light on the nuances in the US–British strategic rivalry. The hypothesis put forth here suggests that the British would welcome American saboteurs and support because their own resources were stretched to the limit. In addition, the inter-service rivalry in both the British and the American special operations and intelligence services themselves were just as strong as the British–American rivalry. However, the British drew a line when it came to contact between the Americans of *Rype* and the British-controlled Norwegian Special Operations Executive (SOE) teams or the Norwegian Resistance because that would mean relinquishing influence in the postwar world. One recurring challenge is that the sources are vague on this point, stating for instance that the "British took a dim view of Operation *Rype*; they didn't like the idea of American troops going into Norway ..."[1] leaving the impression that "the British" were one monolith when they were not.

The operation was also the first and only one in which an American unit parachuted into occupied Europe to operate on skis. There was also a NORSO II, a follow-up force flown in after the German surrender to assist in the disarming of German forces in Norway. NORSO was created following the model of the British special forces. The original members were mainly recruited from the 99th Infantry Battalion (separate) which consisted of the first- and second-generation Norwegian immigrants to the United States. The battalion was attached to the First Army; however, it was labeled "Separate" because it was not attached to a specific regiment. Eventually recruits came from the Norwegian merchant marine.

This account may seem a bit heavy in descriptions of topography and weather, however, both were crucial for the successful execution of the operation as well as for the well-being and security of the men. A shift in the temperatures of just a few degrees could mean they would get wet and cold and require days to cover a distance that in better going would take only hours. Likewise, meters above mean sea level (MAMSL) would be crucial for the same reasons, which is why this data is included in the accounts of their ski marches.

Operation *Rype* was directed against the Nordland Railway and the strategic goal was to stop the redeployment of German troops from Finland, through Norway, and prevent them from being part of Nazi Germany's final battle. To what degree the operation achieved this, is a matter of dispute. In the fall of 1944, the Allies feared that the transfer of German forces from Norway and Finland to continental Europe would extend the war. The Rype team was one of four groups that were to attack the Nordland Railway, the main line between Mo i Rana and Trondheim. The other groups were under the control of Britain's SOE. The insertion, reinforcement, and supply of NORSO became mired in problems. Two aircraft crashed with the loss of the flight crew and all special forces operators. One of the NORSO teams parachuted into Sweden by mistake, where they were interned and prevented from participating through most of the duration of *Rype*. In the end, it was decided to terminate support from the air. Still, NORSO managed to blow up 2.5 kilometers of railway tracks, as well as a railway bridge. Both were repaired by the Germans within a week of the demolitions. One of the other Allied operations groups under British command, Woodlark, would more or less merge with NORSO, which, as we shall see, was much to the frustration and resistance of their superiors in London. Operation *Rype* also had a certain political importance. Through it, the Americans demonstrated that they had the aspirations, the will, and especially the resources to conduct special operations in Scandinavia, which hitherto had been regarded as a British domain. This was also noticeable after the German surrender. The Rype group was involved in a skirmish with a German patrol on May 2 that ended in loss of human life, which was tragic so close to the end of the war. However, the circumstances are unclear and opinions on the incident have been influenced by the various standpoints and interests of those who have provided them.

This introduction, the chapter "Existing Literature," and the supply of sources aim to outline a basis for research. The next seven chapters put the operation into its proper historical, technological, and social context. "Strategic Background" puts *Rype* into the wider perspective of the war in the European Theater of Operations (ETO) while "Norwegian Special Operations Group" offers insights into who NORSO were as individuals, as a group, and how they were selected and trained. To get a more thorough insight into the social background of each member of NORSO I that took part in the operation, see the individual biographies, which are included in a separate section. As several individual members are hardly mentioned in the reports, integrating their biographical details into the main narrative proved to be impractical. For the others who were less involved, their information is included in the remaining chapters where it seems fit according to their entry onto the "stage" of main events. Operation *Carpetbagger* deals with the challenges of supplies being provided by air, which proved to be a formative aspect of *Rype* and "SOE Operations Against the Nordland Railway" provides a basis for comparing *Rype* with other similar operations facing many of the same challenges; both the parallels and the differences can be enlightening. The following 11 chapters constitute the main narrative of Operation *Rype* itself, from the planning, the deployment, the two attacks, and the action and difficulties immediately before the German surrender, as well as the intrigues with the British in the following weeks until the Rype group was sent back to the United States. Names of people and places are written in the original Norwegian form, including the letters æ, ø and å. Although the international audience may find pronunciation difficult, the original spelling improves the likely success of text searches in digitalized sources and map services.

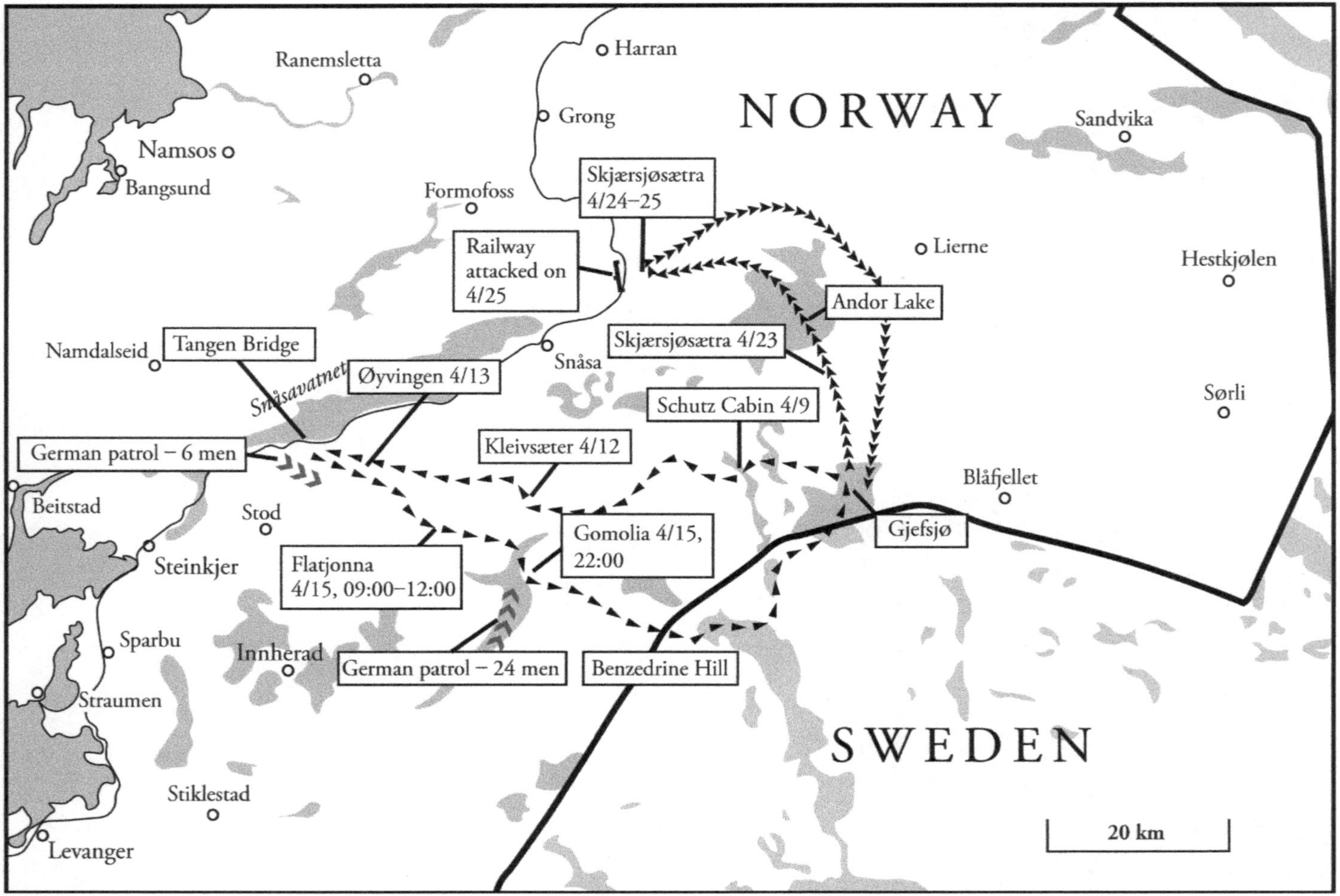
NORWAY
SWEDEN
Harran
Grong
Ranemsletta
Namsos
Bangsund
Formofoss
Skjærsjøsætra 4/24–25
Railway attacked on 4/25
Lierne
Sandvika
Hestkjølen
Sørli
Andor Lake
Skjærsjøsætra 4/23
Namdalseid
Tangen Bridge
Snåsavatnet
Øyvingen 4/13
Snåsa
Schutz Cabin 4/9
Kleivsæter 4/12
German patrol – 6 men
Beitstad
Stod
Blåfjellet
Gomolia 4/15, 22:00
Gjefsjø
Steinkjer
Flatjonna 4/15, 09:00–12:00
Sparbu
Innherad
German patrol – 24 men
Benzedrine Hill
Straumen
Stiklestad
Levanger
20 km

CHAPTER ONE

Existing Literature and Sources

The relevant reference literature for Operation *Rype* may be divided into biographical works on William Colby, general literature on the OSS and on World War II special operations, and finally, Norwegian local literature. In 1978, William E. Colby published his autobiography, together with Peter Forbath, the latter a foreign policy journalist with background from *Business Week* and *TIME* magazine. As with any autobiography—and particularly one written by a man like Colby immediately following his turbulent years as CIA director—context is an important issue in its interpretation. Colby also wrote an account of Operation *Rype*, later discovered in the CIA archives, titled *OSS Operations in Norway: Skis and Daggers*, however, it is not known at what stage in his career he wrote it. Another biography on Colby worth noting is John Prados's *Lost Crusader*, published by Oxford University Press in 2003. Although an independent account, it is at times more defensive of Colby's later and more controversial career in the CIA. Randal B. Woods's account *Shadow Warrior*, published in 2013, was partially based on Prados's research, but focused more on Colby's personal life and psychology.[1] In 2011, Colby's son Carl Colby made a movie entitled *The Man Nobody Knew*, which also focuses mainly on his CIA years.

The general literature on the OSS, as well as biographies of its founder, Major General William Donovan, makes little mention of *Rype*, but it helps put the operation into a wider context. One of the first comprehensive histories of the OSS was published in 1946 by authors Stewart Alsop and Thomas Braden. Both were American journalists who fought in the same British Army unit when they were recruited by the OSS—Braden also later served in the CIA. Their contribution is very much a homage to their comrades in arms but nonetheless offers a vital insight into the workings of the organization. In 1976, documents covering the OSS's World War II activities were beginning to be declassified. One vital item made available was the *War Report of the Office of Strategic Services*, prepared back in 1948 but which had remained classified. It is very much "a general history of," seeking to give a general overview rather than investigating a certain issue or following a discourse. Its basic structure is outlining the origin and organization of the OSS, followed by a geographical summary of its activities. Denmark and Norway are treated briefly in a short sub-chapter of seven-and-a-half pages, a table on supply missions to the Danish Resistance taking up half of it.

In both Colby's and Donovan's biographies, and in much of the general literature on the OSS, the agency is surrounded by an aura of Wild West-like romanticism, portraying operators as a mixture of adventurers and idealists, contrasting them with their cynical British counterparts and the "lethargic" CIA of the Cold War. Their opponents are the evil Nazis, and the natives range from noble savages to deceitful partisan tribesmen. Richard Harris Smith's *OSS, The Secret History of America's First Central Intelligence Agency*[2] is a fine example of this approach. The structure of the book is more chronological than geographical. Its concluding chapter is a direct comparison of the OSS to the CIA. To his credit, he does admit that the "chaotic administration of a dynamic, unmanageable wartime secret service proved dangerous in an era of uneasy peace."[3] *Donovan's Devils: OSS Commandos Behind Enemy Lines—Europe, World War II* by Albert Lulushi, deals with the special operations component of the OSS. It investigates trends in the development of the operations groups through detailed studies of a selection of groups and their missions. Lulushi too finishes with a comparison of the OSS and the CIA, and how the 9/11 attacks had brought special operations command into closer cooperation with the agency "thus reuniting the two halves of the OSS legacy."[4]

A more nuanced insight into the origins and workings of the OSS is provided in *Wild Bill Donovan: The Spymaster Who Created the OSS and Modern American Espionage* by Douglas Waller. Its critical appraisal of the OSS's many shortfalls is tempered by an acknowledgment of the difficult circumstances into which the organization was born, its role as a precursor of the CIA, and the successes it achieved. One of the drier accounts of the OSS is Eugene Liptak's *Office of Strategic Services 1942: The World War II Origins of the CIA.*[5] It is divided into three main parts: organization, operations, and weapons and equipment. A short final paragraph deals with transportation. A more monumental account of wartime intelligence and special operations has been written by British World War II history authority Max Hastings. His *The Secret War: Spies Ciphers and Guerillas 1939–1945,*[6] largely depicts the OSS as amateurs, but no more so than their British counterparts in the SOE. However, he has much appreciation for their research and development branch, which conducted many thorough country studies, as well as developing gadgets. Their major achievement was realizing that where other services relied on expensive, risky, and unreliable spies, the OSS's Research and Analysis branch found it just as useful to go to the Library of Congress and other open sources. At first glance, Roger Hall's *You're Stepping on my Cloak and Dagger* might look like pure entertainment,[7] but the humoristic personal account of this OSS operative provides good insights into the training and preparations for Operation *Rype.*

Hall was attached to NORSO and put in charge of the follow-up force sent in after the German surrender. His book provides a vivid account of the existence of the men left behind in Scotland.

Despite its wide scope, Douglas Waller's *Disciples: The World War II Missions of the CIA Directors Who Fought for Wild Bill Donovan*, dwells on the conflicted relationship between the OSS with both British and Norwegian military leadership. It also gives an insight into the social make-up of the NORSO Group. Jay Jakub's *Spies and Saboteurs* focuses on the British–American rivalry in special operations and intelligence work. Although it touches on the effects on operations in Scandinavia, it does so on a strategic level and does not dwell on the effects on the men on the ground.[8] The only scholarly research on the OSS in Scandinavia during World War II so far is by Tore Pryser. In addition to some articles, his book *USAs hemmelig agenter* (*USA's Secret Agents*) was published in 2010. It gives a comprehensive account of activities of all the branches in Scandinavia. Its most important finding is that the OSS activity in Scandinavia was far more extensive than previously believed. The second part of the book deals with the *Westfield* mission in its entirety, while Operation *Rype* is covered in a short four-page chapter.[9]

The first time the history of Operation *Rype* became publicly known in the United States was through the article "The White War in Norway," written by Thomas R. Henry and published in the November issue of *National Geographic* in 1945. The story of *Rype* covers the five final pages of the article's total of 25 pages. The literature in Norwegian on Operation *Rype* has thus far been limited. In 1995, Arne Sandness and local historian Jarle Skjei co-authored *Operasjon Woodlark og Rype: et 50-årsminne*, an anthology made up of various reprinted accounts from journals of local history. Journalist Olav Solhjell and German wartime veteran of the Snåsa area Friedrich Traphagen co-authored *Fra Krig til fred: Fokus på Snåsa Nord-Trøndelag*, published in 2001. Substantial parts of it deal with *Rype*, and especially speculation on the fate of the German patrol that stumbled into *Rype*'s patrol base on May 2. In 2016, this author published *Kampen om Nordlandsbanen*, a shorter account based on the outline of the Osprey *Military Operations* series.

Operation *Rype* also constitutes an interesting case study on the use of multiple and often conflicting primary sources relating to the same events, as both the sequence of events and the details of single events differ between various accounts. In 1975, the group's telegraphist, Borge Langeland, published the telegrams that were sent and received during their operations in the Snåsa area. Close examination shows that the telegrams do present an authentic reproduction of the communications between NORSO and their HQ in London, however, when reading the comments Langeland added after the war, many discrepancies occur when compared to other sources. These comments deal with occurrences he did not witness himself, such as the initial failed attempts of airborne insertions and details of the retreats following the attacks at Tangen Bridge and Lurudal. The other major discrepancy concerns

Leif Oistad and his group's drop into Sweden, where the accounts by the locals and the Americans differ widely from that given by the local magistrate, Herje Skunke. According to the basic rules of historical method, both Skunke and Langeland fulfill the criteria of being close in time and space to the events described, however, they are not in harmony, with two or more alternative accounts (see Chapter 10).

On the German side, the daily situation briefs from *Der Höhere SS und Polizeiführer beim Reichskommissar für die besetzten norwegischen Gebit*, the highest German police authority in Norway, to the *Reichskommissar* and subordinate police authority provide some insights from the German side. They include only brief accounts of major incidents and the general situation over a 24-hour period, divided into air, land, and sea. However, they list intrusions of enemy aircraft into Norwegian airspace in sufficient detail to make it safe to assume that the missions not listed were simply not detected by the Germans. The Norwegian Resistance Museum in Oslo holds a comprehensive collection of copies of reports from SOE operations in Norway. These include reports written by members of Operation *Woodlark*, which gives vital background for understanding the operational environment NORSO was inserted into. As these British and American groups operated together in the same area against similar targets, it is also fair to assume that the experience of *Woodlark* did have a significant impact on *Rype*.

As *Rype* was an American operation, there are no official reports written by the Norwegian participants. However, recommendations for Norwegian awards for the Norwegians, Americans, and Swedes who took part in *Woodlark* and *Rype* as well as several people who helped with organizing transport and supplies in Sweden was prepared by Herbert Helgesen and amounted to a 58-page document. It was written in two copies; he kept one himself and later transferred it to the archives of the Norwegian Armed Forces Museum, The Armoury, in Trondheim. The fate of the other copy is unknown. The report is modest in style and contains lengthy biographies of the people involved. In addition, Helgesen wrote a more colorful account that was printed in an anthology, called *Partisaner, Soldater og SD* (*Partisans, Soldiers and the SD*) in 1945. His chapter is called "Jernbanesabotage" ("Railway Sabotage"). It deals only with the attack on the railway between Lurudal and Agle. It picks up the story somewhere on the approach to the target and ends before the group returned to Gjefsjø.[10] At some points it might seem too colorful and full of details to be correct, but it is consistent with Colby's more formal reports on the events and any geographical details that could be investigated. At several points, it elaborates on issues discussed only briefly by Colby. Despite the danger of leaving the impression that emphasis has been put on the part of the story it deals with, it simply offers too much vigor to the text to be left out of an account such as the present one. British reports, or reports written by Norwegians to their British superiors, offer valuable insights, either if they mention *Rype* directly or if they deal with operations in similar terrain and against similar objectives. Norwegian Resistance member Kjell

Sørli, who served as a courier for *Rype*, was also extensively interviewed by local historians. There are two major accounts based on his legacy—the one written by a man named Sten Ræder covers 21 pages, but only two pages deals with *Rype*. The second account deals both with Kjell Sørli and another resistance fighter. The part covering *Rype* only amounts to two paragraphs. However, they do add insights into the context in which *Rype* was executed.

Colonel Gerhard Bolland also left a personal archive with two binders of documents, one titled "Military Career" and the other "Office of Strategic Services, Norwegian Special Operations (NORSO) Group. Operation *Rype*. December 1944–May 1945." Both are in the custody of his son, Matt Bolland. In October 1945, Colonel Bolland wrote what was presented as the first comprehensive account of Operation *Rype*, beginning with the words "(s)everal reports of certain phases of the '*Rype*' Operation have been submitted to the Office of Strategic Services, but it is believed that no overall picture of the nature, purpose, and ultimate goal of the operation has been given to date." The report was only four pages long, but Bolland explained the briefness by the termination of the OSS as an organization.[11] In the notes, this collection is abbreviated to "GBP."

Historian of the 801st/492nd Bomber Group Thomas Ensminger also left behind a treasure trove of documents on the OSS at the time of his premature passing in 2008. A total of 672 megabytes of scanned microfilm from NARA's (US National Archives and Records Administration) vaults have been generously provided to this project by Erik Brun. The collection contains the war diaries of the OSS special operations and secret intelligence branches. These were released to the public in 1989. In 1949, the US Department of State composed the above-mentioned OSS war report, since released to the public. They do not offer many details on *Rype* but give many insights into the general workings of the OSS and the relations with the SOE. The most central primary sources that cover Operation *Rype* are held on microfiche by the library of the University of Nebraska at Omaha. The NORSO microfiche call number is J83D249 O.S.S. 311F-314C. In subsequent endnotes they will be referred to by "University of Nebraska Collection," and then the title of the document in question.

Many of the anecdotes from members of NORSO and Operation *Rype* were collected in a publication akin to an American school yearbook in style and composition. It was put together for the 30th anniversary of World War II's end, and contains text contributions, photographs, and newspaper clippings from several of the NORSO members. A central private collection covering the heritage of *Rype* are the archives of Arne Sandness (1924–2016), that have been added to the collections of Norwegian Army Museum, The Armoury (Rustkammeret). Sandness was mayor of Snåsa and a prominent local politician and a point of contact for much of the Norwegian–American activity related to the heritage surrounding *Rype*. He also chaired the committee that established the memorial at Jørstad Bridge in memory of

Operations *Rype* and *Woodlark*. There are also several other items used in this book belonging to the archival collection of The Armoury, abbreviated in the notes as RKT.

Several Norwegian Resistance fighters and SOE operatives involved in Operation *Rype* have left substantial private archives that have proved relevant for this book. These contain personal letters, newspaper clippings, and copies of official documents. The records kept by the Sørli brothers Odd, Kjell, and Øyvind are held by The Armoury in Trondheim. Of the three, both Kjell and Odd were involved in *Rype*. Their resistance work extended throughout much of the war, and *Rype* was only a small part of it. Material not directly related to *Rype* also helps to build a picture of the men involved and the environment in which the operation took place. Another SOE operative, Erik Gjems-Onstad, was not directly involved in *Rype*, however, he operated in the neighboring county of South Trøndelag.

Audio and graphic sources also need to be considered. In the collections of The Armoury, there are three maps printed by the British War Office, presumably used during *Rype*. They have pencil marks indicating the marching route for the Tangen operation. In addition, they provide a grid system that makes it possible to track positions given in operational reports. The place names on the maps are the same as those used in the reports, but these may now be spelt differently, making it difficult to trace on modern maps. Yet, the level of topographic detail makes it easier to retrace the movements of Colby and his men.

The original ownership of the many photographs documenting the operation and its context is not always easy to clarify, however, several of them give a valuable supplement to written sources. Finally, The Armoury also holds two different audio taped interviews with several of the Norwegian members as well as a television documentary on Operation *Woodlark*. Although they do not focus on Operation *Rype*, they do provide insight to the thoughts and experiences of some of those involved.

When referring to documents, this is done according to archival data available. Most of the archival material originating from outside Norway has been received digitally, either from a public institution holding them, or well-meaning private persons. Even the former sometimes do not always provide full data on the location of the items.

CHAPTER TWO

The Strategic Background

When the Germans attacked in 1940, Norway was a young, independent state, although the concept and identity of Norway as a separate people and country dates back over a millennium. Through a combination of dynastic squabbles and economic crisis, Norway ended up as a province of Denmark following the Protestant Reformation in 1537. Caught in the crossfire between Denmark and its archenemy Sweden, Norway experienced a period of almost continuous warfare through the early modern era. After a failed bid for independence in 1814, Norway gained a constitution but became subservient to Sweden after it became a bargaining chip as the great powers settled the scores in the aftermath of the Napoleonic Wars, in which Denmark ended up on the losing side. The 19th century became a political tug of war between Stortinget (the Norwegian parliament) and the Swedish king. In 1905, full independence was finally achieved but not without tensions and a war scare. Throughout the struggle, Norwegian nationalism became synonymous with democracy, individualism, and autonomy. These were sentiments which felt all too real to any Allied commander or instructor put in charge of Norwegians during World War II as they mostly proved to be a handful to lead.

The decade leading up to 1905 had been one of Norwegian rearmament and, as Sweden was the anticipated enemy, emphasis was put on the land army and fixed ground defenses facing east. When World War I broke out, Norway managed to stay neutral. But the constant pressure from the warring parties for special privileges revealed that the main strategic challenges would come from the west and south—across the sea and, to an increasing extent, through the air. However, social, political, and economic crises in the interwar period meant few extra resources remained to take practical measures to deal with these insights. The Norwegian Labor Party followed many of her international sister movements and became revolutionary and radicalized after the Russian Revolution of 1917. However, the Soviet Union's attempt at reining in the international socialist movement in 1920 touched a deeper Norwegian national sentiment and the party broke with Moscow and turned fiercely anti-communist. That did not mean "de-radicalization," and seeing the conventional

Norwegian military as a tool for its opponents in a potentially armed class struggle the Labor Party followed a strict policy of demilitarization.

On the political right, there was also great reluctance to give priority to the military due to a somewhat naïve faith in the ability of the League of Nations and arbitration to keep the peace. As Hitler gained power in 1933 and the threat of war grew stronger, the economic depression caused by the 1929 Wall Street crash hit Norway hard, and the defense budget reached an all-time low. The political fronts hardened, but the 1935 election had seen a reconciliation between the Labor Party and the parties on the right. From 1937, extra funds for the military started to trickle in, but would prove to be too little, too late. The German attack on Norway bore many similarities to the Japanese attack on Pearl Harbor in the sense that it became a sudden national trauma. It was one that a great many people felt could have been avoided by being better prepared militarily and if the signs of what was coming had been correctly interpreted. But, of course, there the similarities ended. Norway had been struck at the nation's economic and political heart and was overwhelmed by an enemy superior in every way in the field. However, for both Norway and the United States, the trauma of attack led future governments to abandon isolationism in the postwar era.

British commando raids against Norway in 1941 (Operations *Claymore*, *Archery*, and *Anklet*) had convinced Hitler that the danger of an Allied invasion of Norway was very real. Large German land, sea, and air forces were therefore transferred to Norway. In addition, Germany used significant resources in building defense works and infrastructure. Many were related to the battle of the Atlantic and German submarine warfare against Allied shipping. However, British Prime Minister Winston Churchill's invasion plans, dubbed Operation *Jupiter*, were rejected by the Imperial General Staff in the same year as the commando raids took place. Still, plans were maintained to regulate the transition from war to peace. On July 20, the Norwegians and the British signed a deal regulating when the civilian Norwegian government would take power following what in effect would be a brief period of British occupation after the Germans had surrendered. The agreement was met with reluctance from the Norwegian Resistance who were not happy with undergoing another period of occupation mostly for emotional reasons. The Americans were not happy either with being left out. In general, they preferred the installment of an Allied Military Government (AMGOT) in liberated areas to take a higher degree of responsibility for civilian society. But not wanting to be sidetracked, they fully recognized British command in a liberated Norway. The dispute was solved by a renewed agreement on May 16, 1944. Thus, there was no real conflict on the political level over who would be in charge in a newly liberated Norway. However, on some levels in the British Scottish Command, whose jurisdiction Scandinavia fell under, the process might have created some suspicion and resentment that might have affected *Rype*.[1]

In the spring of 1943, Lt. Gen. Sir Frederick Morgan was appointed Chief of Staff to the Supreme Allied Commander (COSSAC) and tasked with preparing a return to the continent of western allied forces. In early 1944, the Supreme Headquarters Allied Expeditionary Force (SHAEF)—with General Dwight D. Eisenhower as commander—had as its stated intention to return to Western Europe at the earliest possible opportunity. If the German forces in Western Europe remained intact, Operation *Overlord* would be executed as an amphibious assault on the Continent with subsequent large-scale land operations, as eventually did happen on June 6, 1944, and in the following months towards the war's end. However, COSSAC had been tasked with developing contingency. If German forces showed signs of becoming considerably weakened before Operation *Overlord* was executed, Operation *Rankin*, Case "*A*," would be set in motion. This would entail an "assault on a reduced scale," Operation *Rankin*, Case "*B*," would be put into effect if the Germans withdrew from occupied territory, landing Allied troops "with the opportunity of effecting a lodgment on the Continent, from which the defeat of the enemy forces [can] be completed." This would also include landings in Norway if the Germans withdrew from there, with emphasis on establishing naval bases and taking control of Norwegian waters. *Rankin*, Case "*C*" would be launched "(I)n the event of a GERMAN surrender, the allied armies will, as soon as the Armistice has been signed, occupy selected strategic areas in GERMANY and the liberated countries."[2] Operation *Rype* was partially a Case "*A*" operation, attempting to prevent German troops transiting back to defend the Reich. These operations were mere strategic concepts applicable to a number of geographical contexts and not concrete plans set with landing sites or earmarked units for Norway in particular.

The regular German occupation force in Norway peaked at around 300,000 soldiers, more soldiers per capita than in any other country they occupied during World War II. Soon German forces in retreat from Finland would be added to their numbers. In addition, there was a substantial police force and various other civil servants and support services. Finland had fought a courageous battle attempting to stem the tide of Stalin's legions in the Winter War from November 30, 1940 to March 13, 1940. When Hitler attacked the Soviet Union on June 22, 1941, Finland's leaders made an ill-fated decision to join forces with Nazi Germany in order to regain lost territory. This so-called Continuation War would prove a mistake. As Hitler's fortunes turned, so did Finland's. On June 9, 1944, the Red Army advanced into Finnish territory. Cut off from Germany, Finland's defeat or withdrawal from the war was only a matter of time. After heavy fighting on the Karelian Isthmus, Finland requested negotiations on June 22. On September 4, 1944, Finland signed an armistice with the Soviet Union and declared war on Germany the next day.

This would be the beginning of the Lapland War, which lasted from September 1944 to April 27, 1945, when the last German forces left Finish territory. The German *20. Gebirgsarmee*, also called the Lapland Army, under Colonel General Lothar Rendulic, was forced to withdraw, slashing and burning everything behind them that could be useful to the enemy. On August 5, 1943, Sweden had terminated the agreement with Germany that had allowed for transport of men and materiel along their railway network. This forced the Germans to evacuate their troops into Norway, and the Red Army followed them into Finnmark in October. However, the Soviet forces stopped on the banks of the Tana River on November 6 after advancing only 110 kilometers into Norway. Meanwhile the Germans established a defense line along Lyngen Fjord in Troms, anchored on the shores of the Arctic Sea in the west and the Swedish border in the east. The Lapland Army would be withdrawn behind this line in Operation *Nordlicht*.[3] As part of this operation, they continued the scorched earth tactics employed in Finland and throughout the Eastern Front. Most of the settlements and towns were burned to the ground. However, unlike in the Soviet Union and Eastern Europe, they made an effort to evacuate the civilian population. Nearly 60,000 people were forced to evacuate to southern parts of Norway, where they would be housed in the homes of their compatriots. However, 25,000 hid from the Germans and survived through the harsh winter in mines, cabins, and isolated settlements. Many Samí reindeer herders were ordered by the Germans to bring their flocks behind the German lines, to secure their meat as provisions for themselves and deny it for the Soviets. But the herders led their animals across the border into Sweden instead, and the Germans had no means of stopping them. Into the no-man land between German and Soviet forces, a small number of light Norwegian infantry units trained in the UK and Sweden patrolled in an attempt to establish some sort of law and order. Local Norwegian army units, many of them veterans of the 1940 campaign, were also mobilized in the liberated areas. But the force probably never exceeded 3,000 men and women. Lack of manpower and allied support meant that no control was in effect and the Germans were still able to launch small-scale raids in order to capture civilian stragglers.

At the beginning of 1945, Allied intelligence estimated that there were some 150,000 German mountain troops in the Narvik–Tromsø area that had been driven out of Finland and that the German High Command was organizing their transport southwards through Norway so they could take part in the final battles in Germany proper.[4] SHAEF announced that the arrival of reinforcement in Germany from Norway could no longer be accepted.[5] In response, sabotage orders were issued both from Scottish Command (SCOTCO) to the Norwegian Resistance and the joint Anglo-American SFHQ. How many soldiers the Germans really intended to completely pull out of Norway is disputed, as well as what constituted the decisive bottlenecks in this withdrawal. Was it the railway, rolling stock, fuel, or shipping capacity? In May–July 1944 two divisions had withdrawn from Norway, and another five divisions had been given transport orders. This was duly reported in the Norwegian publication in exile, *Norsk Tidend*, referring to messages from Namdalen in North Trøndelag; the sub-headline read "two–three divisions sent South from Norway—The German forces are smaller than ever and of poor quality."[6] In addition, support staff and crews from the Luftwaffe were also ordered to repatriate to Germany. But the Allied commanders believed that large parts of the German occupational force in Norway were about to be sent to the Continent, and it was perceived as important to stop this. On October 26, SHAEF Europe sent out orders to the special forces HQ that the German troop transports through Norway had to stop. Allied intelligence estimated the speed of the evacuation at one battalion daily if it had run uninterrupted.[7]

The development of the war on the Continent also contributed to Allied fears that the troops pulled out of Norway would be a boost for Germany. The liberation of France went relatively fast and, in the east, Operation *Bagration* had brought the Red Army to the Vistula River in Poland. An almost euphoric mood prevailed in the Allied camp—there was even talk that the war could be over by Christmas. In the summer of 1944, SHAEF expressed the view that assistance in delaying German reinforcements from Norway was no longer required as they could be dealt with more easily when they arrived on the Continent. On October 26, SHAEF addressed the SFHQ, agreeing to a limited number of attacks on Norwegian railways as the Germans withdrew, mainly for the sake of the morale of the indigenous Norwegian Resistance.[8] But when Allied forces crossed the border with Germany, the resistance stiffened. The SHAEF policy on railway sabotage in Norway was revised at the start of December, stating: "We can no longer accept with equanimity the arrival in Germany of troops from Norway. We require urgently to force German withdrawing troops onto the sea where they will be vulnerable to Naval and air attack." It proposed "Norwegian resistance to undertake the maximum railway and road sabotage consistent with it maintaining itself for primary role."[9]

The German offensive in the Ardennes, lasting from December 16, 1944, to January 15, 1945, amplified the fear that troops transported out of Norway to continental Europe would prolong the war, and SHAEF ordered railway sabotage in the country to be intensified.[10] The single-tracked Nordland Railway was identified as a bottleneck for Germany's troop transport, especially the stretch south to Steinkjer, where it passed through deserted stretches where the road was not an alternative should the railway be disrupted. Special forces HQ therefore emphasized the goal of forcing the Germans to use the exposed sea lanes to bypass the area.[11] Not only was the coast mined, a network of agents reported all traffic along the coast and the Royal Air Force's (RAF) strike wings were constantly flying sorties across the North Sea, where the Royal Navy also was patrolling vigilantly. Added to that, German shipping capacity was extremely limited, and the idea was to simply make them run out of ships.

In many Nazi-occupied countries, the resistance was frequently split into rival fractions, sometimes openly hostile to each other. In France, the OSS had to deal with a plethora of groups loyal to various generals as well as the communists. In Yugoslavia, the OSS had begun by trying to prop up Draža Mihailović, who commanded the remnants of the Yugoslav Army, but over time decided to back Josip Broz Tito and his communist-dominated partisans, as they were the most successful in fighting the

Germans. To make matters worse, different OSS commanders championed different factions. In Norway, there were only two factions. The government-controlled MilOrg (*Militærorganisasjonen*) was by far the largest and then there was an autonomous Communist Resistance—despite an image of non-cooperation, recent research has shown that the two cooperated closely.[12] In *Rype*'s operational area, and in central Norway in general, most resistance groups were controlled by the SOE, not the Norwegians. The dominant group was Lark, a group set up mainly to train and arm resistance fighters. Although the Norwegian Resistance was easy to manage, the OSS and SOE still had to deal with some very crafty and well-organized collaborators.

A significant part of the strategic back story to *Rype* is why Britain regarded Scandinavia as their turf or sphere of influence, apart from geographical proximity. The long coastline on the eastern board of the North Sea was strategic for obvious reasons. Since the Viking Age, whoever controlled these shores was in a prime position to launch attacks along the east coast of Great Britain. And you cannot rule the seven seas without control over your home waters. This was obvious also for Britain's enemies. In the age of sails, Britain took a great interest in Scandinavian politics. Not only did a lot of raw materials needed in Britain come from the peninsula, like timber and copper, but whoever controlled the Danish straits also controlled the vital trade with timber and hemp from the Baltics. By playing Denmark-Norway (Norway was ruled by Denmark 1537–1814) against Sweden, they prevented any one power from having total control to dictate trade and tariffs. Napoleon was eager to enlist Denmark-Norway into his continental system, leading to two raids on Copenhagen in 1801 and 1807, setting the city ablaze in the first and capturing almost the entire fleet. Britain allowed Sweden to acquire Norway in 1814 as compensation for Finland that was lost to Russia in the war against Napoleon. However, Britain made sure that there were limits to how integrated Norway could become and supported Norwegian independence in 1905. During World War I, Norway stayed neutral, but the merchant fleet served British interests and Britain had priority in the export of raw materials from Norway. Curiously enough, the British were able to exercise this influence for centuries without ever having to put boots on the ground, until the failed attempt to stave off Hitler's legions in 1940. In addition to the long lines of British foreign policy, Churchill had his particular reasons for focusing on Scandinavia. The ill-fated campaign had very much been his brainchild, so there was an issue of revenge. His focus on the shipment of Swedish iron ore along the Norwegian coast had become a fixation that went beyond its actual strategic importance once the war was going and Hitler had gained control over the ore fields of Alsace Lorraine after conquering France in the summer of 1940. Last, but not least, by the time the Americans entered the game, the British had already invested money, blood and resources into the Norwegian Resistance and intelligence networks and were unwilling to let the new kids on the bloc take over the show.

CHAPTER THREE

The OSS

When World War II broke out in Europe in 1939, the United States did not have a central intelligence service. The closest thing to one was the G-2 at the War Department, except that it was strictly in the service of the Army only. The FBI, which (in theory) operated stateside and in Latin America, and the intelligence services of the Army and Navy respectively, conducted intelligence work mostly on an operational level. In World War I, the United States had deployed agents and spies like any other country, but soon withdrew from the shady business of spying and scheming when war ended. In 1920, Secretary of State Henry L. Stimson closed down the code-breaking units built up during World War I with the words "gentlemen do not read each other's mail."[1] This sentiment continued into the 1940s. After World War II broke out in Europe, President Franklin D. Roosevelt appointed William J. Donovan (1883–1959) as Coordinator of Information (COI) in July 1940, as the first step towards establishing a central intelligence service at the strategic level. Donovan was to report directly to the president, and other government agencies that he deemed appropriate.[2]

Roosevelt also dispatched Donovan as an American envoy to the United Kingdom to study British intelligence and special operations pending the buildup of the United States' own apparatus within the field. That the British were willing to share their secrets within the clandestine arts with another great power was unprecedented in modern history,[3] but this probably reflects the dire straits in which Britain found itself and the expectation that the limitless resources of their overseas cousins might be made available to their full extent in the not-too-distant future. The British themselves had just executed their first large-scale commando operations, among them the Lofoten Islands and the Måløy (Vaagsøy) raids in Norway. At the same time, the SOE had been set up, based on Winston Churchill's vision to "set Europe ablaze." The British commando units were organized to operate independently of the larger unit, with their own organic logistics, and command and control elements. The inspiration came from the British "Independent Companies" organized by the British Expeditionary Corps during the campaign in Norway in 1940. British experience had also shown the importance of including native operators, and several of the first experimental commando raids had been carried out against Norwegian targets with guides, intelligence gatherers, and liaisons from the Norwegian Independent Company No. 1 (NORIC, also called *Kompani Linge*).

At the time, a distinction was emerging between commando raids on the one hand, and special operations on the other. The first took the shape of larger-scale attacks, including several hundred men with access to air and artillery support. Commandos were shock troops operating in advance of, but close to, regular formations to achieve objectives at the operational level, such as securing a bridgehead, taking out enemy fortifications, or seizing valuable terrain. Well-known examples of this were the attack of the US Rangers on the German gun emplacements at Pointe du Hoc on D-Day, or the British commando raid to seize the important island of Walcheren in November 1944. Special forces groups, on the other hand, operated more on the strategic level, conducting interdiction of enemy lines of communication, or sabotaging the production of valuable commodities for warfare. They operated more independently of air support, save in logistics, in smaller groups and deeper into enemy territory. Well-known examples of World War II special operations were the Heavy Water Raid in February 1943, and indeed Operation *Rype*.

Roosevelt's choice of Donovan might be explained both by his dynamic personality and his intelligence and creativity. But there may also have been a political motive. Besides being a World War I hero, Donovan was a Republican and a Catholic, contributing to the much-needed wartime bipartisanship.[4] Donovan has since been known as the father of the United States' intelligence service. He grew up in Buffalo, New York. His parents were first-generation immigrants from Ireland. A trained lawyer, Donovan became a captain in the US National Guard in 1912. During World War I, he was commander of the 165th Regiment of the US Army and earned the nickname "Wild Bill" for his cool appearance in battle and the hard training regime he introduced for his men. At the end of the war, Donovan reached full colonel and was one of America's most decorated living soldiers. When peace finally arrived, he left the armed services and went on to form the American Legion Veterans Association in 1919. In the interwar period, he continued his work as a lawyer.

On December 15, 1941—eight days after the United States had entered World War II—COI had only 596 employees. At its height, the organization of the OSS numbered 12,000 people. The OSS was, and remained throughout its existence, General Donovan's baby. The OSS HQ was run more like a business than a military organization.[5] Many of Donovan's men were very young and their abilities ranged from brilliant to useless. Within the regular army, the eccentricities of some OSS officers earned the service the reputation of being a "bunch of screwballs."[6] Donovan also recruited people with different political affiliations, from socialists to conservatives, as well as people with no strong political convictions. Much of the literature on the OSS describes the organization as full of mavericks; its operators, operational staff, and administrators were a heterogeneous collection of top business executives, academics, and media personalities. Even missionaries and priests found their way into the ranks. Many, like Donovan, had a background in corporate law, and few had any lifelong military careers before entering the OSS. William Colby thus fitted right into Donovan's belief that academia could play an important intelligence role.[7] The "absence of a rigid organizational hierarchy" enabled an exceptional group of men and women to work with great effectiveness under Donovan's leadership, and "standard operating procedures were almost taboo in the OSS,"[8] in the words of historian Richard Harris Smith, himself former CIA. It might be suspected that this homage to avant-gardism could be an indirect lament to the author's views on lethargic bureaucracy of the contemporary CIA but the OSS's "civilian-military" identity also "displeased the old-time West Pointers."[9]

Espionage and subversion were thought to have been an important factor behind the fall of France to the Germans in 1940, and measures to counter this played an important part in the early COI days.[10] In July 1941, the organization for intelligence collection and special operations was reorganized into separate branches, with one section renamed the Office of Strategic Services, while the COI continued as an organization for propaganda. The Moral Operations Branch of the OSS handled the so-called black propaganda, targeting the enemy and its population with fake news and disinformation presented as originating from domestic authorities. The OSS was in turn subdivided into the Secret Intelligence Branch and the Special Operations Groups, of which NORSO was a part.

The OSS was met with much resistance from competing organizations,[11] but the COI was still in an embryonic state when the Japanese attacked Pearl Harbor and thus avoided any share of the blame for the American intelligence failure.[12] In neutral countries, OSS agents were assigned to the embassies under diplomatic cover, which, among other things, caused friction with the State Department and their corps of professional diplomats. With the expansion of the COI into the OSS, Donovan's cohorts would fill the vacuum in various diplomatic fora where the State Department remained absent, such as planning committees involving exiled governments of the occupied countries. The FBI managed to keep the OSS out of Latin America due to ancient prerogatives and General Douglas McArthur refused to let them into his theater of operations in the South Pacific. But besides that, Donovan could spread his wings, perhaps because his close friendship with Roosevelt meant very few people dared challenge him—not that he ever had to play that card. Usually, the value of the assets under his sway persuaded people to cooperate.[13]

A wide range of branches grew out of the COI, some to be merged, others to be attached to other agencies. The Research and Analysis Branch provided the rest of the OSS with reports on a wide range of topics on enemy and occupied nations, covering politics, economy, geography, and psychology. On many topics, libraries and business archives were just as good a source of information as an agent dropped into hostile territory. They also analyzed the information gathered by the COI/OSS. The Censorship and Documents Branch provided the field agents with cover stories and fake papers. During his stay in Britain, Donovan had observed firsthand the destructive rivalry between the SOE and the Special Intelligence Service (SIS), also known as MI6. The Special Operations Branch and the secret intelligence were therefore established to clarify the demarcation between the two functions.[14] The Special Operations Branch oversaw kinetic operations, in theory a counterpart to the British SOE. They would also work with resistance groups and harness their potential in coordination with the overall Allied war effort. Since SO units were operating in direct support of Allied operations, they were often detached to the respective theater commanders, for example, NORSO would report to SCOTCO during Operation *Rype*. The SO consisted of operational groups (OGs), the Maritime Unit, and Technical Development, which in time would develop into separate OSS branches.[15] The Special Intelligence Branch headed classic espionage and were the counterpart of the British SIS. Their activity would be limited to collection of information, mainly on the strategical level.

Some of the operatives in the field sometimes felt estranged from the staff in London, far away from the area of operation (AO) and the realities on the ground. On the other hand, the London staff experienced field operatives as being pig-headed and failing to see the bigger picture of overall Allied strategies. The European Resistance movements often assumed that OSS operatives were preaching the official foreign policy of the USA, whereas in reality they expressed their own personal idealism and initiative, making things up as they went along. To many OSS men the Atlantic Charter was meaningful, and most operatives developed "passionate admiration for their partisan friends." People "burdened with feelings of national superiority or racial intolerance," were weeded out in the psychological selection of operatives.[16] The OSS's relations with their British counterparts in the SIS and the SOE was a complicated one. For the OSS on the ground, it looked as if the British had every intention of keeping Norway within their "sphere of influence," doing so more by subtle procrastination than overt opposition.[17] While welcoming American resources and technology, and willing to share their experience, they were reluctant to accept independent operations into territory they regarded as their own turf. For most of Europe, it was more an issue of the SOE wanting control rather than wishing to exclude their American allies from contributing within the field of intelligence, special operations, and espionage. Operation *Rype* fitted into this pattern. As one US colonel expressed it, "the British were marvelous and opened every door to us."[18] This openness was mainly valid in terms of what could be summed up as "tactical training procedures," that is, how operators and agents were trained, the tools of the trade, and doctrine. Especially in the early stages of this friendship, the British were in desperate need of anything that the Lend-Lease program could offer, which might explain some of what was to follow.[19] According to OSS historian Richard H. Smith, the SOE delayed the insertion of OSS agents into occupied France during the fall of 1943 by insisting that American special operations officers be screened and trained at British installations[20]—one example of how the British wanted to control US intelligence and special operations activities. British reluctance to allow American independence in the field of maintaining an agent network in Europe may also stem from the fact that in the beginning, the OSS office in London was staffed by amateurs with no prior experience in maintaining agents in the field.[21]

As a prelude to Operation *Overlord*, the invasion of Normandy, the SO was operationally separated from the rest of the OSS, merged with the SOE, and put under the control of a joint Anglo-American SOE/SO Headquarters in January 1944, "SO" referring to the Special Operations branch within the OSS. On May 1, 1944, it was renamed Special Force Headquarters—SFHQ, and attached to the G-3 (Operations) of the SHAEF led by American Major-General Harold Bull. There was to be no distinction between British and American operations, and the SO branch was completely detached from the rest of the OSS. The SFHQ was located in London and had coordinating authority in all matters in connection with sabotage and organization of resistance groups and their activities in Norway, Denmark, the Netherlands, Belgium, Luxemburg, France, and western Germany. In addition to planning each mission, this also included general directions of planning, priorities, and intensity of operations.[22] This arrangement would still be in effect during NORSO's Operation *Rype*. The first attempts at a geographical demarcation between the SOE and the OSS was made in the summer of 1942 and tentatively agreed upon by both organizations in September. Accordingly, Scandinavia was to be the responsibility of the SOE until it would eventually become a predominantly US Theater of Operations. In January 1943, the SO branch of the OSS renounced independent operations or independent operational bases in Western Europe.[23]

The first OSS agents arrived in Stockholm in March 1942. Importantly for *Rype*, the OSS established their office in Stockholm in the fall of 1942, with the 50-year-old Harvard professor of government, Bruce Hopper, as its first chief of station. In late 1943, he was replaced by Wilho Tikander, a Minnesota lawyer of Finnish descent. However, the rivalry with the State Department was very much present in Scandinavia too, as an American minister in the Swedish capital, Herschel Johnson, saw American intelligence as "some sort of satanic practice."[24] Part of the British exclusion of the OSS in Norway was an ongoing rivalry between the Norwegian Resistance in Norway (MilOrg) and the SOE—backed by the Norwegian exiled government in London—over the control of sabotage and agents in the country. American interference, it was feared, would only complicate matters. However, this conflict subsided during 1943.[25] Compared to most European countries, the resistance movements in both Denmark and Norway were well unified. Also, the Norwegian intelligence service, the XU, was so efficient that the OSS saw no need to build up their own network in the country.[26] However, most reports on Norway received by the Reports and Registry Division were on shipping in Norwegian waters, hardly relevant for *Rype*.[27] As Operation *Rype* would show, the acceptance of OSS activity in Norway was initially limited to supplying the Norwegian Resistance, which was heavily influenced by the British. Only in the wake of the Ardennes offensive did the British reluctantly allow OSS special operations activity in Norway. Both their long history of trade with Norway and the country's strategic position vis-à-vis the British homeland, might explain why the British were reluctant to allow any foreign influence so close to home.

In early 1943, Scandinavia dominated the planning of special operations, and an invasion in Norway seemed likely.[28] SFHQ/Scandinavia was in theory a joint operation; however, it was very much a British-run show, although the SFHQ in Stockholm was divided into a British and an American section. At the end of 1943, the British were convinced to allow a US special operations unit to establish themselves in Stockholm. On November 7, 1943, the 43-year-old George Brewer Jr., a playwright by profession and former lecturer in English at Yale, left for Stockholm to set up the OSS *Westfield* mission, which was made up of Norwegian, Danish, and German sections, and a logistics and communications section. Its combined staff was 17 people, and it was activated on November 11. While the OSS in Stockholm in general had a strained relationship with ambassador Herschel Johnson, Johnson and Brewer seem to have a good working relationship. Brewer also worked well with the US military attaché in Stockholm, Brigadier General A. Kessler Jr.[29]

The Norwegian section in Stockholm was led by Hans Skabo Erichsen, the grand-nephew of Colonel Skabo. Erichsen was born in 1918 and was quite young to be handling 40 field agents in enemy territory. He had emigrated with his mother to the United States in 1924, and grew up in Brooklyn, New York, and Pennsylvania. He returned to Norway for studies at the University of Oslo in 1935–36, and then continued them at Swarthmore College in Pennsylvania. His subjects were history, political science, languages, and economics. Before the war, he had worked in the Department of Agriculture. Erichsen worked with shipping intelligence before he joined the OSS and relocated to Stockholm, where he arrived on April 1, 1943. The purpose of the *Westfield* mission was to provide intelligence for SO operations, as well as communications and liaison with the underground networks in Norway, Denmark, and Germany to assist in the execution of special operations.[30] The condition was that the OSS operated in northern Norway, leaving the southern part to the British. Where the demarcation ran is unclear, but a report drawn up by Lieutenant Colonel Bolland on *Rype* after the war suggests that the line was drawn through Trondheim;[31] the official OSS war report stated it was the "northern tip of Norway."[32] *Westfield* was under the direction of SFHQ in London, and thus independent of the OSS in Stockholm. Norwegian historian Tore Pryser has described *Westfield* as one of the most successful OSS operations.[33]

Together with the SOE, the SO branch of the OSS supplied MilOrg groups and worked with Section IV of the Norwegian High Command who controlled those groups. An OSS representative was also added to the Anglo-Norwegian Collaboration Committee, which, among other things, ensured that any activity was in accordance with the interests of the parties involved. At the OSS office at Grosvenor Square in London, Commander Unger Vetlesen was appointed head of the Special Operations, Norwegian Desk, on November 11, 1943. This was a strategic move, since Vetlesen was both a millionaire and a personal friend of King Haakon VII and highly influential among the vital shipping industry and the Norwegian forces in exile. Major Fredric Cromwell was appointed SO Area Operations officer for Norway on May 10, 1943.

NORSO arrived in Britain on December 13, 1943, then numbering 69 men and 12 officers under command of Lieutenant Colonel Harold P. Larson. Larson would be replaced by Lieutenant Colonel Hans E. Skabo in February 1945 after the former was relieved of duty after refusing further parachute jumps after sustaining an injury.[34] The OGs would be responsible for irregular warfare, conducting raids, and sabotage directly against enemy forces. They would also protect important infrastructure against German scorched earth tactics, as well as train and operate alongside resistance groups. In Scandinavia, preventing the southward movement of German troops back to continental Europe was also part of the mission given by SHAEF. The OGs were established as a separate branch in May 1943. Unlike other branches of the OSS, the OGs would always operate in uniform in the field. The OGs were formed along ethnic lines, making use of the unique language skills and cultural savviness of America's diverse immigrant communities. From August 1944, the OGs in Europe were collectively identified as the 2671st Special Reconnaissance Battalion (Provisional). The OSS also wanted its personnel to enter Norway and Denmark immediately after liberation to continue the close relationship with domestic intelligence services and to direct intelligence and counterintelligence operations aimed at Germany from there. Also, they were to provide updates on the political and economic developments in Norway and Denmark.[35] NORSO was not mentioned specifically but, for all practical means, they would constitute the main bulk of OSS manpower on the ground in Norway.

SOE regarded Scandinavia, as well as the Balkans, as their exclusive domain, and tried to limit OSS activity in these areas.[36] According to Douglas Wallers's biography on Donovan, the SOE was more than willing to share its secrets in the beginning, wanting to secure American support for the war effort. Then, as the OSS grew and asserted itself, the relationship became frostier around 1943, before it thawed again towards the end of the war. Further, Wallers explains that the OSS–SOE relationship was far more cordial than that between the OSS and the FBI and the intelligence services of the US Army and Navy.[37] There was also a general trend that the British wanted to control operations even where American contributions were welcomed, including obstructions made by MI6. But inter-service rivalry and factionalism among the clandestine British services was also strong,[38] and it would be simplistic to view the obstructionism as driven by differing state interests. On their side, by building one unified organization from scratch, the Americans avoided much of the inter-service conflicts of the British on the strategic level—but on the operational level they still had to face the respective Army and Navy intelligence services, as well as the blatant refusal of McArthur to allow the OSS to operate in the Pacific at all. Also, Latin America remained the sole domain of the FBI. The first agreement of cooperation between the OSS and the SOE was struck in January 1943. It seems that the SOE in general accepted American special operations as a necessary evil, and that their cooperativeness could be seen as an effort to control it. To make the picture more complicated, the exiled government of the occupied countries had their own interests, spies, and special forces operatives.

Although the Americans were relative novices to the shady world of secret intelligence and special operations, that exact quality did provide some advantages the British did not enjoy. Up until the beginning of World War II, the United States had pursued a mostly isolationist foreign policy, thus it was not burdened with a legacy of great power rivalry or colonialism that would frequently complicate Britain's relationship with other nations. Thus, the Americans could benefit from a clean sheet when dealing with resistance movements and exiled governments. They also enjoyed a far better relationship with the Swedish Security Service, Säpo, and the intelligence service (C-byrån), than the SOE. Early in the war, when German victory seemed within reach, the Swedish secret services had given British operatives a hard time, arresting and expelling several. However, by the time the Americans got into the game, the tides of war had turned. While the Swedish–British relationship remained strained, the Americans and the Swedes enjoyed more cooperative relations.[39]

CHAPTER FOUR

Norwegian Special Operations Group (NORSO)

The original crews picked for the NORSO group were mostly volunteers from the US Army 99th Infantry Battalion (separate). The forming of this type of unit was an important part of the development of American special forces during World War II. By July 1942, the US Army had grown from 269,000 to more than 2 million since the attack on Pearl Harbor. Immigrant groups were recognized early on as a source of "information and services of importance to our military effort and our diplomacy."[1] At this point, it was calculated that 360,000 men with foreign citizenship eligible for military service resided in the United States and that there were even more first- and second-generation immigrants who presumably had retained networks, cultural knowledge, and language skills which might be useful during the liberation of Nazi-occupied Europe. President Franklin D. Roosevelt had pointed out the opportunity to exploit the ethnic diversity of the United States in the fight against the Germans, and the OSS would offer a prime opportunity to accomplish this. It was also of important propaganda value for the civilian population in the occupied country, and it was believed that an ethnic element would strengthen the ties between individual European nations and the United States.

The British experiences with Norwegian operators during commando raids on German targets in Norway may have been one of the reasons why Norwegian Americans were one of the first groups to be included in the forming of operations groups in the OSS. Contemporary stereotypes may also have had some influence. Norwegians appeared as hardy people who could survive in the wilderness with limited supplies. Polar explorers such as Fridtjof Nansen, Roald Amundsen, and Bernt Balchen were well known in the United States. Norway had also made a clean sweep as the best nation at the first Winter Olympics in Chamonix, France, in 1924. In 1925 during the diphtheria outbreak in Nome, Alaska, Norwegian sledge drivers (one of them Kven—the Finnish minority in Norway) had delivered life-saving medicine to the hard-hit population.

For President Roosevelt in particular, Norway also stood as a symbol of the follies of isolationism and appeasement that he had been addressing at home. As a small democratic country with no legacy of empire, Norway was nevertheless attacked by the Nazis, as emphasized in his "Look to Norway" speech, held on September 16, 1942, on the occasion of the handover of the naval vessel KNM *King Haakon VII* to the Norwegian Navy in exile:

> If there is anyone who still wonders why this war is being fought, let him look to Norway. If there is anyone who has any delusions that this war could have been averted, let him look to Norway; and if there is anyone who doubts the democratic will to win, again I say, let him look to Norway.[2]

Although not particularly conspicuous to non-Norwegians at the time, Crown Princess Märtha of Norway and the future King Harald V were Roosevelt's personal guests during the years of occupation, which may have lifted Norway's plight on the president's agenda.

After Ireland, Norway was the country from which most people had immigrated to the United States, relative to the size of the original population at home. A survey done in the 1920s concluded that 1.2 million people living in the United States had Norwegian ancestry only, in addition to the 700,000 of mixed Norwegian and other origin. Norwegians had preserved their language, culture, and traditions to a greater extent than many other comparable immigrant groups such as Danes and Swedes, despite the fact that Norwegians could blend in with the Anglo-Saxon majority population, being Northern Europeans and Protestants. This meant too that the few cultural differences that existed had little potential to create friction or conflict with the majority population. But since the War Department did not allow the staging of foreign troops on American soil, the immigrants had to at least have applied for "first papers"—that is, register as immigrants—before they could serve in the US Army.

An operations group would consist of professionally trained volunteers who stood at the disposal of the Allied High Command to be sent on sabotage missions or conduct guerrilla warfare. Personnel were selected based on physical fitness and competence in this type of operation, as well as knowledge of the area and the language of the enemy, or the people where they would operate. Each OG had a service headquarters and a site command—for NORSO this was in London. These were in close contact with the operations team in the field, and controlled reinforcements and reserves. Three main types of missions were initially outlined for OGs. The first was the support for the major operations of a crucial character (*coup-de-main* operations); the second was support for resistance groups; and the last was to carry out raids to prevent the Germans from conducting scorched earth tactics. In other words, they were more adapted to an operational environment when the war ended to support liberation and to prevent more rebuilding in the aftermath of the war than necessary. This was a somewhat different operational profile than that of the SOE which, in Churchill's words, was meant to "set Europe ablaze." In the OSS, knowledge of local culture and language carried higher priority than in the British special forces.[3] To illustrate this, during the design of the operations group's doctrines, the books of T. E. Lawrence were studied, and lessons drawn from his experiences working with the Bedouin Arabs during World War I.[4]

The 99th Battalion, into which many of the would-be NORSO men were initially inducted, was formally created through a memorandum from Lieutenant General Lesley J. McNair, commander of the US 2nd Army, in April 1942.[5] The event was to take place at Camp Ripley in Minnesota—in the middle of the Norwegian–American heartland. The force consisted of 931 privates—of these 884 were infantry, 36 medics, and 11 transport and service personnel. Officers had to be of Norwegian descent and able to speak Norwegian, although some correspondence reveals concerns that other ethnic groups were also included in the unit.[6] The men were quartered in tents, but after these were swept away by a snowstorm, the unit was moved to Camp Snelling in October 1942. In December, the unit moved again, this time to the newly built Camp Hale in Colorado. There they began rigorous training in mountain warfare to prepare them for operations in Norway. In a personal letter, Leif Oistad would later reveal that he started skiing at the age of four, quite normal for a kid growing up in many areas of Norway. But not everybody would be so proficient. During training at Camp Hale, it was not uncommon to see men fall flat on their faces and not be able to get up again. The next day they would call in sick because of blisters. Later, during the NORSO training, those who were already proficient skiers could devote their time to night jumps, language studies, and map reading.[7] The tradition of cross-country skiing was not particularly strong among Norwegian Americans as many immigrants had left the old country in 1860s and '70s, at a time when the popularity of skiing was at a low point. Back in Norway at that time, construction of roads and railways meant skiing was no longer a necessity, and it had not yet become a prized leisure activity. In addition, Norwegian immigrants to the United States settled mostly in the Midwest where the terrain is relatively flat and did not provide any slopes. Many also came from coastal areas with little tradition or climate for skiing. Training fields at Camp Hale, however, had excellent skiing conditions and brought the men up to altitudes of about 4,500 MAMSL.

The raising of a separate Norwegian unit, however, did not happened entirely without reactions from the Norwegian government-in-exile in London. From communications with the War Department in July 1942, is obvious that the creation of the 99th Battalion happened without coordination with—or even knowledge of—the Norwegian London government. On the American side, they thought the Norwegian ambassador was informed, but the Norwegian government-in-exile in London was first informed about the creation of the battalion through the American press. They were then quick to point out that no one should be recruited from the Norwegian merchant marine, something the Americans complied with in the beginning.[8] But as the submarine warfare claimed its victims, Norwegian tonnage was not replaced as fast as it was sunk, and several of the later additions to the 99th Battalion, and subsequently NORSO men, were stranded Norwegian merchant mariners.

In the summer of 1943, Camp Hale was visited by officers from the OSS. Together with their Norwegian colleagues Otto Hjersing Munthe-Kaas and Arne Dagfinn Dahl they would select men to form the Norwegian Operations Group (NORSO). Munthe-Kaas and Dahl had previously assisted in selecting operators for the British SOE and had some experience in what to look for in prospective recruits. In addition to physical qualities, they would also set out the psychological profile of the volunteers to weed out those who were unsuitable. Besides the Norwegians, there were also other Scandinavians in NORSO. It was among the first ethnic operation groups formed; the others were Greek, French, and Italian. The rumor traveled within the 99th Battalion that those picked would be trained as special forces operators to be dropped behind enemy lines to conduct sabotage against the targets of economic and military value for the Germans and that they would operate independently of the local resistance movement. In the interview, they got to know NORSO sought volunteers for extremely perilous missions behind enemy lines in Norway and that they had to undergo parachute training.

But who were these men that set out to choke the German's line of communications in Norway in the final months of World War II, under their uniforms? (See Biographies for individual bios.) Except for Colby and Farnsworth, most of the men sent to Norway were of Norwegian or other Nordic ancestry. Not many had any upper secondary education, and even fewer had gone to college, quite usual for the basic demographics of the time. But surprisingly few of them came from big farms in the "Scandinavian" Mid-West with any experience in agriculture or forestry that would be useful when operating in the harsh mountain environment of Norway. Most were born in Norway, many in the southern and western parts of the country and had either emigrated with their families or come to the United States as sailors during World War II. Many had work experience in the shipping industry, ranging from stock clerks to fitters, and most had lived urban lives before enlisting. And though men such as Leif Oistad and Tom Saether had been active skiers, not even they had much life experience that prepared them for surviving in the mountains of mid-Norway during wartime. Of the men who were dropped into Norway, only Einar Eliassen had a career as a professional soldier prior to World War II.

When on leave, they often ended up in brawls with the military police, and the officers had to bring their men out of the stockade, but the individuals seldom suffered any consequences. Some of the men claimed in retrospect that they had a secret number they could call to get out of predicaments and avoid a court martial. But usually there were only minor offences, such as not saluting an officer. As logistics Sergeant Clifford Kyllo put it, when they did not salute General Donovan, why would they salute a lowly ensign from other units? During the interviews, OSS operatives were rated on "Motivation" (energy, effort, initiative, interest in assignment);

"Practical Intelligence" (speed and accuracy of judgement, resourcefulness in solving problems); "Stability" (emotional control and maturity, absence of nervous symptoms); "Ability to work with others" (teamwork, tact, absence of annoying traits); "Leadership" (organizing ability, ability to win cooperation); and "Physical Ability" (agility, daring, ruggedness, stamina). The ratings from top to bottom were: superior, excellent, very satisfactory, satisfactory, and unsatisfactory. For *Rype*, this assessment was done by Colby and two other officers from the OSS.

About 80 soldiers and 12 officers were selected from the 99th Battalion and transferred to Washington D.C., where they were accommodated in "Area F," part of the Congressional Golf Club used as a training ground for the OSS. There, NORSO was activated on July 28, 1943. One of the training fields, known as "Area B," would later become Camp David, the official country retreat of the United States president. They received close combat and urban combat training, weapons training, and they were trained for night patrols. One of the instructors, Major W. E. Fairbairn, had been a police chief in Shanghai and was well trained in martial arts. He developed a unique fighting style devoid of any gentlemanlike consideration, which was passed on to Allied special forces. A telegram from March 1945 suggested that his dealings with NORSO were not over after the initial training. Obviously, his services were requested for the training of those going to South China:

> Understand you have requested Col. Fairbairn for OG instruction when available from present assignment with rescue group for Norway. This will be done if you feel there will be no embarrassment because of his status as British officer.[9]

NORSO also trained at Martha's Vineyard and Poponesset, in Massachusetts, where physical education, demolition, map and compass reading, as well as the landing exercises were on the curriculum. In one exercise, they were to knock out a radar station guarded by a detail of US Marines. They were transported by submarine to Gay Head on the western side of Martha's Vineyard, but when they came ashore, they discovered that the installation had a high-power electric fence. There was only one way in—through the main gate. On Saether's suggestion, they went inland, hijacked a Marine truck, drove straight in, and marked the target as "destroyed." Once back on the mainland, they called the Marines to tell them where they could find the original truck driver and passengers.

By the time NORSO left Fort Hamilton in December 1943, there were only 72 men and 12 officers left from the original set of volunteers from the 99th Battalion. As some were relegated from the group, new candidates were added—so-called "fillers." The force was then divided into a staff and two groups. Each group consisted of two sections of 16 men each. The sections were again divided into two squads. The squads contained a signaler and a squad leader, among other positions. While basic training was done stateside, most advanced schools were located in the theater of operations. NORSO arrived at Swansea in Wales, then continued to Scotland on

December 17, 1943, where they were temporarily accommodated in Lord Lovat's hunting residence at Forest Lodge. HQ was located near Inverness. Six months of ski and demolition training awaited them at SOE's facilities at Aviemore; a month later they moved to more permanent quarters in Stronelairig, not far from Loch Ness. On the curriculum were:

1. demolition of rail lines, high bridges, power installations, telephone and telegraph communications, etc.;
2. weapons, map reading, compass reading and Morse code;
3. scouting and patrolling;
4. unarmed combat; and
5. parachuting and rubber boat assault exercises.

NORSO trained with operations groups from other nationalities, such as Greek, French, and Italian. They subsequently received their parachute training at the British Army Parachute School at Ringway Air Force Base outside Manchester; NORSO was the only American unit allowed to wear both the British and the American parachute wings, however, they had to wear the wings on the upper right sleeve, not the left breast as the British did. Exercises were held at the SOE-run Special Training School 51, located outside the village of Altringham. Leif Oistad later said that jumping out of an aircraft did not scare him as the noise of the engines had a hypnotic and calming effect.[10] They had about two dozen practice jumps over the fields of Tatton Park, using British bombers. The training was rigorous, but they had a saying—"you've got to be tougher than the Germans, because if you're not, you won't be coming back." At the same time, the OSS set up an office in Stockholm where Sverre Ellingsen was the liaison with the Norwegian authorities. In addition, Ellingsen had a similar function with the SOE, which probably facilitated the cooperation that developed between *Rype* and *Woodlark*.

At Stronelairig, NORSO got more basic training and physical education. Then followed the technical education at various schools under the auspices of SOE. In addition, more close combat and weapons training was followed by patrol and ranger training. Demolition skills became more advanced as they learned how to blow-up railway lines, bridges, power supply lines, and telephone communications. They were taught to hit hard and disappear quickly, and then reassemble a few kilometers from the target. The missions, the conditions, and the opponent were recreated as closely as possible during the exercises to add realism. As NORSO was prepared to be inserted by sea, they also received training in the use of six-man rubber attack boats. In May 1944, the Norwegian Operations Group was transferred from Stronelairig and Killin Lodges to Brockhall, Northamptonshire, (designated "Area E") leased through the Ministry of Works. It consisted of a house, stables, garage, and 25 pyramid tents.

Meanwhile, in September 1943, the 99th Battalion, from which many of the NORSO men came, had also arrived in the UK. On June 17, 1944, they landed in Normandy and were placed directly under the command of the US 1st Army. They participated in the liberation of Cherbourg and fought through the northern part of France, Belgium, and the Netherlands. During the battle of the Ardennes in December 1944, they were the first Allied unit to arrive in Stavelot-Malmedy and held out for 30 days against SS armored units. At the end of January, they were pulled out and were merged with the First Service Force (the "Devil's Brigade") into the 474th Regiment. The 99th Battalion was earmarked for insertion into Norway if it became required. They also escorted the transport of the so-called "Nazi Gold" found in Merkers, Thuringia, Germany, in April 1945. The battalion was located in Regensburg when Germany capitulated. On May 29, they were transferred to Norway to participate in the disarmament and expatriation of the German occupation force in the country. The 99th Battalion also served as the Honorary Guard for King Haakon when he returned to Norway on June 7, 1945.

Towards the end of 1944, it was clear that the 99th Battalion had suffered huge losses, and there was a halt in the recruitment into NORSO from the unit. It was mainly this that led to non-Scandinavians in the NORSO ranks. Without any prospect of operations in Norway in the foreseeable future, NORSO was sent in on the *Jedburgh* operations in France, where small groups under the OSS commandos were dropped behind enemy lines to coordinate the Allied advance from Normandy with the French Resistance movement. Each team would consist of one OSS or SOE officer and one French, and one British or American enlisted man as radio operator. For fear of revealing the invasion, the Operation *Jedburgh* teams were not inserted until after the Allies had landed. This caused much frustration among the NORSO units when they learned that the invasion had taken place without them. When they jumped in June 1944, they expected to be in the field until the spring of 1945. However, France was liberated quicker than expected, and the Jedburghs would often find that their operations had become redundant before they could be sent in, or even found that the area they had landed in had already been liberated. The expected casualty rate had been 40 percent, but it turned out to be less than 20 percent.

CHAPTER FIVE

German Forces in the Area of Operation—Grong to Snåsa

On October 31, 1944, the German Army Command in Norway (AOK) sent out orders to plan for the securing of the railways. The order was not limited to the territorial occupational forces but also extended to the units in transit to Germany from Finland and northern Norway. This included the crack mountain troops of the Lapland Army (*20. Gebirgsarmee*), which by now were in a pretty bad shape. Field Order No. 1 to Operation *Rype*'s advance party included an estimate of enemy strength locally, but did not indicate what units they belonged to, nor their quality. The German force in Namsos was calculated at 700 men and the Americans counted on a further 150 men at Grong. There were also some Germans stationed on Formo and Ekker, listed as a "few men." At Formofoss there was a guarded ammunitions depot, no number of troops given, and a patrol base was located at Nordli with 23 men. At Agle in Lurudal, the list includes "hutments" without specifying what that implied. At Krossgarden in Snåsa, the estimate given was 500 men, a camp, and an ammunition dump. Several of the tunnels on the stretch of railway were also guarded.

Twice a day, the Field Order estimated, a German patrol on a draisine traveled along the line. At "Maelsester Tunnel" (Melaseter on a modern map) there was a railway guard.[1] There were no further remarks on this estimate in the Field Order No. 2 sent to the main force, except for the notice of one "Quisling" (collaborator) at a position east of Snåsa and the location of a German air observation post at Imsdalfjell Mountain, manned by 12 men. It is worth noting that these estimates only stretched south to Snåsa village and were relevant for the intended operational area that lay further north than the place which would become the actual operational area. Detailed intelligence of the enemy further south would be unknown until they could confer with Norwegian assets on the ground as the operation got underway. The Norwegian Nazi Party, *Nasjonal Samling*, did have some supporters and the party had 130 registered members in Snåsa, with a core of four to five who were most active. One of them was the local veterinarian who undoubtedly could acquire wide knowledge about the people of the community through his profession. Another was the mayor and the sheriff. But most *Nasjonal Samling* members were passive, mostly farmers who joined to protect their property against German confiscation.[2]

During May–July 1944, there was a reshuffling of the German units stationed in Norway. According to intelligence coming out of the Namdalen area, a whole division was in transit on their way to the Continent. Rumors had it that Norwegian veteran volunteers from the German forces (*frontkjempere*) and Norwegian Nazi "stormtroopers" from the Hird (the Norwegian Nazi Party's version of the German *Sturm Abteilungen*) were going to replace them. It was also reported that German replacements were of poor quality, "partly only kids."[3] The OSS had no estimate of German forces to offer as of early January 1945 due to their "extreme state of flux," but the issue had to be carefully studied as the operations were mounted, reports urged.[4] As far as units went, the Snåsa area was controlled by the *722. Grenadier Regiment*. The regiment was subject to *702. Infanterie Division* under *Generalleutnant* Ernst Klepp, with their HQ in Trondheim. The *722. Grenadier Regiment*'s area of responsibility was bounded by the county border with Nordland in the north and a line crossing Lake Snåsa at Strindmoen in the south. Their neighboring unit to the south was the *742. Grenadier Regiment*, of unknown status and number. Operational strength of the *722.* would have varied though out the period of the operation.

There are two major sources to the numbers, qualities, and strength of the unit and its sub-units at the end of the war. The first is from Friedrich Trapphagen, a German *leutnant* at the time, who served in Snåsa. He later stated the number of "German men" stationed in the area was 1,422 on May 23, 1945—probably the date of departure from Snåsa following their surrender. He also lists 31 German women and 84 non-German men and 2 non-German women—a total of 1,539. The physical source is a letter written by the said German in Norwegian in 2004, based on a mix of his own recollections and studying the available material in the Bundesarchiv.[5] It is interesting that he lists several "Volksdeutsche" within the ranks. A *Volksdeutsche* would be somebody of German descent, but not a resident of the German Reich, predominantly from east and central Europe's many German minorities. These seem not to be included in the category "non-Germans." In his company, the source lists a total of 15 *Volksdeutsche* from Poland, France, and Italy.

Among the units he lists was the *702. Panzerjäger Abteilung*, with 395 men (366 Germans) based in Snåsa. Their weaponry and combat value are uncertain, but at full strength such a unit would comprise 550 men, 12 guns, and six machine guns. Extrapolating the number of guns from the actual number of men, the *702.* probably had no more than eight guns of unknown caliber, but most likely 37mm or 75mm PAK anti-tank guns. There were also two companies of *Landesschützen* at Snåsa. These units consisted of men aged 30–45 or who for other reasons were unfit for frontline service. They were mostly used for security duties and were known for poor leadership, low morale, and poor discipline. The *1. Kompanie, Landesschützen Batallion 309* consisted of 165 Germans and three "non-Germans." The *2. Kompanie* from the same battalion consisted of 150 men, all Germans. It is fair to assume that these two companies were those responsible for guard duty and patrolling the area where *Rype* would operate. Also, there was one labor battalion and an additional labor company in the area. These consisted of Soviet or Yugoslav prisoners of war (POW) working as slaves and their guards, and while the guards would have their hands full with looking after their captives to go out and search for saboteurs, their activity would complicate *Rype*'s mission and increase the risk of being detected. In addition, there were numerous support units of various sorts, such as bakeries and hospitals in the area, but it is difficult to assess what potential they could have had of interfering with *Rype*'s operations. However, one of these was a detachment from the *702. Panzerjäger Regiment*, numbering 12 men at Sandness, a few kilometers south of Snåsa community center. There was also an armored train based at Grong.[6]

In local Norwegian military archives, a map is preserved, showing the interment plan of the German forces at Snåsa at the war's end. Upon surrender, the Germans were ordered by the Allied commander to pull out from their positions and gather in central camps. This would prove impractical because they were still needed to guard weapons stores, ammunition dumps, and various installations against looting. But it might be assumed that the units listed in this undated map were gathered from the whole *722.* AO. There were two main camps in Snåsa. "I Lager Snaasa" was located on the south side of the road from Krossgarden Farm, just east of Snåsa Church and the railway line. According to the map, there were a total of 1,147 men in this camp at the end of the war. This included the above-mentioned *702. Panzerjäger Abteilung*, here listed with 454 men. The second unit listed for "I Lager Snaasa" and not mentioned by Trapphagen, is *I./A.R. 702.* (1st Battery of Artillery Regiment 702) with a stated strength of 286 men. Batteries and companies in Wehrmacht regiments were numbered continuously; from this, the battery should have initially been set up with four 105mm field guns pulled by horses. But especially so late in the war, it is very uncertain whether this was the reality. The map also places 249 men from *Kriegsgefangenen Arbeitsbataillon 206* and 70 men of the *2. Kompanie* of *Kriegsgefangenen Labor Battalion 70* in "I Lager Snaasa." There are also 88 "Verschiedene," i.e., "miscellaneous" listed. What kind of personnel this may have been is not known. The other large camp was located close to the shore of Lake Snåsa and was called "II Lager Viosen." Here we find the *1. Kompanie* with 188 men, and 192 from the *2. Kompanie* of the *Landesschützen Battalion 309.* Also listed in the same camp but not mentioned by Trapphagen is *Feldlazarett 662* with 43 men and 151 "Verschiedene." A total compliment of 574 men for the whole of "II Lager Viosen."

In addition to the two larger camps, the map includes several minor encampments and single buildings used by the Germans. Just north of the railway station and on the east side of the line was a supply camp. Between it and Krossgarden was the "Waffenmeisterei" armory, and at what is probably Forberg along Øverbygdsvegen further east, a stable has been marked. Just east of Snåsa Church there is an *Offizersheim*—an officer's home. This location is a little misleading as the officer's home lay more north of the church. On the other side of the road from the church is a building called *Frauenheim*—women's home. Exactly what this notation meant is unknown. It may have been home to women who had contracted STDs after relationships with German soldiers and officers in the area (such an institution was established in Trondheim) or simply billeting for women serving with the Germans.

In accordance with the orders from the AOK, units from *722. Grenadier Regiment* held training courses in the Grong–Steinkjer area during spring and summer of 1944 to prepare to meet Allied saboteur groups. The regiment also regrouped from being deployed to meet a possible invasion on the coast, to facing the new threat against their troop transports that was expected to come from the border area in the east. Several alarm drills were held to heighten alertness. To the German soldiers, their opponent was presented as the Communist Partisans with little support in the local population. After some time, the terms "agents" and "saboteurs" came into use, which may indicate that the German leadership realized that the threat came from groups under Allied command. The security plans from November onwards took into consideration threats from both the resistance groups and Allied sabotage teams.

CHAPTER SIX

Operation *Carpetbagger*

Air transport support for *Rype* was organized through Operation *Carpetbagger*, which was flown by the United States Army Air Forces (USAAF). "Carpetbaggers" was a nickname for people from the northern states going to the South following the American Civil War (1861–1865). Some were idealists, but many went to make money exploiting people's destitution. Operation *Carpetbagger* delivered agents, supplies and special forces operatives to France, Belgium, the Netherlands, Denmark, and Norway. With their black-painted aircraft, the operation is considered to be the origin of the US Air Force's special operations. Aircraft were mainly decommissioned B-24 bombers that had been pulled from anti-submarine duty at the end of 1943, when the Allies thought the battle of the Atlantic was won once and for all. These planes had greater range and better carrying capacity than the Short Stirling used by the British on similar missions. Before they were put into the *Carpetbagger* operations, the B-24s were modified. The belly turret, nose gun, and the oxygen supply to the crew were removed to reduce the weight so that the planes could carry more cargo, and to improve speed and range. Colby once described the inside of these aircraft as "spacious but uncomfortable."[1]

The hole in the floor left by the belly tower was used by agents and operatives when parachuting out of the aircraft. The bomb racks held supplies packed in specially designed supply containers, which were parachuted out of the bomb bay. The planes did not carry marks, and the crews wore civilian clothes. The aircraft entered in the squadrons that eventually became the 801st Bomb Group. The *Carpetbagger* operations started on January 4, 1944, and in April the squadrons moved to Harrington, a secluded airbase ideal for staging covert operations in England's East Midlands. Forward bases at Leuchars and Kinloss in Scotland were used extensively for refueling during flights to Scandinavia, but they did not have the capacity to carry out heavier maintenance or to prepare the missions. Prior to the Normandy landings on June 6, 1944, the group was expanded with an additional two squadrons, and the remains of several squadrons were added in August. After heavy losses in May, the group was reconstructed and redesignated 492nd Bombardment Group.

In the beginning, *Carpetbagger* operated on behalf of British SOE, but soon coordinated with the newly created joint British–US SFHQ. The first *Carpetbagger* missions to Norway were flown in February 1944, with an average number of two flights per month until focus was turned almost exclusively towards Belgium and France during summer and fall of 1944 due to the Normandy landings. Then, from July 17 to September 28, 1944, Colonel Bernt Balchen's detachment of six Liberators flew missions over Norway from Leuchars—a total of 63 sorties of which 35 were successful, delivering 52 tons of supplies. Balchen (1899–1973) was born in Norway and joined the French Foreign Legion during World War I but arrived at the Western Front near Verdun just too late to see action. He then fought with the White Guards during Finland's Civil War in 1918. Balchen represented Norway as a boxer in the 1920 Olympics, and in 1921 he became a pilot in the Royal Norwegian Navy Air Service. As an aviator, he took part in the unsuccessful Amundsen–Ellsworth Arctic Relief Expedition in 1925, the beginning of a long and outstanding career in polar aviation. Balchen held dual Norwegian–American citizenship, and in 1941, he joined the USAAF.

In 1944–45, Balchen's Operations *Sonnie* and *Where and When* evacuated Allied pilots who had crashed in Sweden, ferried supplies and Norwegian police troops to the liberated parts of Finnmark, and managed to smuggle weapons and explosives through Sweden to the Norwegian Resistance and groups similar to *Rype*. As Air Transport Command's representative in Sweden, he also led the OSS's courier flights to the United Kingdom from Bromma Airport outside Stockholm. The "instigators [*sic*] of this scheme," in addition to Colonel Balchen himself, was Commander George U. Vetlesen (1889–1955).[2] Vetlesen was born in Oslo, the son of a surgeon. Despite his family's social standing, he signed up as a crew member on a ship bound for Copenhagen, Denmark, at the age of 11. He studied naval architecture and mechanical engineering in London and worked in shipbuilding before emigrating to Canada to work as a miner. In 1916, he emigrated to the United States to continue work in the shipbuilding industry. In 1932, he married the widow of a wealthy mining executive. When World War II broke out, Vetlesen became central to the resurrection of the Norwegian Air Force in exile. In 1943 he joined the US Navy before serving with SFHQ. After the war, he continued working in shipping and was one of the founders and the first chairman of the board of the joint Norwegian–Danish–Swedish publicly owned airline company, Scandinavian Airline Systems.

From the middle of September 1944 and throughout the rest of the year, the *Carpetbagger* group continued to be preoccupied with supporting Allied operations in France, dropping supplies, and extracting Allied pilots who had been forced to bail out. A couple of squadrons were also retrained for bomber operations. In October, a discussion was held within SFHQ on the requirement of airlift capacity in support of the resistance in Norway and Denmark. At that point, these missions were flown exclusively by the RAF from Tempsford (No 138 Squadron, which had specialized in flying for the SOE). They would fly only at night in moon periods due to Air Ministry regulations, something that greatly limited the time window for the operations in Norwegian airspace. In a letter to the United States Strategic Air Forces (USSTAF), the OSS complained somewhat cryptically that "Facilities will always be available for non-moon period drops, and for certain targets north of latitude 62° which Sterlings cannot attempt and which 38 Group may not particularly care to undertake." The No 38 Group, RAF flew in support of British airborne units with Short Sterling and Handley Page Halifax at the time, but the prospect of them serving special forces or the resistance might have come up at some point or it was simply a mix-up with the No 138 Squadron. In a letter to USSTAF, SFHQ requested specifically that Balchen be put in charge of supply missions to the Norwegian Resistance, probably because nobody in Allied service had more experience in navigating in Arctic airspace than he did.[3] But *Carpetbagger* missions to Norway picked up again towards the end of 1944. From January 1942 to May 1945, some 1,241 sorties were flown in support of the Norwegian Resistance or Allied sabotage groups in the country. 717 of these were successful, but at a great cost. A total of 23 RAF crews and 5 USAAF crews perished, two of the latter while supporting *Rype* alone.[4]

SFHQ had planned for 100 sorties to Norway between October and December 1944 and 400 to Denmark in the same period. They also warned that in case the situation in these countries deteriorated due to famine, revolt, or German scorched earth tactics, the need for airdrops would increase dramatically. If the SFHQ groups and Norwegian groups were deployed, the latter probably pointing to the Parachute Company, Commandoes, and/or *Kompani Linge*, the number of sorties required during that period would increase to 400 for Norway alone. To broaden the timeframe for air drops and the latitude at which the drops would be undertaken, the OSS recommended to USSTAF that 10 B-24 Liberators be earmarked for support to the resistance in Denmark and Norway. If there was a general uprising in Norway, the estimated number of sorties needed would rise to 2,400 to both serve Allied and Norwegian groups, as well as the resistance and civilian population. In that case, the aircraft available would "in all likelihood" be insufficient, even included the ones requested.[5] At the time, the number of resistance fighters in Norway was estimated at "15,000–25,000." In the spring of 1945, *Carpetbagger* operations picked up again with drops of agents and sabotage teams across the Netherlands, Denmark, Norway, and Germany. At the end of the war, *Carpetbagger* missions also included the return of important people from exile to the recently liberated countries. From the end of April 1945, the operations were scaled down. The 492nd Bombardment Group was dissolved and returned to the United States in July 1945.

Special operations required a support system that in scope and the number of people involved far surpassed the number of operatives on the ground.

This included everyone who provided leadership, planning, intelligence, facilitates insertion, reinforcement, and resupply and who would be located miles away from where the real action took place. In the spring of 1945, the increase in airdrops led to a shortage of personnel at Harrington, and some Royal Engineers were brought in to relieve the situation. This shortage would certainly not have encouraged further operations in Norway when various difficulties meant few supplies would be dropped despite much effort being made. Operations along the Nordland Railway were particularly challenging. The operational area lay outside the reach of the Allied fighter bombers like the Mosquito and Beaufighters that operated against German shipping along the coast of western Norway, so any lumbering transports were completely on their own. In western Norway, sabotage groups could also be inserted and resupplied with Motor Torpedo Boats (MTBs) or subchasers, a luxury not allotted to those operating in the interior of mid-Norway. While conducting air supply missions in Norway, dangers resulting from topographic and atmospheric conditions, as well as terrain, proved far greater than German air defenses. Over Denmark, the Low Countries, and partially over France, the pilots could come in low over the flat landscape and navigate with relative ease following recognizable landmarks such as rivers, lakes, and railway lines.

Over Norway, topography made low-level flight dangerous, if not impossible, and the mountain ranges and peaks could be difficult to see even on the brightest nights. Several of the flights were canceled or aborted due to bad and unstable weather and even claimed the lives of several Allied aircrews. These difficult conditions could in general be ascribed to the warm seawater of the Gulf Stream meeting the cold fronts from the Arctic. This results in a lot of precipitation and mist. Light conditions also proved problematic. Even if not above the Arctic Circle, from late April until early August the nights were so short it was not possible for a World War II heavy bomber to get in and out of Norwegian airspace under cover of darkness. The prospect of crossing the coastline, silhouetted against the sunset in the west and thus highly observable to enemy air defenses, was not very favorable. But Balchen's men did manage to fly four successful sorties north of 61 degrees latitude in the latter part of July in support of the Norwegian Resistance. From September to May, the nights were long enough for aircraft to enter and exit Norwegian airspace under cover of darkness. But then, weather frequently also made flying supply missions all but impossible, save for the most skilled and daring aircrews. Another problem with Arctic flying was that of icing on the aircraft's fuselage and wings. Rains and storms coming in from the Atlantic were prevalent along the western coast during the winter months. Inland, there would be low cloud cover due to the broken terrain, frequently covering the land surface completely. And of course, the snow would erase contours of landmarks and the curves of mountains, as well as making rivers and lakes hard to distinguish from the landscape surrounding them. Even further north, Norwegian Resistance groups were completely dependent on getting what weapons and supplies they needed via Sweden.

The Allies also complained that the maps available for Norway were inaccurate and contained insufficient details. Despite all the radio navigational devices developed during the war the obstacles of navigation over Norway were never fully overcome, resulting in a high percentage of unsuccessful sorties, especially for inexperienced crews. The great distances were also a challenge, leaving the margins of error perilously narrow. From bases in Scotland, there would be some 640 kilometers before the aircraft crossed the Norwegian coast, and flights of up to 2,400 kilometers were not uncommon. This meant cutting down on the payload to save fuel. In other words, the same quantity of supplies that could be delivered into Belgium by only one aircraft would require at least two to be delivered in Norway.[6] There is also the issue of magnetic deviation, which increases the further north you go. The compass points to the magnetic North Pole, not the geographical one. Over France this would not matter much, but over Snåsa, the deviation is significant. It is not stable over time—in 1940 it was -3 degrees, in 1945 it was -2.3 degrees. It was hard to calculate the deviation from take-off, as it would gradually increase during flight. Lack of landmarks, combined with shifting and unpredictable winds that made it difficult to assess speed and distance traveled, made it all but impossible to find a lake with a surface of 46 km^2 covered in snow after flying 1,216 km to some point in the middle of nowhere in Sweden, turning due north and flying a further 20 km north and into Norway.[7]

But air drops were not the only way to deliver cargo through the air. During the winter of 1944–45, Balchen's men flew supplies into Sweden as diplomatic pouch to prevent them from being searched and seized by Swedish authorities as they included weapons and explosives. The supplies were brought to the US Embassy in Stockholm into stores codenamed Twinkle. In the spring of 1945, weapons were also procured legally through the Swedish Army. The weapons were transported further overland to be allocated to the Norwegian sabotage groups with the Swedish police's and the Swedish State Department's tacit consent (Operation *Planet*) or flown to Kallax to be distributed into the areas evacuated by the Germans in Finnmark and Troms counties (Operation *Blizzard*). Containers were placed in hollow trees or logs and transported to the border by trucks, from there the supplies were taken over by skiers and sledges to the bases in Norway. Getting supplies through Sweden was complicated for political reasons, but from the beginning of 1943 Sweden's policy of neutrality was changing due to Nazi atrocities in occupied countries and because the tide of the war had turned in favor of the Allies. The Swedes had closed a zone along the border to foreigners, even though Norwegian saboteurs usually had a residence permit in Sweden, however, the American soldiers from Rype did not have this permit. Local officials might look the other way though when faced with the activities of Allied sabotage groups, but it required knowledge of who they were and an almost personal relationship between saboteurs and the officials in question for it to be exploited. And when clandestine activity became too obvious and ceased to be clandestine, Swedish authorities were forced to react—as happened when Helgesen was expelled after his group had arrested a Swedish policeman inside Sweden. (See Chapter 7 for the details of this incident.)

Though it was never said openly or put into reports, Colonel Balchen felt beyond any doubt that British were not interested in American interference in Scandinavia,[8] and at first the *Carpetbagger* missions were not even allowed to use the airport at Leuchars until after Balchen had brought the matter to the attention of the Foreign Minister of the Norwegian government-in-exile in London, Trygve Lie, of whom he was a personal friend, in March 1944. But it proved impossible even for the British not to recognize the contribution of the two strategic bomber squadrons in the logistics support of the resistance and clandestine operations in Europe, and the *Carpetbaggers* became an icebreaker that would lead to the reluctant recognition by the British of the Americans as a partner.[9] Two strategic bomber squadrons available for dropping supplies and agents into occupied Europe were also an important asset vis-à-vis the British SOE, when they offered General Donovan's SO Branch a merger into the joint SFHQ.[10]

Despite the British doctrine of dropping supplies on moonlit nights when aircraft could navigate by coastlines, waterways, and railway lines, about 60 percent of the US drops was either done in daylight or on nights without moonlight. Though the calculations were done by the navigator, the bombardier had perhaps the most exhausting task of keeping his eyes glued to the ground for large parts of the mission to keep track of known landmarks. A final check point would be reached 10–15 kilometers from the dropping spot, from which there would be a straight run. Descending to a drop zone (DZ) was especially nerve wracking, as the plane's speed was reduced to 200 km/h, running the risk of stalling or being hit by small arms fire. Then they descended from 10,000 feet down to 500–700 feet, and the pilot could never be certain whether they would crash into a hill. Although weather could be predicted, the urgency of operations was often such that the missions had to be attempted no matter the conditions, which would sometimes be quite unfavorable, adding to the danger. On their way, the aircrew had to look out for any sign that the DZ was compromised, such as lights of automobiles or any unusual activity, and if there was the slightest suspicion, the drop would be canceled.[11]

An OSS survey of the B-24 crews performing these missions revealed that most had no previous operational experience from ETO, and they were transferred directly from the USA to the 492nd Bomb Group. One of the most experienced crews, that of First Lieutenant George Bledsoe, with over 30 OSS missions to Norway, France, and Germany under their belt, was interviewed in depth in order to extract lessons learned. The main difference between flying bombing missions and covert ops, they revealed, was that the latter was a "lone wolf proposition," where the crew were responsible for planning and performing their own navigation, and as background intelligence, the OSS only provided the position for the drop and the areas in their path that were infested with flak. In regular bomber operations, the formation would follow the lead plane which contained the most skilled navigator of the unit. The crew differed on the perceived danger, and opinions varied from black ops being more dangerous to just as dangerous as normal bombing operations. But in dropping agents and supplies, the natural hazards were often more intimidating than enemy action. This was especially so in Norway, where they were "flying up and down the Fjords, sometimes below the level of the cliffs."[12]

In the cargo bay the dispatcher or the jump master, the enlisted man in charge of the drop, resided. It was his responsibility to look after the equipment to be dropped and to ensure that the static lines releasing the chutes were properly hooked up. He would also need to have a strong personality and good people skills as many agents had last-moment hesitations about jumping into the void and had to be talked back into line. Sometimes, agents froze at the edge of the hole and had to be "nudged out the door." However, if they actively resisted, verbally or physically, the jump would be aborted. This problem would sometimes also affect trained paratroopers, and one dispatcher commented that he thought that in many cases, the "j-hole" was opened too soon, and when he or she looked down on the countryside whistling by, many a jumper had second thoughts about what they were doing.[13] Once the cargo or agents were clear of the plane, the B-24 would immediately start to gain altitude. The rear gunner would have the best view and could tell if the chute had opened or not. According to the OSS records, in 1944, a total of 471 containers were packed for Norway, though it is uncertain whether *Carpetbagger* was responsible for all of them. A total of 154 sorties were flown, and 67.75 tons of supplies and 88 personnel were dropped.

CHAPTER SEVEN

SOE Operations Against the Nordland Railway

The Norwegians began forming a resistance almost immediately after the surrender on June 10, 1940. Weapons caches were hidden and discharged units kept in touch, expecting the fighting to be renewed at some stage. However, the first attempts at organizing a Norwegian Resistance proved there was no experience nor culture for clandestine work in Norway. Too many knew too much about the organizations they were part of. Many of the first leaders were former officers of the army, whose doors were the first the Germans came knocking on. With the help of Norwegian collaborators, the Germans had arrested most of their leaders by summer 1942. Especially in Central Norway, the resistance was hit hard, both because the Germans were particularly effective in the area which had a high priority due to its strategic significance, and because of the most ruthless and successful Norwegian collaborator, Henry Oliver Rinnan. With British help, the Norwegians learned how to organize the hard way, in small cells where few people knew anything about other cells. The motto was "Your first duty is silence." These lessons also explain why there was a lot of skepticism of liaisons between the resistance and Rype.

Resistance to the occupation in Norway was a fight for the soul of the Norwegian people. When the Germans arrived, they claimed to be friends that had come to help resist British pressure. German soldiers had strict instructions not to anger the Norwegian population by shouting orders to them. This sentiment originated with Nazi ideology and their perception of Norwegians as the purest of the "Aryan Race." In an effort to win over the Norwegians, the Nazis deployed their propaganda machine. With the help of their Norwegian Nazi puppets, the Nasjonal Samling (National Unity Party—NS), they hoped to spread their teachings and reorganize the country culturally and politically, just as they had done with Germany since 1933. Thus, civilian resistance was by far the most important in the early stages. The Germans banned all political parties except for the NS, independent newspapers, trade unions and sports associations, but few Norwegians accepted their substitutes. Especially hard "battles" were fought over the curriculum of the schools and the preaching of the Norwegian Lutheran Church. Despite deportations and threat of executions, the teachers managed to resist, and when the bishops and ministers were replaced by pro-Nazi ones, people just stopped going to mass.

By autumn 1942, the Germans had had enough. Following the confiscation of huge weapons stores where three German soldiers were killed in a shoot-out with resistance members at Majavatn in Nordland County, martial law was declared throughout large parts of central and northern Norway on October 6, 1942. A total of 34 people were executed, and others were arrested and sent to concentration camps as reprisals without having any connections to the resistance. At the same time, deportation of Norway's Jews began. Mounting resistance and sabotage in the occupied areas had made Hitler enact the infamous German "kommandobefehl"—"Commando Order"—on October 18, 1942. This said that all Allied agents and special forces operatives should be shot if captured after having been interrogated. This regardless of whether they wore uniform and otherwise conducted themselves according to the laws of land warfare. This major shift made resistance work and clandestine operations riskier and civilians less likely to be of assistance. Although the war was clearly coming to an end when Rype landed, this was the environment in which they would operate.

As the Norwegian Resistance formed, two main organizations evolved. SivOrg organized passive resistance to the German occupation. That included anything that would make the German administration of occupied Norway more difficult. They provided support for families of people arrested by the Germans, forged identification papers, sabotaged German requisitions, and organized illegal newspapers and other prints countering German propaganda. The military resistance was organized into MilOrg, which again set up district commands all over the country. However, due to the distance to the United Kingdom, resistance work in northern Norway was difficult. Especially in the northernmost county of Finnmark, many patriots gravitated towards the Soviet Union. Not necessary because they had Communist sympathies, but rather out of necessity. Unlike many other occupied countries, the Norwegian Resistance was disciplined and under control of the government in exile in London, whose legitimacy remained largely uncontested. MilOrg's main mission was being on standby in the event of a German withdrawal. It was expected that the occupational forces would employ scorched-earth tactics, and the resistance would secure vital infrastructure, stores and supplies to prevent these tactics from being executed.

Sabotage work in the form of blowing up railroads, factories and powerplants was mainly reserved for special forces of the Linge Company, named after their first commander Captain Martin Linge, who had been killed in Operation *Archery* in December 1941. These men had escaped Norway and were trained by the British under the command of the SOE. Towards the end of the war, some were also trained in Sweden. Their high degree of training heightened the chances of success and lessened the risk of collateral damage and unnecessary deaths. Among the most famous attacks performed by these men were the attacks on heavy water production to prevent Hitler from acquiring an atomic bomb (Operations *Grouse* and *Gunnerside*). On missions, they would always be in British uniform. After the enactment of the Commando Order, that would not prevent them from being shot by the Germans if caught. However, it proved to spare the local civilians from reprisals as it appeared that those performing the acts of sabotage came from Britain and were not locals. The discipline and restraint exercised by the Norwegian government in exile also included some basic principles for attacks on targets in Norway, either from the air or sabotage on the ground. The risk of civilian casualties, collateral damage or reprisals against the civilian population of any operation had to be justified by the goals they sought to achieve. By and large, the Allies abided by these principles.[1] However, holding back young men and women eager to participate in the fight proved difficult, and from the autumn of 1944, the Home Forces were allowed to take more part in sabotage missions.

Operation *Rype* was part of a larger sabotage offensive against railroads in Norway by the end of WWII. Groups under the leadership of the British SOE had already completed several acts of sabotage against Norwegian railways between October 1943 and March 1944 but, up until then, these had been restricted out of fear of German reprisals against Norwegian civilians. After SHAEF ordered an intensification of attacks on the railway network in Norway in the autumn of 1944, about 50 sabotage missions against the Norwegian railways under the auspices of the SOE were carried out between December 9, 1944, and April 29, 1945—the great majority under the collective name Operation *Concrete Mixer* in southeastern Norway. In a series of coordinated actions on March 14, Norwegian railway and port infrastructure was destroyed at 750 locations. Other important goals in the battle to cripple the German transport capacity in Norway were oil storage facilities and wood pellet factories (for wood gas generators). Groups that directed their operations against the railway network in mid- and northern Norway were Lapwing, Grebe, Fieldfare, Freethorpe, Lark, Woodpecker, Woodlark, Cramlington, Waxwing, and Coton. The last four, like Rype, targeted the Nordland Railway between Brekkvasselv River and Steinkjer, and operated January–May 1945. Because of that, they are important references to assess the conditions and the implementation of *Rype* and will be dealt with later in some detail.

The first of these attacks against the Nordland Railway was carried out by the Woodlark group made up by men from *Kompani Linge*, who originated from all over Norway. The group was led by Second Lieutenant Herbert Helgesen and belonged to the part of the group that was infiltrated by sea in September 1944. He would later play a crucial role in *Rype* too.

Herbert Helgesen was born in Trondheim in 1918. He became a butcher by trade. Before and after the war, he was active in the city's sporting community. Helgesen was familiar with the outdoors and raised sledge dogs. Due to an accident in his childhood that left him blind in his left eye, he was not accepted for military service before the war (Norway had conscription), however, he had some experience from the Leidangen, a government-sponsored paramilitary organization. When the Germans attacked Norway, he and his friend Johnny Pevik had just returned from a five-day skiing trip in the Snåsa Mountains in north Trøndelag. Helgesen volunteered with Infantry Regiment 14, and, as a driver, saw action both in Trøndelag and around Narvik. After the Norwegian surrender, Helgesen got involved in the Norwegian Resistance, probably from the summer of 1940, and he was central in the MilOrg in Trøndelag. His family's butcher's shop was appropriated by the Germans while they still ran it, and Helgesen made sure that some of the meat intended for occupants was handed over to the resistance. Helgesen was the liaison between MilOrg and those loyal in Trondheim police. He joined the resistance group Lark and escaped to Sweden in late 1942 to early 1943 after the Gestapo blew his group's cover. His wife Anna Elisabeth died tragically as she crossed the border mountains with other refugees in 1943. The loss of his childhood friend Johnny Pevik at the hands of Gestapo torturists was another heavy personal blow. Despite personal problems that could have incapacitated the best of people, he carried on his work for the resistance. Helgesen crossed back to Norway several times, and together with Johnny's brother Arthur Pevik, he made an attempt at assassinating the infamous collaborator Henry Oliver Rinnan, who had built up a whole organization to help the Germans infiltrate the resistance. Helgesen's experience with the resistance is too extensive to elaborate on in full but in February 1944 he made a dramatic journey from Sweden to England aboard the British gunboat HMS *Nonsuch*. In April 1944, he was inducted to the famous *Kompani Linge*. In a roster completed by Lieutenant Colonel Bolland after the war, Helgesen is listed as S-2 (intelligence officer). Helgesen died in 1981.

On September 12, 1944, Helgesen, together with Ole Valderhaug and Oddvar Østgaard, landed in Jøssundfjorden in Flatanger. They crossed the mountains to Steinkjer and hid their equipment near Stod Church, north of the town. In Engdal they met resistance fighter Harald Larsen from Steinkjer, who helped to transport the equipment to Sveet Farm. The four of them then went east up the mountain to Gomolia to establish a base there, where they would fuse with the other half of the team being infiltrated from Sweden. Larsen had gathered a group comprising Agnar Andersen, Jon Moan, and Ludvik Kruksve, all of whom would end up with *Rype* too.

Harald Larsen was one of the driving forces behind the resistance in his native Steinkjer area. Before the war he had been a regimental tailor with the Norwegian 13th Infantry Regiment, earning him the nickname "Schneideren"—meaning the tailor in pidgin German. As with many resistance fighters, he began his career as a courier; he worked especially in the Ongdal and Skjækerfjella areas. Larsen had also worked as a guide with the SOE group Lark. The 28-year-old was arrested on February 27, 1943—due to Henry Oliver Rinnan's activities—and incarcerated at Vollan Prison in Trondheim. On July 12, 1943, he was sent to Falstad Prison Camp. His comrade Knut Sand had managed to get hold of a pair of pliers and together they managed to cut through the fence, and they escaped on July 20. Larsen never got to the UK for training there, but arrived in Stockholm on December 18, 1943, and received sabotage training (probably the SOE course at Ählby). Larsen returned to Norway in September 1944, to go into the Skjækerfjella Mountains to organize a resistance cell there. Colby was especially fond of Larsen and expressed the view that without him the attack on Tangen Bridge would have been more difficult, if not impossible to execute. After the war, Colby even recommended Larsen for the Silver Star, which was not awarded. In addition to his skiing skills, Larsen had a physical capacity that enabled him to carry more than his weight. He was easygoing, emotionally stable, and disciplined, as well as an experienced woodsman.[2] He would later serve as "acting soldier," the status given to resistance fighters who had not received full training in the UK, whereas in Bolland's postwar roster for Rype Harald Larsen is listed as "attached" to the HQ.

Agnar Andersen began working on the National Railway in 1940, at the age of 22 as an apprentice engine driver. In February 1943, he was asked by the Norwegian Legation in Stockholm to take part in the important courier traffic between Sweden and the resistance in Norway, as his line of work took him to the border and the employees of the railway were hardly ever checked by the Germans, not even for papers. Herbert Helgesen, who was his recruiter, noted that he did not hesitate to accept this risky mission. Secret messages were carried in the lining of uniforms or in lunch boxes. But in February 1944, he was warned that his contact in Trondheim had been arrested by the Germans and he escaped to Sweden. Andersen had gotten married in 1942 and had to leave his wife and little daughter behind when he fled. Agnar Andersen joined the "police troops," but soon received sabotage training as well. After Agnar Andersen fled to Sweden, his wife moved in with her sister. His wife was soon dragged in for interrogation by the Norwegian Nazi State police, but she did not know where her husband was and could not reveal anything about the missions he took part in. Agnar's detailed knowledge on the railway, its hardware and routines would prove useful both for *Woodlark* and *Rype.*

In Sweden, Andersen was transferred to a camp where he was trained in sabotage techniques, most probably the so-called "Linge Light" training at the SOE school at Ählby outside Stockholm. Helgesen described Agnar Andersen as capable, brave, disciplined, and unrelenting. He was also observant and had a good memory. Andersen was sent to join *Woodlark* in November. As later with *Rype*, his intimate knowledge of the railway was invaluable, but he hurt his hand and ended up at a hospital in Östersund, Sweden, therefore he missed the demolition of Jørstad Bridge. Andersen took part in the reception of NORSO and later remembered the Americans with fondness. Andersen took part in both of *Rype*'s attacks and continued to serve up to the fall of 1945, when he returned to work for the railway.[3]

Ludvik Kruksve was born in 1918 and grew up on a smallholding in Leksvik by Trondheim's fjord. During the campaign in 1940, he fought at Narvik. Together with

Jon Moan he helped numerous Jews, Russians, and Serbs as well as Norwegians escape from the clutches of the Nazis. His career in the resistance began when a Jewish mother and her four-year-old daughter knocked on the door of the Moan family's farm. Together with Jon, Jon's younger brother Kristoffer, and some other friends, Ludvik escorted them from Leksvik to cross the Swedish border in December 1942, a trip of 131 kilometers. During the German crackdown on the Norwegian Resistance, known as Operation *Oleander*, in the Fosen region—across the fjord from Trondheim—Ludvik, Jon, Jon's elder brother Johan, and sister Borghild fled to Sweden. Ludvik also received the so-called "Linge Light" training at the SOE school at Ählby. In September 1944, he returned to Norway and joined Woodlark, and took part in the attack on Jørstad Bridge on January 13, 1945. Helgesen, in his recommendation for an award, described Kruksve as self-sufficient, never refusing any task or mission he was asked to perform, and as "absolutely reliable, easy going, brave and dauntless." Kruksve was a woodsman and an excellent skier and shot, having practically grown up in the Norwegian outback. After the war, Ludvik married Jon's sister Borghild and continued his humble way of life as a farmer, lumberjack, and road worker. He was awarded the St. Olaf's Medal with Oakleaves.

Jon Moan was also born in Leksvik, in 1919. As Ludvik Kruksve's close friend, they shared many of the same experiences. In his commendation, Helgesen lauded Moan for having shown righteous conduct throughout the war, with great efforts for the national cause. Further, he was confident, easy going, calm, and a terrific shot.[4] He too took part in the shepherding of refugees across the border to Sweden. In the winter of 1943/44, he hid four Russians in a cabin, keeping them fed. In the end, Jon himself had to flee after the infiltration by a Nazi collaborator named Karl Adding, who had been a childhood friend of his and Kruksve's. In Sweden, Moan entered the training program at Ählby, where he was headhunted for Woodlark by Harald Larsen. In Colby's reports from the field, he mostly referred to Moan as "Jens Leksvik"—his wartime cover name. After the war, Moan started a dairy, while he continued his service with the military as an area commander (*områdesjef*)—a captain's position—in the Norwegian Home Guard (*Heimevernet*) that was established after World War II. Moan died in 2011.

Helgesen felt that Woodlark's first base at Gomolia, was unsafe so they moved to Burvatnet, some 150 meters into Swedish territory. Østgaard objected to this move because he felt it was wrong to move so far from the railway, and this disagreement was to be the start of a long and conflicted relationship between the two men that would badly affect the group's ability to operate. At Burvatnet they occupied the hunting cabin of a Swedish shipping magnate named G. Dahlmann, a resident of Goteborg, with permission from his ground supervisor Svein Andersson. There was some discussion on whether they should rent it officially, but the conclusion was that it was an unnecessary risk, no matter how favorably disposed Dahlmann might be, as they reckoned they would to be able to stay without interference throughout winter.[5] Helgesen on his part argued that there was reason to believe that Swedish troops would patrol the area south to Gaundalen, implying that it would be a mistake to occupy the lodge without permission if they were detected.[6]

Woodlark's initial mission was to train Norwegian Resistance fighters, as well as to reconnoiter DZs for reinforcements and material. Detailed plans were made for week-long courses for recruits. They would have preferred to billet 25 men permanently at the base but doubted that it would be possible to supply that many men at the base.[7] As SHAEF's policy on large-scale railway sabotage in Norway changed, *Woodlark* received amendment to their orders on October 26, 1944, adding attacks on the Nordland Railway to their portfolio. That Woodlark had received orders to sabotage the railway was first mentioned in an outgoing report dated December 20, 1944. This order must have come just a few days after the Germans launched the Ardennes Offensive on December 16, heightening the fear of a prolonged war if occupational troops could be sent from Norway as reinforcements to the troops on the Continent.

Grana Bridge in Snåsa was the most lucrative target, an intricate trade network construction that would take a long time and a lot of resources for the Germans to repair. Early plans also included blowing up the railway line in a tunnel to force a derailment inside, which would have caused major damage and made any rescue work very cumbersome and precarious. But all plans had to be approved by London. In October 1944, Oddvar Østgaard and Agnar Andersen reconnoitered a stretch of railway line from just north of Grong down to Snåsa as part of the selection of targets for the forthcoming operations, a distance of about 50 kilometers. Here, Andersen's special knowledge of the railway came in handy, and it was probably on this expedition that he even entered one of the heavily guarded locomotive sheds at Grong. They also made detailed investigations of the security measures around Grana Bridge and noticed that there were barbed wire barriers and Germans in the area, but there did not seem to be a permanent guard post there at that time.

However, the supply situation for Woodlark worsened. The group waited 24 nights for an airdrop that did not materialize. They tried to augment their provisions by hunting, but the area was full of Germans and Norwegian Nazis, who hunted in the border mountains. The harvest had also been poor in the fall of 1944, and the local population had little to offer.[8] Some reindeer were shot to supplement their diet, which led to friction with the local Sámi. They finally had to buy supplies in Sweden, and even explosives had to be obtained from Stockholm. During one of the transport runs, Helgesen, Valderhaug, and the new addition to the group, Erik Gaundal, were apprehended by a Swedish border guard and arrested with explosives in their backpacks. They were released after intervention from the Norwegian Diplomatic Legation in Stockholm. The group also received assistance from Swedish nationals, such as police officer Bergström and Mrs. Hildur Hoberg in Järpen. Woodlark members had a residence permit in Sweden, but the border zone was off limits to all foreigners, so such connections were useful. In one incident, Østgaard, who did not have a proper permit, was arrested with Jon Moan. On their way to the refugees' reception area, they managed to jump off the truck, put on their skis, and head back to the base.

Before they executed the attack on Jørstad Bridge, Woodlark received further reinforcements in the form of an additional signaler, Yves Øgaard, as well as Georg Løkkeberg, Jørgen Havig, and Robert Andersen. The latter two would also serve with Rype.

Robert Andersen was born near Halden in southern Norway. He was arrested by the Germans on December 29, 1941, and spent seven months in the notorious Grini Prison Camp. After his release, Andersen became engaged in escorting refugees to Sweden and found his way into the MilOrg through his local sports club, Gimle. He also had a day job at a ceramic factory. In the summer of 1944, the Germans busted his group and he had to flee to Sweden. He was trained at Åhlby from September 24 to November 1, 1944, and attended an advanced course at Skjeberg (also in Sweden) from November 2 to December 15. Andersen then joined Woodlark and took part in the demolition of Jørstad Bridge. Andersen continued to serve in the Norwegian forces until June 1945 and later joined the police force in Trondheim. For his efforts, Andersen was awarded the US Medal of Freedom. In his certificate for Robert Andersen, Colby wrote:

> This is to certify that ROBERT ANDERSEN of Halden, Norway served as a member of this unit from 8 April to 15 June 1945. His experience in living and working in the mountains of North Trøndelag was of invaluable assistance to this unit in the accomplishment of its mission. No effort was ever too great for him to make if it would assist the unit in its task or make the labor of its members easier. Though without special military training, ROBERT ANDERSEN showed himself the equal to the regular American troops in courage, resourcefulness, and discipline. This certificate is intended to commend ROBERT ANDERSEN for his extremely arduous but excellently performed work for the liberation of Norway. It is also intended to express, in the name of the Army of the United States of America, the deep appreciation felt by every officer and man of this unit for the invaluable assistance given to them by him.[9]

Herbert Helgesen also wrote Andersen a most favorable recommendation, describing him as being of great physical strength and ready to ease the burden of others, as well as being brave, emotionally stable, and level-headed. He was not among the greatest skiers, although that did not stop him from keeping up with the rest.

Johannes Havig was born in Trondheim in 1918. He was a graduate of the Norwegian Artillery Officer School before the war. His name is not mentioned in any American report, but he is frequently named as part of *Rype* in Norwegian sources. He escaped to Sweden, but returned to join Woodlark in November 1944, thus sacrificing the career opportunities in the Free Norwegian Forces in exile for a meager existence in the mountains as a resistance fighter. During the approach march for the attack on Jørstad Bridge, Havig became sick and had to turn back.

According to Helgesen, he then took part in the Lurudal attack, and Colby wanted him more closely attached to *Rype*. In his commendation, Helgesen described Havig as full of initiative, knowledgeable, and always ready to assist.[10] After the war, he continued his career in the military and rose to the rank of colonel in the Royal Norwegian Air Force. He died in 1997.

The radio connection with London varied due to atmospheric conditions, and it was also necessary to have a courier service with the Norwegian Legation for longer dispatches. A model of the Grana Bridge was made for *Woodlark* to assist in the planning of the attack on it. Allied intelligence had done meticulous work in mapping the Norwegian railway network, and the Inter-Service Topographical Department presented a dossier in May 1944 on the Nordland and Meråker lines. It included data on sidings, gradients, curves, and detailed description of bridges. It even included photographs from several station areas that would be heavily guarded by the Germans. The report listed Grana as one of eight "principal" bridges on the Nordland and Meråker lines. The bridge was 114 meters long, supported by six pillars. At most, it stood 30 meters above the river that ran through the valley floor.[11] The mission was reviewed and practiced on down-to-the-minute details. The plan was to attack on Christmas Eve, but mild weather and a flood made the execution of the plan impossible. On December 30, they headed out to make a new attempt, but turned back after 5 kilometers because of broken skis. On New Year's Day they tried again but the heavy backpacks were too much even for trained skiers. In the evening, a blizzard brewed, and the snow was loose and heavy. One of the men also called in sick. The next stage was to cross the road and they started in the evening to be able to exploit the cover of darkness. They planned to attack the bridge at midnight. But weather conditions had deteriorated even further and at midnight between January 2 and 3, they were still so far away from the target that they had no hope of reaching it before dawn. The leader of the group, then Second Lieutenant Helgesen, chose to cancel the attack, but Valderhaug and Øgaard protested. They threatened to report Helgesen for what they regarded as insubordination and demanded that he should resign as leader of the group. Another argument to call off the attack was that with an additional stop and delays, the chances were that the ski tracks they had already made would reveal that an action was underway before they were able to get away or even launch the attack. Considering also that the Germans had beefed up security around the Grana Bridge, it is doubtful whether the operation would have been successful anyway. They were 12 men, but only armed with three carbines, five Sten sub-machine guns and three Colt pistols, and it is highly unlikely that they would have succeeded in defeating a well-entrenched guard force around the bridge. On the way back to base, the unused explosives were hidden away in a shieling while Valderhaug and Øgaard went to Stockholm to file their complaint against Helgesen.

The morale within Woodlark was low at this point but future events would soon solve the personnel problems. After they returned to the Burvatnet, Jon Moan was sent out on reconnaissance to find out if their movements had been detected. He saw no one but discovered unknown ski tracks near the cabin. They went out to investigate and ran into a Swedish soldier and a state policeman. The Swedes had picked up their radio communications and sent a patrol to investigate. The two Swedes were captured by the Norwegians, but since they were inside Swedish territory, they found it best to switch roles and surrender to the Swedes instead. Only Helgesen was taken in for questioning right away. He was later expelled from Sweden and put on a plane to the United Kingdom. Jon Moan promised to go in for questioning later. The incident showed that there were limits to Swedish patience even this late in the war.

Østgaard now assumed command of the group. They got the go-ahead from London to carry out attacks against targets other than Grana Bridge. The top five skiers were picked for the task, after the lessons learned from the previous attempts when they had to turn around because of the difficult snow conditions. The five were Harald Larsen, Jon Moan, Ludvik Kruksve, Robert Andersen, plus Oddvar Østgaard himself. The target was changed to Jørstad Bridge, as they now knew Grana Bridge was too well guarded. Jørstad Bridge is 30 meters long and 5 meters high, a smaller but more accessible prize. The just-over-50-kilometer-long ski march from Burvatnet passed without drama, except that Harald Larsen broke his skis and had to repair them. They found the explosives where they had hidden them after the previous attempt and stayed overnight at Kjendstadsetera.

On the evening of January 12, they were in position at the bridge span. They made a reconnaissance and secured the area, but no Germans were to be seen. Four men began to place charges on the steel girders while the remaining one stood guard. But it was hard work in the cold. The first thing they had to do was to knock the ice off the beams, and while they were at it, two trains passed by. Both times, the charges became loose, and they had to start all over again. After two to three hours, the charges were all placed, using tape and twigs. Originally, they were going to use time pencils, but they were too unreliable in the cold and took a lot longer to burn. Luckily, they were provided with a traditional fuse along with the explosives, although it was a bit too short for comfort. The others withdrew before Østgaard lit it. At about 02:30, the charges went off. Fragments from the bridge flew around them and it was a miracle that no one was injured in the explosion. Jørstad Bridge was completely destroyed, its elements crashing into the river below. As the team moved out, they left some British effects to show that this had been done by soldiers under Allied command to reduce the risk of the local population being subjected to German reprisals. The retreat was without event and there were no signs that anyone had followed in pursuit.

But the drama had not yet reached its peak. Back at the base, they learned of the effects of their mission over Swedish radio. For one reason or another, a train that had left Grong Station at 06:10 had not been notified that Jørstad Bridge had been blown up. The train consisted of 31 cars weighing a total of 370 tons, with over 170 Germans aboard. In addition, there were nearly 50 horses, plus tanks, vehicles, and other materials. All the staff manning the train were Norwegian. It had passed Jørstad Station at approximately 08:20 and just after, the locomotive and the front 17 carriages drove straight down into the river at a speed of approximately 60 km/h. Smoke rose from the wreck, wounded soldiers and horses were everywhere—several had to be cut loose from wreckage with a blowtorch, while others had ended up in the icy river water and were hypothermic. A member of the Norwegian staff made his way to a farm and called Jørstad Station and told them what had happened. The ensuing rescue work was chaotic, but both civilian Norwegians and Germans helped to get the wounded out, and a medical train arrived from Trondheim at 16:20.

The final tally was 78 German soldiers killed, about 100 wounded, and 48 horses died either in the actual accident or were put out of their misery afterwards. The Norwegian locomotive driver and stoker also died. In addition, a local Norwegian was killed during the rescue. The event remains the worst train accident in Norwegian railway history. German mountain troops and the Norwegian State Police were dispatched on a search but failed to find the saboteurs. The local population was interrogated. However, the Germans appeared to be more concerned with how the train had not been notified of the demolition than with who had executed the sabotage. Many people must have heard the explosion, but no one had notified the Germans or the public Norwegian Railways, NSB. Few sources are available from the NSB or the Germans covering the incident—most are said to have been removed just before the liberation. But the Germans seem to have been at a loss about what had happened—whether the train had triggered the explosion or whether it had taken place on board the train. Pioneer units, Russian POWs, and Norwegians worked strenuously to build a new connection across the river. The evening after the attack, a footbridge was constructed so that personnel could walk between trains on either side of the break. A new track was constructed parallel to the existing one, across a makeshift bridge, and on January 19, the first train could roll over, but it is uncertain what weight limitations the repairs had. The Germans were naturally furious. *Reichskommissar* Joseph Terboven, the top Nazi bureaucrat in Norway, demanded that 10,000 Norwegians be executed in revenge, but this did not get approval in Berlin.

After the attack, Moan dutifully turned himself in to the Swedes, as promised. Courier traffic to the base at Burvatnet was halted for a while. Moan was not allowed to return, but neither would the Swedes send patrols towards Burvatnet. The Swedish attitude was apparently that they accepted that the Norwegians used bases in Swedish territory, provided the required discretion was observed. At the same time, the Norwegian and Swedish governments negotiated the establishment of Norwegian weapons depots on Swedish territory, but an agreement was not arrived at before April 21. According to a report by an SOE psychological operations (PSYOPS) group called Durham, led by Second Lieutenant Erik Gjems-Onstad, the Norwegian civilian population initially rejoiced at the casualties that had been inflicted upon the Germans but, on second thoughts, they regretted that Norwegian lives had also been lost, questioning if the attack had been worth the sacrifice. Thirdly, they were even more worried that similar actions in the future would provoke German reprisals. The report concluded laconically that while people were welcoming sabotage, and felt the more they hurt the Germans the better, they would not like to be involved.[12]

There were also other groups attacking the Nordland Railway. On January 6, 12 men from *Kompani Linge* formed special operations group Coton. Five of the members had roots in Helgeland in northern Norway, close to their AO. Lieutenant Arne Hægstad, their leader, was from Drammen in the south of the country. He already had the attacks against the Thamshavn Railway in 1942 under his belt. On January 9, they arrived at the Atostugan, a disused Sámi school just across the Swedish border from Hattfjelldal. After they established themselves, they had to heat the building for several days before the plastic explosives could be shaped into the railway charges. The building was also located so far north and far from bases in the United Kingdom that air supply was out of the question, so everything they needed had to be smuggled in from Sweden.

On January 11, Johan Simskar and Lorentz Langaas, Coton's second in command, skied from Majavatn across the border to conduct reconnaissance against the Holmvassåsen Bridge that crosses the Vefsna River. They crossed Børgefjell Mountain Massif at Orrvatnet and spent the night in a hunting lodge at Vapstjärn, whose Swedish owner placed the facilities at *Coton*'s disposal. In the Remdalen, still on the Swedish side, they met with wolf hunter Johan Walfrid Enochson, who advised them not to cross the mountain at night. They therefore took to the Tjokkola fjällstuga cabin for the night—it would not be an easy march the next day. It had rained in the mountains around Christmas and the slopes were icy. On January 14, they reached the bridge, but did not find it worthwhile to blow it up, probably because it would not cost the Germans much of an effort to repair it. On their way back to the Atostugan, they went by Enochson's cabin, and he agreed that they could use it in the future as a forward base for storage of explosives and rations. On January 17, they were back at Ato.

For the next attack, they had chosen a stretch of railway line north of Majavatn and Sefrivatn Station where the line curved. By attacking there, they reasoned that it would take longer to repair the damage since the rails had to be custom-made to fit the curve. They were going to place the charges a ½-meter from the joints of each rail. One man would secure the area while the others placed the charges. The charges were split up before they moved out and the plan was to lock the charges into the profile of the rails with tree branches.

On March 1, they received orders to meet in Stockholm to pick up weapons and equipment. Eight days later, Trygve Brunsell visited the Norwegian Legation and met an engineer who had the drawing of the Trolldalen Valley Viaduct, north of Trofors, that was supposed to be the group's primary target. Brunsell was commissioned to calculate the size of the charges. When they returned to Ato, Coton were all together for the first time, and consisted of Arne Hægstad, Lorentz Langaas, Arthur Gundersen, Aamund Salveson, Svein Losnegård, Lorange Sandin, Alf Andersen, Johnny Hansen, Odd Dyrnes, Trygve Brunsell, Sverre Pedersen, Ole Moen, Gunnar Nordahl, and Johan Simskaret. The explosives were stored in a *goahti* (sod house—a cabin made of earth and timbers) located about 20 meters from the schoolhouse. With the help of the drawings Brunsell had made, a wooden model of three columns on the bridge was made. From this, they calculated the size and shape of the charges and the length of the fuses. Brunsell gave the following description of how the charges were rigged:

> A detonator and the pull switch igniter was attached at each end of two black powder fuses. These were bound together and were going to light up and burn at the same time to each blast cap, which gave double security for a good result. In the same execution they had two detonating fuses that would go from the black powder fuses and terminating in the pre charges (aut. transl.).[13]

On March 15–16, they went over the equipment and explosives. It was carefully considered how much they could take in terms of weight. The weapons were light, US carbine and Colt pistols. Provisions were wrapped in canvas bags—they took oatmeal, half a loaf of bread, soup powder, dried milk, sugar, and packs of Kreyberg rations. The latter was a form of field ration developed for Norwegian special forces in World War II, which consisted of boiled macerated sheep meat. For the preparation of food and melting snow for water, they carried a spirit burner and a liter of spirits. They were careful in the selection of apparel, ensuring it was clean and nicely packed in sacks. Ski wax, shoe polish, and laces were also emphasized. Ski poles and skis were painted white, and the men wore snow camouflage from head to toe. The skis were wide, to be able to carry the weight of men with loads of 30 kilograms. Their skis had steel edges and sturdy Kandahar bindings "important for the time of year," probably considering the snow crust because the sun was starting to get warmer. During the march, the US carbines were placed on the backpacks along with a sleeping bag. Nordahl had, however, a longer sniper rifle (probably an M/1903 Springfield) and experienced some trouble when they skied through bushes and scrub.

Coton was split up into three groups, a demolition team and two teams that would defeat the guard force that was expected to outnumber them at the bridge. On March 18 at 04:00, they set out for the attack. Lorange was left at the base, so they were 13 in all. The ascent towards the border was heavy going, but they crossed into Norway at 06:15. For many of them, it was the first time they had been in their home country for years. The terrain was probably not much different than what it was on the Swedish side, but emotionally it was a different world.

They remained at high altitude, away from settlements—there was not a soul in sight and not a sound other than that which the skis made as they slid through the crust. At night they passed the Røsvatn, where they made their ski tracks crisscross to confuse any stalkers. At 05:00 on the night of March 19, they went forward to a cabin. They had traveled 65 kilometers since they started. It turned into a long rest, and they did not start again until 15:00. Just after that, they happened upon a young man out hunting. They asked to see his border pass, noted his name, and said that it would have consequences if he told anyone that he had met them. But the going had become wet, and progress was slow that day. After having spent the night in two barns near Heringbotn, they started again at 05:30. But going was still wet and heavy. The next day progress improved. They approached Liaseter, from where they were to deploy in front of the attack. They were just 3 kilometers from the populated area and could hear the train when it passed, and German trucks on the main road. This meant that they had to keep quiet and not use any heat sources. They arranged security, reconnoitered escape routes, and went through the attack plan. On March 22, it was snowing in the morning, turning into rain throughout the day, so the attack was postponed. It was no better the next day. Reconnaissance revealed that the ice had broken up on the Svenningdal River in front of them. They could not reach the target, and with heavy hearts they decided to cancel the attack and hide away the explosives. Late in the evening, on March 25, they were back at the base.

From Stockholm, they got a new mission—they were to blow up the tracks of the Nordland Railway. Brunsell prepared 70 charges of plastic explosives and was careful to sculpt them so they would provide maximum effect. Each man would carry 10 charges. They had, however, clear instructions not to cause any loss of Norwegian life. At the same time, they listened to radio broadcasts and knew that the war was nearing its end. On April 12, the group was briefed. In the morning of the next day, they went on to reconnoiter, and access to local knowledge of Salveson came in handy. Just before they were due to go, five Norwegian refugees came to the base, two women, two men, and a small child. They gave them food and coffee and the clear message that they had not seen them. At 07:00 on April 15, Langaas, Losnegård, Nordahl, Andersen, and Brunsell started out for Majavatn. The going was relatively good to begin with, but in the middle of the day it thawed and became hard. The next day they did not head out until 09:30 when it was snowing heavily, and everybody was under the weather from illness. They only made 16 kilometers that day. On April 17 they reached Enochson's cabin, just 5 kilometers from the border where they could stay overnight and leave provisions for the return journey. Losnegård had become snow blind, and the operation's fate was in the balance. The next day Andersen, Nordahl, and Brunsell skied towards Børgefjell with the charges to make the trip the day after easier. But they did not get far before the weather turned so bad that they had to turn back after having buried the explosives. Losnegård recovered sufficiently from his snow blindness so they could continue at 07:30 the next morning.

The route around Børgefjell Mountain was tough. They picked up the hidden charges, and their rucksacks now weighed more than 35 kilograms. On April 21 they were finally approaching the target. They came around a mountain and were just 3 kilometers from the main road and could see the German barracks below. It was Saturday night, and the sound of the festivities could clearly be heard. At 22:20 they separated into two teams. Team North—Salveson, Andersen, and Nordahl—turned northwest while Langaas, Losnegård, Simskaret, and Brunsell went south. In the moonlight and with the crusted snow, it was difficult not to be noticed. Along the railway line, the background was dark, so they took off their camo suits and skis. The charges were fitted with primers and fuses before they moved down to the line. The team split yet again—Langaas and Losnegård went south, while Brunsell and Simskaret went even further north. When Brunsell had three charges left, Simskaret ran the up the hill to secure the area. At 01:00 they began pulling the pencil fuses. Soon a cacophony of explosions rang out through the valley. In total 65 charges went off, destroying 1,600 meters of rails. In Team North, Salveson was thrown backwards down a slope when one charge went off as he stood bent over it—miraculously his only injury was a burst eardrum. The return trip was uneventful, but exhausting. Around 14:00, on April 23, they were back at Atostugan. The trip had lasted for 11 days and they had covered a total of 310 kilometers. At the beginning of May, Coton prepared another 70 charges for the next attack, but peace beat them to it. They celebrated by blowing up the remaining charges and, as a result, they got a call from the nearest Swedish military camp where they wondered if they were under attack.

About New Year 1944/45, rumors circulated in mid-Norway about a large-scale Allied operation that would cut Norway in half. This rumor was mainly connected to a group named Waxwing. A total of 200 men from the Norwegian Brigade in Scotland, complemented by police troops from Sweden, was supposed to be sent in to occupy Røyrvik Municipality prior to a general liberation of Norway. The rumors also said that British companies were going to be sent in. *Rype*'s Field Order No. 2 listed Waxwing's number at 40 men. The operation, however, was restricted to blowing up Nordland Railway at two locations in the Majavatn–Namskogan area, as well as a telephone signal amplifier and railway switch at Namskogan Station. Operation *Waxwing* was planned much in parallel with *Rype* and is mentioned in some of the documents that related to the American operation.[14] It was first proposed in October/November 1944 but shelved because of lack of air transport. But as the execution of *Rype* was proposed at a conference, this operation was again put on the table by Major Jens H. T. Nordlie in a letter to the second in command of the Norwegian Armed Forces, General Wilhelm von Tangen Hansteen.[15] Nordlie had actually been member of the Norwegian Fascist Party, *Nasjonal Samling*, before the war, and it is fair to assume that he harbored some skepticism against allowing the Anglo-Saxon powers to operate independently on the ground in Norway.[16] There is also reason to believe that *Waxwing* was launched as a counterweight to *Rype*. Two copies of the letter were made and, for some reason, one of them ended up in the OSS archives. Nordlie recognized the weakness of the resistance north of Trondheim and wanted to alleviate this by using paratroopers and the police force from Sweden to assert Norwegian sovereignty when the Germans surrendered.

The AO outlined by Nordli was the stretch of railway between Grong and Majavatn, which is immediately north of the original AO for *Rype*. The group was put under control of SFHQ and commanded by Major Ole Jacob Bangstad (1917–2010). Born in Harstad in northern Norway, he had attended the Norwegian Military Academy before the war, became a lieutenant in 1939, and had commanded an infantry company in Trøndelag and northern Norway during the 1940 campaign. Bangstad commanded the Parachute Company of the Norwegian Brigade in Scotland from 1943–1945. He continued his military career after the war, rose to Major General in 1966 and headed the Military Academy, Norway's Southern Command, and was Inspector General of the Norwegian Home Guard and of the Army at the time of his retirement in 1979.

The Norwegian Army Brigade in Scotland did not see action as a unit, something that almost led to mutiny on one occasion and many members sought service elsewhere. The Parachute Company was activated on April 25, 1942. The company received "independent" status in June 1943. Besides Operation *Waxwing*, men from the Parachute Company also saw action during operations on Svalbard (*Alvsjo I* and *II* and *Gearbox*). Units from the company also acted as vanguard UK air and land forces that arrived in Stavanger and Oslo on May 10, 1945.

The intelligence basis for Waxwing was extensive. All the bridges and roads on the stretch Grong–Majavatn, as well as water stations, were accounted for. Cabins and other accommodations that could be used as a "safe house" for the force were also surveyed. The village of Grong was carefully described, as well as a German armored train that operated in the area. Attitudes of individual civilians were also recorded, whether they were collaborators or friendly to the resistance. Potential base areas that were mentioned were Gjersvika and Skorovass. The number of men to be accommodated ranged up to 600–700, however, once it got underway, the scale of the operation was downsized to a small sabotage party. The target considered was the railway bridge at Fossland in Grong, but that was found to be too well guarded. Another group named Cramlington had previously been ordered to blow up the railway bridge at Brekkvasselv in Namskogan. This consisted of leader Second Lieutenant Ryen; second in command Second Lieutenant Hansen, Second Lieutenant Kvarme, and Sergeant Øgo. Ryen had flown to Stockholm where the rest of the group joined him. As they were leaving for Norway on January 22, Swedish law enforcement stopped them, and their equipment was seized. After the loss of supplies and equipment, they were redirected to Orrvatnet on February 22 where they would later make up the reception party for Waxwing.

On the afternoon of March 24, in parallel with Rype, Waxwing boarded three Short Stirling bombers. A fourth aircraft of the same type carried equipment containers. In addition to Major Bangstad, the group consisted of Lieutenant Knut Sand as second in command, Second Lieutenant Hafstad, Sergeant Lund Simensen, Corporals Larsen, Aanonby, Kvarfordt, Bredesen, Gotvassli, and Block, and the medic, Lieutenant Sanderud. Sanderud had almost finished medical school and was not part of the company, but Bangstad had insisted that he should be in the team. Their signaler was Lieutenant Hellberg. A little before midnight, the first plane arrived over the DZ at Børgefjell. On the ground was the reception party led by Second Lieutenant Ryen, and *Cramlington* was placed under *Waxwing*. The Norwegian courier Per Ørnulf Øien was also ordered to Orrvatnet to assist in the reception. In all, 85 parachutes with equipment and personnel were released, all landing within a 5×100 meter square. With *Cramlington* added, *Waxwing* now constituted 16 men.

The security situation, however, was uncertain. A group of Swedish reindeer-herding Sámi was passing through the area, but they probably did not detect the tents and the tracks after the drop. Waxwing had specific orders to avoid contact with the local resistance movement. The danger of infiltration was regarded as especially high in Trøndelag, probably because of the activities of the infamous Rinnan Gang. The temperature was another challenge; at night it could drop to 20 degrees Celsius below zero, while at noon it would rise to around zero—so the snow melted, and equipment and clothing were soaked. This would then all freeze at night. The base at Orrvatnet was established in a valley to reduce visibility, with tents and snow huts to receive the rest of the company. On an island on Orrvatnet they placed a guard post that had a good view to the west and the most probable approach routes for German patrols. The composition of the supplies dropped with Waxwing is either a testimony to chaotic support, or that the intention of the operations was something more than "just" blowing up the railway. They had received plastic explosives in bulk but no primers or fuses. Yet, at the same time, they had also received 100 guns and food in five containers, the latter probably with the intention of recruiting and training resistance members for "cutting Norway in half."

The operation was under constant reassessment and gradually scaled down. Not until two weeks after the insertion was Bangstad informed that the rest of the force would not come. A follow-on force of 20 men from the Parachute Company was admittedly ready at a base on the outskirts of London, but it did not get under way before the German surrender. According to the British, they needed all available air transportation for the campaign on the Continent and could not spare aircraft to insert the rest of the Parachute Company. Bangstad decided to carry out the sabotage despite the lack of manpower (one local resistance fighter was added to the group), but reduced numbers had to be part of the calculation in the selection of a target.

Bangstad decided on three different attacks against the railway—to blow up the 500–1,000 rail lengths at Smalåsen and Trongfoss, as well as destroying tracks and switches at Namskogan Station. The group was divided into three attack teams. At 16:00 on April 12, Group 1 with six men, which included Bangstad himself, left Orrvatnet. In front of them lay a difficult mountain ski march through snow and sleet towards the Smalåsen–Majavatn railway line, a total of 85 kilometers.

After five hours, they had gone no further than 14 kilometers, and spent the night at the Sipmeksjøen. On April 13 at 07:00, they broke up and continued west over the mountains. That same afternoon the team had a fatal accident when a Sten gun went off and hit one of them in the left lung. The man died of the injury and the incident put its mark on the rest of the group. The march continued to a lake, about 5 kilometers from the railway line, where they made themselves ready to carry out the attack. At 08:00 on April 14, they continued towards the target. The snow was crusty. A silent approach was all but impossible but, luckily, they were not detected. A kilometer from the target they split up into pairs to lay the charges on the tracks. After about 10 minutes the fuses were lit and about 600 meters of rail was destroyed. The explosion rang out sharply in the narrow valley and soon vehicles with searchlights could be seen coming towards them. At 04:00 the following night, they ascended the mountains near Majavatn. But the going turned difficult as the weather got warmer. After 24 hours of continuous ski march, they arrived at Sipmeksjøen on the night of April 15, after covering 80 kilometers. On April 18, a German seven-man patrol came near the base. They had probably followed Group 1 on their way back to base, but they failed to locate it.

Group 2, consisting of five men led by Lieutenant Sand, started from Orrvatnet at 09:00 on April 13. They went south along the Swedish border to the Hudningsvatnet Lake where they spent the night. The next morning, they turned south to Jomafjellet and Limingen Lake. The weather was bad and the going was miserable. They were also low on food and had to enter Sweden to get supplies. They did not reach the target area until April 23. By then the weather had also improved. They reached the rail line 2 kilometers north of Trongfoss. After a one-hour rest, they readied the equipment for the attack. At 20:50 they approached the target and placed the charges, and about 21:30 set off an explosion that destroyed about 800 meters of rail. They withdrew without incident, but did not stop for 34 hours while negotiating difficult terrain. They continued to Orrvatnet the next day and arrived there at 18:00. The entire mission had by then lasted 12 days.

The third group consisting of five men, was led by Lieutenant Sanderud. They left base on April 26 with the mission to derail the maintenance train that was expected to come up from Grong. The target area was south of Steinåa Bridge in Namskogan. On April 27, at 06:45, they were only 1.5 kilometers from the railway line. They were in hiding in the forest, just east of the bridge until about 17:00 when they advanced to a point 35 meters from the target and made the final preparations. The charge was placed and rigged to be set off by a cord from a parachute. The train was supposed to have passed at 17:00 but failed to appear. That night they were hit by a terrible rainstorm. At 08:00, a draisine passed by, but still the train was nowhere to be seen. They had removed the charge out of fear that they would not hear the train coming in the storm, but an hour after the draisine had passed, they replaced it. Then the draisine returned, and the German soldiers on top of it caught sight of the charge. The Norwegians yanked the cord and the force of the explosion threw the Germans into the air. On the team's way back over the mountain, the weather was so bad that they had to dig a snow cave for shelter. They arrived at Orrvatnet on April 29 at 13:15.

The remaining five men of Group 3, led by Lieutenant Sanderud, were targeting Namskogan Station. Intended points of attack were the telephone signal amplifier and a railway switch. Although not targeted by *Rype*, a telegram from March 30 stated that "[s]witches and crossings are bottlenecks due to repair difficulties."[17] They came to Namsvatn where they spent the night and got the latest news from the settlements down in the valley. At dawn they continued; by the afternoon they reached a point 6 kilometers from the target where the charges were prepared. They arrived at the target on April 22 at 03:00. Three of them were going to blow up the signal amplifier, and if necessary, kill the guard with a silenced sub-machine gun. The other two were going to blow up the switch. As they placed the charges, they saw that the light was on in the second floor of the station building and they feared that they had been discovered. They ran for their skis, but realized it was a false alarm and continued to rig for the demolition. Four minutes later, the charges were set off. According to the NSB archives, some of the charges failed to explode and were removed by the Germans.[18] Since the two rails were destroyed, there is reason to believe that it was the charges on the switch that did not explode.

On April 27, another German patrol closed in on the base. The circumstances are unclear, the reports only states that they were "disposed of," whether that meant they were killed in battle or executed afterward remains uncertain. The list of Germans fallen in Norway has no entries for April 27.[19] On the other hand, there are three Germans listed as killed on April 26. Neither location nor unit for these men are provided, but there is reason to believe that the Germans "disposed of" are among these. When it became evident that the war was ending, the many surplus weapons were temporarily moved into Sweden. On May 3 they received orders to suspend all sabotage, and after VE Day, they returned to their former target area to prevent the Germans from executing any scorched earth tactics.

The British also planned to insert another group, practically on top of Waxwing. On March 25, Second Lieutenant Erik Gjems-Onstad from *Kompani Linge*, was ordered to assemble a reception team and infiltrate into Norway and prepare the drop of 11 men from the British Special Air Service north of Store Namsvatn in what was dubbed Operation *Ibrox*. Their target was another railway bridge at Snåsamo.

By special operations standards, the area was now becoming quite crowded. The more people inserted into one area, the bigger the risk that the Germans would detect them and intercept their movements or base areas. Gjems-Onstad and his men even had specific orders on which route to follow back to Sweden, probably just to avoid bumping into Waxwing, whom they visited anyway. In the end, bad weather meant that *Ibrox* was canceled.[20]

CHAPTER EIGHT

Planning of Operation *Rype*

The strategic foundation for Operation *Rype* was laid down by Colonel Russel J. Forgan, a banker by profession and General Donovan's deputy commander. In a letter dated February 26, 1945, he drew up 12 objectives to guide OSS activity in the ETO for the remainder of the hostilities. Two would affect operations in Norway and Denmark—the development of intelligence, and to "promote sabotage and resistance" in said countries.[1]

Working with the Norwegian High Command and the SOE, Special Operations Scandinavian Section had drawn up plans for an attack on the pyrite mines on the western Norwegian island of Stord. On January 24, 1943, Norwegian commandoes under British direction had staged a successful raid against these mines, codenamed Operation *Cartoon*. The force comprised 50 men in two MTBs with a further three vessels in support. But production in the mines had since resumed, albeit not on the same scale.[2]

Plans for a new raid were approved by Colonel Joseph Haskell, Chief of SO in London and Chief of Staff to Supreme Allied Commander, in January 1944. Operation *Barter*, as the proposed NORSO attack was dubbed, called for the demolition of the mining machinery at Stord Litlabø, and the loading machinery at Grunnavågneset Quay at Sagvåg. The planning soon ran into problems because there were too many parties with an interest in the operation: SFHQ, Norwegian High Command, Anglo-Norwegian Collaboration Committee, SHAEF, and SCOTCO.[3] However, the execution of the plan hung on the question of transport. The planners counted on making use of the same Norwegian MTBs based at Lerwick that had ferried the Norwegian commandoes across the North Sea the year before. The request for their use was made by Lieutenant Colonel J. S. Wilson, chief of SOE's Scandinavian Section. However, the commanding Allied naval officer of the Shetland and Orkney Islands, Admiral L. V. Wells, replied that all MTBs were engaged in anti-shipping operations. Admiral Wells suggested that they instead used the American-supplied subchasers that frequently ferried agents and resistance fighters to Norway. This was not acceptable to Wilson since it would mean that they would not be available for taking agents and supplies to Norway for the British. Ironically, the subchasers named *Hitra*, *Hessa*, and *Vigra* had been secured by the OSS for operations between the Shetland Islands and the Scandinavian Peninsula in the first place. The subchasers were handed over to their Norwegian crews on October 12, 1943, with an understanding between the Norwegian High Command, SOE, and SO that they "remained American Property on loan to SOE ..."[4] Now Donovan himself got involved, requesting the use of subchasers for the operations to his counterpart in the SOE, Director Major General Sir Colin McVean Gubbins. SOE's reply to Donovan was signed by the SOE's deputy director, Lieutenant Colonel Henry Nathan Sporborg, which some might have seen as a suggestion of British superiority towards their American brothers in arms. In the end, Operation *Barter* stalled on this lack of transport.[5] The question that remained was if the denial of use of both the MTBs and the subchasers was a deliberate British obstruction of an American presence in Norway.

With *Barter* out of the picture, NORSO remained unemployed, and as of April 1944, there were still no plans for their use. The question was whether they should be kept in reserve for future operations in Scandinavia or if they were to be deployed in support of the forthcoming Allied invasion on the Continent. In May 1944 it looked as if there was going to be another operation into Norway on the initiative of officers from the Norwegian Army and Navy. However, on May 11, SHAEF decided to deploy NORSO in support of Allied ground operations following D-Day. This would be the operations known as *Jedburgh*, for which NORSO was transferred from the control of the Scandinavian Section to the commanding officer of the OSS OGs, Lieutenant Colonel Serge Obolensky. Obolensky came from a Polish aristocratic family and was born in Tsarist Russia. He fought for Russia in World War I and for the Whites during the subsequent civil war. Obolensky emigrated to the United States and served as a paratrooper before he transferred to the OSS. He retired in December 1944.

In June 1944, four French OGs had been transferred from Algiers, but were poorly trained and needed to be beefed up. As a result, NORSO became subject to SFHQ. General Andrew Thorne, Chief of SCOTCO, also hoped to get the Norwegian OG transferred to his control, in case it became necessary to execute Operation *Rankin B*. He argued that these troops would be best used in the Scandinavian theater, for which they were intended and trained. However, SHAEF believed that it was too unlikely that *Rankin B* would be required for that to happen.[6] According to Lieutenant Colonel Bolland, this splitting up into smaller units and their use behind the lines in France "practically destroyed [NORSO's] identity."[7] The very nature of the OSS also contributed to this as its parts operated fragmented into small entities and the unit as a whole did not have longstanding tradition as an organization.

The *Jedburgh* operations were executed from August to September 1944. Late in the year, NORSO was withdrawn from France. Lieutenant Colonel Hans Skabo was tasked with selecting about half of the group for operations in Norway, which would subsequently become Operation *Rype*. Skabo was a regular army officer who thus far had proved invaluable in resisting British attempts at keeping *Rype* on the ground. He handpicked about 50 men who "sincerely wanted to work for Norway and who could ski well."[8] They were transferred from the OGs to the OSS Special Operations Section, and sent to Dalnagar Castle in Perthshire, Scotland, for intensive training. The remaining 29 were sent back to the United States to train for jungle warfare, then deployed to southern China to work with local guerrillas in their fight against the Japanese.

The group sent to Scotland got at least 16 days of intensive ski training but even with the mountain training many had received from the 99th Battalion, this was "sufficient barely to qualify the men for their operation," according to Colby's later report.[9] One reason might be the lack of snow.[10] Also, there was only room for 35 men (plus Colby) on the upcoming mission. There was a further screening, based on "general soldierly character and their ski ability." The remaining men would stay in Scotland, under the command of Major John M. Olmsted, to act as a reserve or to be sent on a separate mission later in the spring when skis would not be of use anyway.[11]

At night, on January 26, the NORSO men intended for operations in Norway were whisked away to Peterborough in the English Midlands to get closer to their point of departure, Harrington Air Base. In mid-February, NORSO was joined by Lieutenant Roger Hall, a non-Norwegian, son of a lecturer at the Naval Academy in Annapolis and an Officer Candidate School graduate. Hall took a dim view of their accommodation, stating in his biography *Don't Step on my Cloak and Dagger* that the castle looked as if it had "fallen flat and then been reassembled by a gang of lunatic apprentice stone masons."[12]

The groundwork for the operation was laid well before the final months of the war. In 1943, direct links between the Norwegian Ministry of Defense in exile and the OSS were established,[13] thus effectively bypassing any obstructions the British might place at the strategic level. In 1943–1944, intensive work was done by Allied intelligence in a detailed mapping of the railways in Norway. In mid-Norway, much of the work was done by the SOE team Lark. In May 1944, the joint British Army and Navy Inter-Services Topographic Department had published an extensive dossier on the Norwegian railway lines, stations, and bridges as well as gradients, curves, and terrain.[14] An excerpt from this dossier covering the area from Agle to Formofoss in Nord-Trøndelag was included in a dispatch from Harold P. Larson to Vetlesen, dated January 1, 1945,[15] and from that it can be assumed that the dossier was part of the intelligence basis for Operation *Rype*.

Putting together this information must have been a laborious task, done by men who must have envied those who would do the actual sabotage work and get all the subsequent credit. To illustrate the bravery of these anonymous agents, on one of the pictures of Grong Railway Station, then under construction, a group of German officers are seen on the platform about 30 meters from the man with the camera. Long distances of railway were sized up—far into Namdalen Valley—by Norwegian Resistance fighters looking for choke points, advantageous topography, and weaknesses that could be targeted, as well as enemy strengths and positions. These reconnaissance missions were not done only with *Rype* in mind, yet a lot of the effort put into this work would never result in any mission, as many of the targets and lots of the terrain that was mapped out would never see as much as a fuse or an ounce of explosives.

The Field Order No. 2 to the *Rype* main force contained the following formulation of the mission:

> Primary target: Railway tunnels in Formofoss-Lurudal sector. Tentative Target: Røhylla [Raudhylla on modern maps] tunnel and northern tunnel of Svortfossan [Svartfossan] series to be attacked simultaneously if supported by reconnaissance. Maximum rail destruction specially to flanks of tunnels without detracting from tunnels. If a surprise attack is possible, the initial attack will be delivered with the movement of a maximum amount of demolitions up to the targets prior to the attack.[16]

Zooming in on the map, the choice of target area seems obvious. From just north of Landsem, the railway ran for miles through uninhabited areas with few parallel roads to support an eventual German salvage operation. Likewise, the terrain would offer saboteurs good opportunities to approach the target area and withdraw without much chance of running into civilians. The dossier noted that between Lurudal and Formofoss—a 15 kilometer stretch of railway—there were 15 large and small tunnels, the longest being the 370-meter-long tunnel at Melaseter. There were also three large bridges and several culverts along the same stretch, and special note was made of the 8-meter-long stone span bridge at Raudhylla that followed immediately north of a 135-meter-long tunnel. At Trongfoss and Brekkvasselv, it was noted, railway and road bridges ran close to each other, providing good opportunities to kill two birds with one stone by disrupting both lines of communication and transportation in one attack. At some points, the roads were cut into the mountainsides, offering good conditions for mine explosions.

The Svartfossan series of tunnels must have referred to six tunnels, beginning with the 100-meter-long tunnel at Embrigtfossen, and ending with the 160-meter-long tunnel at Merkesbekken, just above Svartfossan.[17] The rail line at these points was cut into the mountainside and ran close to the Namsen River. This would provide ample opportunity for creating much damage and make salvage difficult for the Germans. However, one might point out, it also made a quick getaway difficult for the saboteurs. That the Namsen River ran between them and their proposed base area made it even less tempting, especially as the river ran through a series of rapids that would not freeze to create any ice to cross over, even in the dead of winter.

In other words, they would have to cross the bridges in order to return to base, with the risks that would entail of being detected and cut off by the Germans.

After the attack on these targets, Rype was to withdraw to the secure rear area to avoid enemy countermeasures. It was also where supplies not brought along on the attack would be cached, perhaps with follow-up attacks in mind. After the primary targets were attacked, the Rype team would move to targets further south. Grana Bridge was listed on top of this prioritized list, followed by the rails from Lurudal to Jørstad, or any other targets that would have to be reported to SFHQ before an attack was launched. The order set a northern limit, being Grong, but no southern limit to the AO.[18] Lieutenant Colonel Bolland wrote in his report that the operation was limited to the area north of Trondheim "due to political considerations" but did not elaborate on what these considerations were.[19] The OSS war report stated that Norway was recognized as an SOE domain, but an agreement from June–September 1942 specified that the northern tip of Norway could become an American special operations domain if Western Europe became a predominantly US Theater of Operations.[20] It might also be pointed out that south of Lake Snåsa, the railway ran through more open and populated areas, perhaps seen in itself as a tactical limitation on any acts of sabotage.

According to the official OSS war report, the overall purpose of *Rype* was to "prevent German redeployment of 150,000 troops in northern Norway, which was being accomplished at a rate of a battalion a day."[21] The importance of stopping the extraction of German troops in Norway was also explicitly noted in the SO program for Norway:

> The facilities for withdrawal of large numbers of German troops estimated at thirteen divisions, are limited in Norway. Railway communications in Norway are few and run through wild, hilly country. Many parts are not vulnerable to air attack. This increases the necessity for ground attack and sabotage from within.
>
> …
>
> <u>Implementation</u>
>
> a) SO/ETO, in cooperation with SOE, will continue to provide in approved amounts—arms, equipment and supplies for sabotage and resistance activities in Norway and Denmark and will assist in their delivery.
> b) SO/ETO will furnish such personnel to assist in the planning, direction and execution of sabotage and resistance activity in Norway and Denmark as may be necessary to the support of military operations.[22]

In other words, no suggestion of an US special operation without conjunction with the native resistance.

In January 1945, the Stockholm Mission of the OSS produced only two cables giving partial coverage to German troop withdrawal from Norway.[23] In mid-January, the Allies assumed that the pace of the evacuation of the German troops in Norway was increasing, and together with the recognition that spring would come dangerously close before any operation could be put into motion, this created a sense of urgency.[24] The objective set was "[t]he disruption of road and rail communications and the harassing in general of the enemy in the area, in connection with the policy as set forth by SHAEF …"[25] A letter to Unger Vetlesen from Harold P. Larson[26] from January 1945 identified the Nordland Railway as a choke point in the German troop transports. Special attention was given to the bridges, most notably the Grana Bridge.[27] As noted above, this would force the Germans to use sea transport, thus making them vulnerable to Allied sea power along a stretch of sealine of communications that lay open to attack from the sea to the west. The letter also noted that the target area lay close to Sweden and offered several escape routes for sabotage groups in case an emergency extraction became necessary. In the appendix, Larson listed several weak points that offered opportunities for attack, including tunnels, bridges, and drainage systems between Agle and Formofoss with detailed information of each object, topography, weather statistics, and the population.[28] Colonel Larson concluded that a US operation against the railway and road between Formofoss and Snåsa was indeed feasible but identified access to airlift capacity both for insertion and resupply as the crucial factor. Major Nordli had come to the same conclusion—there were many weak spots which could be successfully attacked.[29]

However, the Norwegians did have a more optimistic view on how large a force could be inserted and sustained in the AO. The largest unit size mentioned by Major Nordlie in his advocacy for *Waxwing* was that of a battalion, drawn from the Norwegian Parachute Company and the police forces trained by Sweden, inserted at an advantageous position between Trondheim and Mosjøen in Nordland. However, as Nordlie was going through the details, he was down to one troop from the Parachute Company only.[30] Larson recommended the size of the party be 10–15 men, and even that was far below the number that would be attempted to be dropped. A smaller number would also reduce the risk of detection and enhance the commander's tactical control.[31] Nordlie, on the other hand, recommended that one troop be used to secure a temporary "dominion in the operational territory,"[32] in addition to those groups laying the charges. It must be emphasized that Major Nordlie probably had no previous experience in the detailed planning of sabotage missions with the SOE. The exact date of Larson's letter is uncertain. The word "January" is barely legible in the upper right corner of the first page. However, it does mention a sabotage mission carried out by the SOE group Lapwing under Second Lieutenant Reidar Kvaal on December 10, 1944, but not the following attack carried out by Woodlark against Jørstad Bridge on January 13, placing the letter most likely in between those two dates. On December 16, 1944, the Germans launched their offensive in the Ardennes. On December 20, 1944, Woodlark confirmed that they had received orders to switch focus from training local resistance groups to sabotaging the railway (the original orders are nowhere to be found).[33] Thus making the offensive a highly likely catalyst for the implementation of Operation *Rype*.

In January 1945, Lieutenant Colonel Gerhard L. Bolland was assigned to the detailed planning of *Rype* and then given command of the operation by Colonel Skabo. The original plan of the operation called for the insertion of two teams, each 35 men strong and commanded by a major. While Colonel Skabo held overall command from London as chief of the NORSO groups, Bolland was to hold field command of the two groups. According to Bolland's later report, the initial mission was to "retard the movement of German troops in northern Norway on their movement south over the Nordland Railway," however, with a flexibility to changes from sabotage to arming, organizing, and training of the resistance, running escape routes for refugees from Norway to Sweden, and supporting an eventual armed liberation of Norway.[34] Colby's requests to put this latter part into practice would cause much conflict with the operations staff in London during the later stage of the operation. The team, commanded by Major Olmsted (NORSO II), was never sent until after the war ended. Command of this group was by then transferred to Lieutenant Roger Hall, and Olmsted himself was sent to France in February to recruit additional operatives for Norway. Olmsted managed to enlist 12 men originally belonging to the Greek OGs with experience from the confusing and volatile Greek, Italian, and Yugoslav AOs. One of the operators was hospitalized in Paris with malaria, and 11 turned up in London, however, without Skabo being able to meet them and they were never sent to Norway.[35] They did train extensively with the part of NORSO under Lieutenant Hall's command, who remained in Scotland after Colby and his men left for Norway.

During the planning of *Rype*, it was noted that the resistance north of Trondheim was weaker and harder to supply than their brothers in arms in the south. Sabotage here would therefore have to be done by groups dropped from Britain (or infiltrated from Sweden as it turned out). The ground conditions for such an attack would be ideal until late April, as deep snow would render certain areas very suitable for airborne landings.[36] *Woodlark* was a natural tactical reference point for the *Rype* planning. At the time of planning, there were eight Woodlark operatives at the hunting cabin by Burvatnet, and it was noted they were linked by courier service to Stockholm. But they were "under difficulty." This is probably referring to their recent encounters with Swedish border guards, leading to Helgesen's arrest and deportation.[37] However, sabotage against the railway had been presented to Woodlark only as an alternative mission before leaving the UK, and its execution was based on local knowledge and on-the-job planning rather than prior staff work. But the tactics outlined may also have applied to *Rype*. Two major doctrinal options were discussed. One was large-scale attacks against bridges and similar targets, possibly tunnels. The other described attacks on a small scale by mobile detachments against the tracks themselves in so many places that the north–south transport would be prevented, or the Germans be forced to ship the troops from Namsos, exposing them to Allied naval supremacy.[38] In December, Woodlark had advised against the small-scale approach. First, the Germans had made dumps of sleepers and rails along the whole length of the line, and according to railway personnel, it would not take more than 3–4 hours to repair a single break. On the other hand, such attacks would result in tightened security and probably also martial law in the district. In short, much inconvenience for the local population with extraordinarily little achieved.[39]

The original plan was to insert an advanced party to reconnoiter a DZ for the main party, as well as targets along the railway line between Formofoss and Lurudal, prepare the reception of the main party, and then remain in hiding until the main party could be deployed.[40] The advanced party drop was scheduled for the moon period of late January, and the main body was to follow during the next moon period. The advanced group would be led by Lieutenant Tom Saether, and include Second Lieutenant Borge Langeland as signals officer, and Staff Sergeant Listeid.[41] In Langeland's comments, Helgesen is also listed as part of the team that was assembled in January, but this is contradicted by other sources.[42] The initial DZ was intended to be located at Gauptjønna, a small lake some 20 kilometers east of the railway line at Agle. From the center of the lake the intended base was about 1.5 kilometers to the southeast. They were supposed to establish them in a shieling, or a "seter" in Norwegian. There is no exact equivalent word in the English language that fully covers the meaning, but the Scottish term shieling is what comes closest. The *seter* is a kind of traditional farmstead in miniature. Every spring, Norwegian dairy farmers used to lead their livestock to these farmsteads in order to exploit the pastural resources in the highlands and leave the grasslands in the lowlands to be harvested for winter fodder. As fall neared, the shieling would be abandoned until next spring. Shielings were scattered all over the Norwegian outback, thus, during World War II, they would provide plenty of opportunities for resistance groups and saboteurs to hide in areas not easily accessed by the Germans during winter.

The field order did state that the advanced party would be contacted by members of Woodlark at Gauptjønna, and if the point proved to be unsuitable, they would notify SFHQ of an alternative site. The DZ for the main party would be picked out within a 133 square kilometer box between the rivers of Sandøla and Grana. The maps that were available to them were on scale of 1:100,000 which proved to be lacking in sufficient detail during the operation. But what was perhaps the riskiest part of the plan was that the box was only 1.5 kilometers from the railway line at some points, and 4 kilometers from populated areas of Snåsa in the southwest. They would also attempt to find a base area for the main force near the DZ, concealed from air observation, work out a security plan with position of guards, and reconnoiter routes from the DZ to the target area. The commander's critical information requirements were what German guard system existed along the railway line, and the schedules, if any, of trains—civilian as well as troop trains. SHAEF discouraged attacks on locomotives as it was feared that it could make the food supply situation difficult for the Norwegian civilians in the long run.[43] Rype's reconnaissance was also required to investigate the most favorable points of attack, as well as provide information on measurements and construction of the points to be attacked, such as masonry, soil character, and weak points. The information sent back to SFHQ was to be supported by sketches and photos. This would all be included in a report in code sent through the courier of the Woodlark party to Erichsen in Stockholm, who would forward it to London by diplomatic dispatches. If that was not possible, the essentials would be radioed directly to London, saving the report until the arrival of the main party.

The insertion of the main party was scheduled for the period beginning on February 20.[44] For identification signals used in the DZ, they would rely on the "C-system" and the Eureka/Rebecca system. The "C-system" must have been in reference to signs laid out on the ground, like the burning logs in the case of *Rype*. The British Eureka/Rebecca system was technically based on the same principles as radar. The Eureka (transponder) would send out a pre-arranged signal that was picked up by the airborne counterpart, the Rebecca. The signal would be sent to a conventional radar display, enabling the navigator of the aircraft to estimate distance and direction to the target. The system had a range of 80 kilometers in good weather. It was introduced in the winter of 1944–45, and practically revolutionized the air supply operations of World War II.[45] However, optimal conditions seldom existed over mountainous Norway, especially in winter, something *Rype* would pay the price for. Given the atmospheric conditions and general difficulties of navigating this close to the magnetic North Pole, a good deal of dead reckoning would be required until the aircraft could get close enough to pick up a signal.

In advance of the drop, the BBC would broadcast the message "Foxtrot i mastetopp" ("Foxtrot in the masthead") between 14:00 and 17:30 GMT to notify the advanced party that the main party was going to be dropped that night. During World War II, the BBC used to send news broadcasts in the native language of all Nazi-occupied nations of Europe. At the end of the broadcast, the presenter would read out cryptic messages like this that made no sense to anybody except for those for whom they were intended. Upon receiving the main party, the advanced party was going to take Colby along on a final reconnaissance of the target area. Field Order No. 1 for the Rype advanced party suggested that if the original target area would prove unsuitable, they had to be prepared to make reconnaissance of other targets in areas to be announced by radio from SFHQ.[46] If captured by friendly forces on suspicion of being infiltrators, they would request by wireless telegraphy (W/T) the following message to be sent by the BBC "Katt og hund er gode venner" ("Cats and dogs are good friends"), which would be transmitted the following day between 14:00 and 17:30 GMT. If SFHQ suspected that Rype were under duress, that is captured and forced by the Germans to transmit and receive messages on their orders, they would ask what skis they took to the field worked the best. If they were ok, they would transmit that the flat ones were the best. If captured, they would answer the ribbed ones they just had received.[47]

Despite the success of *Woodlark* against Jørstad Bridge, Skabo reckoned that the party was too small and that deploying the OG in the same area was necessary to create a second and more thorough break in the rail communications. In this he was supported by the G-3 of SHAEF.[48] Skabo also expressed concern about the incident that caused Herbert Helgesen to be expelled from Sweden, fearing it would deprive Rype of the much-needed reception party and guides. In the worst case, the advanced party would have to go in blind—i.e., without any reception party—a risk Saether, Langeland, and Listeid declared they were willing to take. Assistance from Woodlark would still be needed and contact with the reminder of the group would have to be made at the earliest point possible.[49] Knowing about *Woodlark* and that Helgesen was present in Sweden, Skabo made a request to the Norwegian FO IV—Forsvarets Overkommando, the Norwegian High Command—that Helgesen be transferred to the UK. Helgesen had supposedly also taken part in the planning of *Rype* through *Westfield Mission* up to that point.[50] Helgesen arrived in London, and after some conferring, he was attached to Rype and sent to Dalnagar for parachute training.[51] He not only brought detailed knowledge of the terrain NORSO would operate in, but the notes from his basic SOE training also reveal extensive knowledge of the German units and native Nazi organizations in Norway, their appearance, equipment, and status. In a progress report, dated April 4, Colby wrote of him:

> I wish to make a record of this unit's appreciation of the helpful assistance given by Lt. Hans Hoel [Helgesen's cover name]. He has handled all liaison with Norwegian citizens of the area, has organized the transport of supplies to the unit from Sweden, and has given much valuable advice on routes and areas in the surrounding territory.[52]

It is interesting to note that Helgesen used the alias "Hans Hoel," even within Rype. His transport cases that were shipped from the United States to Norway after the war were also addressed to "Hans Hoel." Other than Helgesen, Colby would also be surrounded by several Norwegians who probably had just as much local knowledge, but who did not have the same military training and English language skills. And it was this combination that made Helgesen an invaluable asset to Colby.

A technical planning meeting held in London on February 2, had both Colonel Skabo and Lieutenant Colonel Bolland present, as well as a Lieutenant Thorn from the Norwegian Army. The target was defined as a "stretch of railway … containing a number of tunnels one or more of which are to be attacked with explosives; extensive rail cutting is also to be carried out. A 7-span steel bridge is to be an additional target if circumstances permit." Still, most attention was on the tunnels. Lieutenant Thorn had worked as an engineer on that stretch of railway and brought detailed drawings of them, including the masonry in the arches as well as the drainage system.

The type and size of explosive charges was discussed too, showing that the planning of the operation had reached a later stage.[53] At a meeting with representatives of the SOE and the Norwegians from FO on February 1, the stretch between Lurudal and Formofoss was confirmed as the AO for the First NORSO Group. The Americans suggested that the second group be inserted north of Grong, but the British and the Norwegians pointed out that this would intrude upon the AO of the Norwegian paratroopers in what would become Operation *Waxwing*. A destination south of Trondheim for this latter group was also considered, but none was found suitable. This of course would also violate the principle of leaving the area to the resistance. It was decided that the target area of the second group would be the railway south of Agle Station, and again Grana Bridge was pushed up the list, probably since Rype was intended as a much larger group. It was noted that *Woodlark* had abandoned this target because it was too heavily guarded for such a small group, and they instead had attacked Jørstad Bridge. Repairs were now completed there, thus still making it a target. Also, Woodlark itself now remained inactive in Sweden, and NORSO's focus on this area would not infringe upon any other operations.

The conclusions drawn from this meeting seem a bit unclear, but from the premise put forth and later events, it seems that the AO for the First NORSO Group was switched to south of Agle, with the Grana Bridge being the main target, and the rail lines between Snåsa and Agle as the secondary target in case the Grana Bridge proved too well guarded. According to Helgesen's report, he had been in contact with the "American office"—probably *Westfield*—and upon his recommendation, the target was switched.[54] The main argument for switching targets was that the First Group (approximately three officers and 32 enlisted men) contained the best skiers, and that the topography in this area required the best skiers available. However, it is not hard to guess that Helgesen's advice was perhaps marked by his personal desire to set things straight and go after the target he himself had to give up so ingloriously back in January. The main preparations for the operation seem to have taken place at Dalnagar. Special maps would also be drawn, and the members of Rype were briefed on the terrain, the population, and weather conditions.[55]

No specific targets were thus assigned for Second Group (approximately two officers and 20 enlisted men), and at the end of the document, they are assigned to an AO south of Trondheim.[56] The latter is consistent with Lieutenant Colonel Bolland's report, but at odds with principles outlined for these operations. Colby's final report—dated June 30, 1945—also states that "it was decided that no uniformed operation could be undertaken south of Trondheim in order to avoid exciting the Norwegian Resistance and subjecting it to elimination by the Germans before its mission could be fulfilled."[57] The fear of "exciting the resistance" to make premature moves towards liberation had deep roots in the recent experiences of the OSS. There were bitter lessons learned in Italy, France, and Yugoslavia, where taking and holding territory led to horrific reprisals against the civilians if the Germans retook the areas, as they often did. This had happened in the enclave around Vercors, which was temporarily liberated by the French Resistance being inspired by the presence of OSS operators, only to be crushed in a Nazi counterattack on July 23, 1944. Men, women, and children were murdered indiscriminately and their bodies hung from meat hooks.[58] A message to Rype, dated April 28, explicitly made the reference by stating "[r]emember the Vercourt [*sic*] Plateau in France" (Vercourt is in the Somme region, and we might quite assume that it was a mix up with Vercors).[59] It is suggested that the Norwegian High Command were especially worried about such an outcome.[60] This fear of inciting a revolt that would result in reprisals is also confirmed by SOE archives, which also added that the Norwegian Resistance were very anxious to strike a blow at the enemy on their own south of Trondheim, unaided by outside forces.[61]

The Snåsa area, into which the Americans would drop, was a small rural community. The Norwegian term *bygd* is sometimes translated into "village" in English, but that is highly inaccurate. A classical European "village" is a cluster of houses, while a Norwegian *bygd* consists of homesteads more widely spaced, maybe with only a church or other community buildings at its center. Farming was the main livelihood in Snåsa, but the forest industry was also important, and the Nordland Railway went right through the community with Snåsa Railway Station positioned at about 75 MAMSL. In a census from 1946, the population numbered 3,158. In the latter half of the 19th century, Snåsa had a high rate of emigration to North America—some 500 people left in just two generations. Knowledge of, and ties with, the United States must have been high as almost everybody had relatives living there. In addition to ethnic Norwegians, the Snåsa area had a Samí population, and although there could be conflicting relations between the two groups in some parts of the country, this does not seem to be the case in Snåsa. During World War II, the Samí proved to be loyal citizens who did their share of resistance work.

The border area with Sweden in these parts seems barren and devoid of people, save for three or four mountain farms, but that is deceptive. Although hunting was banned for most people, the general supply situation in wartime meant that people would forage in the outback for fish and berries to supplement their diet even more than in peace time. Also, the landscape was dotted with shielings, where farmers would take their animals to graze during summer. Although *Rype* came to the area in winter, the risk of running into people ice fishing on the lakes, cutting timber and firewood, or fetching fodder stored in mountain barns was always present. According to Arne Sandness, an adolescent during the war and later mayor of Snåsa, the resistance was not particularly active in the area. A recurring pattern with the Norwegian population was that the hate for the Germans was particularly high in the coastal areas, which fostered a lot of sailors, due to the U-boat warfare in both world wars, but Snåsa had few, if any, sailors. However, its geographical position meant that Snåsa had strategic importance for the resistance in mid-Norway in general.

XU, the Norwegian intelligence service, was especially active there. Prominent members of the resistance in Snåsa included the district surgeon and the aforementioned deputy sheriff. The area also became a vital transit point on the "underground railway" into Sweden for both refugees and agents from all over mid-Norway. There were two main routes into Sweden from Snåsa, one across the Skjækerfjella Mountains and Gaundal, and the other across Gjevsjø. And the movements of refugees were also a potential security issue, as experienced by *Woodlark*.

CHAPTER NINE

Deployment Phase and Supply

Based on map studies, planners in London had picked out Gauptjønna as the DZ. The coded sign to be laid out on the ground, if a reception committee were feasible, was to be an "F." The coded message sent by the BBC was "Kålrabien er lekker" ("The Swedish cabbage is delicious"). Two men, unknown, were to travel from Stockholm with a W/T operator to join them with a Eureka set. With this device, Skabo hoped, even a non-moon drop would be possible. The password call of the reception party would be "Hvordan star det til på den andre siden av dammen?" ("How is it going on the other side of the pond?"—"the pond" being an affectionate nickname for the Atlantic Ocean). The advanced party would respond "vi ser lyst på fremtiden" ("We are optimistic about the future"). The advanced party would then wait at Gauptjønna for the men sent from Stockholm and not make any contact with Woodlark. If they were forced to escape across the border, their story before Swedish authorities would be that they had been captured by the Germans but had managed to escape. Upon arrival in Sweden, they would report to SFHQ by W/T and, if possible, send a written report in code through Stockholm, addressed to "Vaudeville," the codename for Hans Skabo Erichsen. The mission of the advanced party remained the same as during planning, specifying that after the initial reconnaissance they would remain in hiding until the main party arrived, which was estimated to happen on the first favorable night of the following moon period, beginning on February 20, 1945. Gasoline for a power generator would be dropped with them, as well as K-rations, British mountain rations, various field engineering tools, skis, radio sets, six-volt wet batteries, and Eurekas.[1]

The order to deploy the NORSO advance party, Field Order No. 1, was signed by Colby on January 29, from which point the group was ready to go. The party was scheduled to be inserted on February 19. In the early planning stage, it was hoped that the advance party could be dropped in the moon period January 20–February 4, and the main group during the next, lasting from February 17–March 3. February 22 was also mentioned as the earliest date of insertion. In the sources there is a gap between the orders and notes issued up to and including February 3, and when the first telegrams started ticking in from the field in March, so there is not much information on details of the adjustments that were made due to the delays. For instance, changes made to the load plan are not known. Originally, the advance party was supposed to be dropped with:

1 container of gasoline
1 container of "K" rations
1 container of miscellaneous base equipment
9 containers of British Mountain Rations (40 rations per container)
2 packages Eurekas
1 package B-2 radio set
1 package gasoline generator
3 packages of rucksacks
2 packages of skis (3 pairs per package).[2]

The advance party would be dropped with the 10 containers of rations, shotguns (probably to supplement their diet through hunting), an axe, a saw, hand grenades, and more, as well as a generator. The coded message from the BBC and the call-and-response password remained the same as given above. The main force would then arrive with the orders to carry out sabotage against the Nordland Line between Grong and Steinkjer. They were supposed to be dropped with:

40 10-lbs drainage channel charges
700 1-lbs rail charges
100 10-lbs Cramlington blocks standard charges
1,500-lbs bulk explosive
Ancillaries
16 extra sets of skis
4 extra rucksacks
1 Nichols radio set

In addition, there was base equipment, uniforms, and personal equipment. Everyone would be provided with Norwegian escape kits and 100 Swedish kroner in emergency funds. The unit would be provided with additional funds of 50,000 Norwegian kroner and 400 Swedish kroner. On the ground, the advance party would transmit the letter "P" and light a sign on the ground forming the letter "C" when the main force came in to be dropped.

Because of his experience in France, Leif Oistad, and probably the others too, felt confident. But Operation *Rype* would have a difficult start, marked by delays. By early February, the assistance they hoped to get from Woodlark hung by a thread. Although Swedish authorities were keenly aware of the base on their side of the border, what they considered "high-handed proceedings," culminating in the arrest and expulsion of Helgesen, led to irritations. Also, the Allies were entering difficult negotiations on the establishment of bases on Swedish territory, and calm was needed for these to succeed. This would make courier services very difficult, even on the

Swedish side. Also, the services of Kjell Sørlie was required in Stockholm, and a replacement was badly needed.[3]

The advance party was separated from the rest of the group and was standing by at Area H (Harrington) from January 29 to the end of the moon period on February 5, but the first scheduled drop was canceled due to bad weather. Meanwhile, events took place in Norway that suggest that it was for the best. Harold Larson's letter to Vetlesen recommended an initial reconnaissance by an advance party, possibly inserted through Sweden.[4] Odd Sørli, former leader of the *Lark* operation, the elder brother of Kjell, a childhood friend of Helgesen, and now attached to the Norwegian Legation in Stockholm, had been tasked with organizing the resistance work in mid-Norway. In December 1944, he asked his brother Kjell to lead the reception of NORSO. The chief of the Norwegian High Command's 4th Office with responsibility for operations in Norway, Bjarne Øen, questioned trusting the mission to somebody that young, but Odd assured him that he was not too young at all. An American "general" present (presumably station chief Brewer) just chuckled and approved Kjell's assignment.[5]

Kjell Sørli was born in 1923 and was only 17 years old when the war broke out. He was then a student at the Trondheim Cathedral School (an upper secondary school). Despite his youth, Kjell Sørli was experienced in fieldcraft, and was lauded by Colby for his outback skills. Helgesen described him as full of initiative and outspoken. Both his elder brothers, Odd and Øyvind, were called up to take part in the 1940 campaign and would become pioneers with the resistance in mid-Norway during the occupation. Odd started as a courier and a guide for refugees, and Kjell often carried the messages on the last leg to his brother's contacts inside Trondheim after meeting Odd at a safehouse in the forest. One of Kjell's earliest coups was acquiring blueprints for the U-boat nets that protected the German battleship *Tirpitz*, which was moored in Trondheim's fjord in 1942. He would also take part in the failed attempt to hit the battleship with mini submarines, bringing messages to the various groups taking part in Operation *Title*.

His parents' house became an operational center for the resistance, and Kjell foiled an attempt by one of Rinnan's collaborators to infiltrate it. Due to German crackdowns in Trondheim, he was forced to move to Oslo, but his apartment there was raided by the Germans. It turned out that they were looking for Odd, and they released Kjell after a day, but not before they had taken his picture and fingerprints. Once in the Gestapo's records, Odd ordered that his little brother be extracted to Sweden. In spring of 1944, Kjell finally took his exams in Uppsala, Sweden. In the meantime, Kjell's father had been arrested and sent to the Grini Prison Camp. In Sweden, Kjell underwent a courier course, learning orienteering, climbing, and interrogation in addition to combat training. From then on, he was a courier in his own right. Incredibly, the whole Sørli family survived the war despite their heavy involvement in the resistance. Later, Kjell studied medicine in Copenhagen, Denmark, and then practiced at various places in Trøndelag. He died in 1998.

Kjell brought with him Erik Gaundal who had long-time experience as courier and knew the Snåsa area like the back of his hand. Erik came from a small community, just 4 kilometers from the border. Living that close and being a loyal Norwegian, it was almost impossible not to be dragged into the underground railway of guiding refugees out of Norway. In the fall of 1944, he was forced into hiding himself.

Gaundal and Kjell Sørlie left Stockholm on February 2, loaded with American equipment and a radio receiver on which to listen for coded messages from the BBC, according to Helgesen, at the same time as he left for England. In Östersund, they met an officer from the criminal police who followed them through the forbidden border zone around Kallseidet. They then continued alone to Björkede, where they encountered a Swedish military patrol who let them pass. From there, only 2 kilometers remained until they reached the border, and they crossed to spend the night on Gjefsjø Farm on the Norwegian side.

In the mountains they observed a person they were pretty sure also had spotted them. Therefore, they decided to make contact, and the person turned out to be Hans Leirmo, an old acquaintance of Gaundal's who later would be involved in Operation *Rype*. They spent a lot of time at Leirmo's *goahti* at Plukkutjønn Lake. As an authorized wolf hunter, Leirmo was one of the few reliable Norwegians in the area with permission to carry a hunting rifle and to move about in the border area. Harold Larson had emphasized that "guides with a knowledge of the area would prove invaluable and are almost essential for the success of the operation",[6] and Leirmo would indeed prove essential to *Rype*. He was orphaned as a child and had more or less grown up in the mountains where he was sent out as a shepherd at a young age. He spent most of the year at the *goahti*. Leirmo had already guided several refugees across the border. His sister-in-law was one of the many civilians who offered Rype help. According to Helgesen's report, she opened her home for meetings, sheltered people, and relayed messages, but he offered no details of her efforts for the resistance.[7] Gaundal and Kjell Sørli told Leirmo about the drop and that they were going to received it near the shieling at Gauptjønna Lake. Leirmo informed them that the shieling had been torn down 50 years ago. There was a cottage near the lake, but at the time it was being used by two grouse hunters known to be "politically unreliable" (ironic, since "Rype" is Norwegian for grouse), according to the report that Kjell Sørli later wrote. They were also told there were many other grouse hunters roaming the area, which increased the risk of being detected and reported to the Nazis. But Gaundal and Sørli decided to continue to scout the area anyway in an attempt to find to find a new suitable DZ.[8]

On Leirmo's recommendation, they went to the National Forest Service lodge at Seisjøen Lake, about 4 kilometers south of where the shielding had stood at Gauptjønna. There, they spent about a week and made reconnaissance of the surrounding area in the direction of Langvaten and Vivaten, about 5 kilometers to the south. Subsequently, this location was picked as the new DZ. On the evening of February 6, they received the coded message "ri ikke på kosteskaft" ("Do not ride the broomsticks") on the BBC, which was the then current message telling them that the Americans were on the way. For the next three days they searched around Gauptjønna for three men from the advance party who were supposed to have jumped out but found nothing but the tracks of the grouse hunters in the area. Those men must have seen their tracks too, making it even more dangerous to stay in the area. Finally, they gave up and went back to Gjefsjø where they met Thoralf Lian, a local resistance leader who brought new orders to them. Kjell Sørli's report does not specify what these consisted of, but they probably included a new coded message to be expected from the BBC that was now "kålrabien er lekker" ("The Swedish cabbage is delicious").

As with many of Rype's Norwegian helpers, Lian's introduction into the resistance was the "underground railway"—to hide and guide refugees into safety in Sweden. He ran Hegge Farm, which became a stopping point where those on the run hid in the loft. The main building was divided in half, and while Lian's family supported the resistance and hid refugees in the loft, the other family threw parties for local Nazi dignitaries. One of those who sought refuge with Lian was Judge John Lyng, who would briefly serve as prime minister of Norway in 1963. Sometimes Lian followed the refugees into the mountains, but in October 1944, he too had to flee. According to Helgesen, Lian could have settled for a safe position in Sweden, being married with three children, but he felt compelled to report for duty with the resistance. He was also part of the original reception committee assigned to receive the Rype advance party. In a recommendation for an award after the war, Helgesen described Lian as sympathetic and able.

To avoid the grouse hunters around Seisjøen, Gaundal and Kjell Sørli stayed at Hans Leirmo's *goahti* with Hans, who was to act as a guide. On Thursday February 15, they went to Edevik, about 10 kilometers inside Sweden, to buy food. On the way back they saw the traces of three skiers who had been at Holden Farm, a known hotspot for collaborators. From Sweden, Erik Gaundal and Kjell Sørli must then have returned to Seisjøen.

At 02:00 on the morning of February 16, Gaundal and Sørli were suddenly awoken at Seisjøen by Hans Leirmo banging hard on the door. He had been down in Snåsa and heard that the Germans had asked around about Seisjøen Lodge and Gauptjønna. Leirmo told them that 17 Germans were on their way towards them, and it was not hard to guess where they were going. They burnt all the papers and promptly headed towards Sweden to report that DZ was compromised. They had just put about 5–6 kilometers between themselves and the lodge when they could hear heavy automatic weapons fire behind them. It was the Germans who riddled the lodge they had just been sleeping in with bullets. On the way to the border, they narrowly escaped three skiers, whom they suspected to be frontier police, and who only gave up the chase as they crossed the border. Then they had another 24 kilometers to the nearest phone in Bjørkede on the Swedish side. They later learned that the frontier police visited Gjefsjø Farm too. Kjell had to contact his brother Odd in Stockholm to cancel the drop. He feared, however, that the phone line was tapped so he would have avoided saying so directly. But they had not agreed upon any danger code to notify that the drop had to be canceled. So, Kjell called and said "ikke send kålrabien, den er ikke lekker" ("Do not send the Swedish cabbage, it's not delicious"), which was enough for Odd to realize that the operation had to be stopped, and he relayed the message to the US embassy in Stockholm.

Erik Gaundal and Kjell Sørli reached Stockholm on February 19. After this, Gaundal was dropped from the reception committee, replaced by Kjell's brother, Odd. According to Helgesen, this time the advance party was planned to be inserted just 24 hours before the main party and the drop was called off after warnings about Germans in the area, as had happened another time previously for the same reason.[9]

At the suggestion of Kjell, the DZ was moved to Gjevsjø. The mountain farm (actually, two separate farms of the same name) consisted at the time of a farmhouse, a smaller house, and a barn. The farm was quite remote, without electrical power or a phone, and it was several kilometers to the nearest road link on the Norwegian side. According to Helgesen, this was a far more suitable base area, offering better quarters, being easier to defend, and with better opportunities for resupply.[10] The animals there consisted of a horse and several dairy cows. The owner, Alfred Anderson, was a legendary hunter of the border areas. Even though he was originally a Swedish national and came to ownership of Gjefsjø Farm through marriage, he remained a loyal Norwegian and true friend of the resistance. During the war Gjefsjø Farm became a stopping point for refugees fleeing the Nazis. Alfred also had a radio receiver hidden up in the woods on which he listened into news from London and Stockholm. Ownership of radios for ordinary people had been banned by the Germans in 1941, and even being in possession of one was a huge risk. Alfred owned firearms but, as a licensed hunter, he had a carrying permit.

German guard patrols stopped at the farm from time to time. Before Rype arrived, a patrol of eight men searched thoroughly through all the rooms in every building on the farm but found nothing illegal. This may have been the patrol chasing Kjell Sørli and Erik Gaundal on February 17. With family on the other side and a short distance across the border, it would have been no problem to cross over to safety and comfort in Sweden, but Alfred chose to stay until March 1945—he left only after Rype had arrived. However, the war did not prevent Alfred from crossing the border into Sweden and Björkedet to shop and send mail, although it was not entirely risk-free, and on one occasion he and his brother Nikard were almost detained by a Swedish police officer.

According to the biography of Alfred Anderson, *Gjevsjøgubben* (*The Old Man of Gjefsjø*), the farm was visited before the deployment of Rype by "the great saboteur" Herbert Helgesen, who informed them that the farm would be the base for the Americans during the "liberation of Norway." This could not have been the case since Helgesen was expelled from Sweden and was already in the United Kingdom when it was decided to have the DZ at Gjevsjø Farm. Either it did happen right after they landed, or someone else, probably Kjell Sørli, could have notified the people on the farm about the plans in advance. The latter does seem unlikely as it would have been a security risk. Andersson, in his biography, is said to have nodded as a sign that he understood the situation. And, further, that it was already decided that residents should evacuate after a while, as the place would become quite crowded.[11] Kjell Sørlie, Thoralf Lian, Jon Moan, and Ludvik Kruksve then returned to Norway to act as the reception committee for the drop.

In the meantime, in the UK, the USAAF had advised a non-moon drop for the advance party. But bad weather continued to hold them up. On February 19, Helgesen joined the advance party group too because of his knowledge of the terrain. A new attempt was scheduled for March 2, and the four men proceeded to Harrington, where problems had already begun at the briefing. The time over the target was estimated to be between 22:00 to 02:00, but the air crews were briefed to be over it between 01:00 to 05:00. They took off, and made the planned pitstop at Leuchars, and proceeded to be over the target at 02:30 hours. The pilot could not get a visual of the target and the Rebecca did not receive any signal from any Eureka on the ground. Not being certain of their position, Saether decided not to do the drop. His men protested and demanded they go through with the insertion anyway. Fuel supply on the Liberator aircraft was carefully allocated and being forced to turn around with the plane still full of equipment and people, after making several attempts at finding the DZ, had to mean trouble. Strong headwinds also increased fuel consumption. As soon as they were over the open sea, all equipment was thrown overboard including machine guns, parachutes, and personal equipment. They landed at Leuchars with only 50 gallons of gas remaining.[12]

The sources differ, however, when it comes to the timing of the first drop attempt. The telegraphist Borge Langeland, in his published telegrams, places their attempt at the same time as Sørli and Gaundal had to escape the base on Seisjøen:

> The men heard the plane fly over but due to snow and zero visibility, were unable to jump. This was fortunate as they discovered later. The Germans apparently had some advance information about the drop. A large German ski patrol from Steinkjaer proceeded directly to the drop zone the same night. They were observed by a member of the Norwegian underground forces, Lt. Harold Larsen who also knew about the intended drop. Lt. Larsen was a fantastically fast skier, and he soon outdistanced the German patrol. He was able to warn the Norwegian members of the resistance forces who acted as a reception committee at the drop zone.[13]

Firstly, it must be noted that Langeland, relying on secondhand information, mixes up Harald Larsen and Hans Leirmo. Kjell Sørli, on the other hand, assigned the attempt to another occasion but does not specify a date when aircraft was heard flying above and that it had to turn back because of the weather. According to the phases of the moon, it was most likely around January 27 when there was a full moon. More is added to the puzzle by Bolland's report stating that the "The operation was mounted and waiting from 29 January 1945, but the USAAF reported repeatably that flying conditions were not suitable until 24 March 1945." No mention is made of any aborted attempts, nor any turn-backs in midair. Colby on the other hand does mention the "arrival of a German patrol in the area selected for the drop" in addition to a newspaper article "which seemed to indicate that the security had been violated ..."[14] However, Colby does not state any date, nor that the incident led to the last aborted insertion.

The move of the drop site even further south meant that attacking the tunnels listed in Field Order No. 2 became "impracticable,"[15] and the drop site decided the possible targets instead of the other way around. These changes meant that all intelligence and mission specific preparation became redundant. But they were not completely in the dark about their targets. The shift brought them right into the AO of *Woodlark*. Their prime target was initially changed to Grana Bridge, which was also the original prime target of the British-controlled Norwegian group. Woodlark had, as it might be recalled, abandoned it due to it being too heavily guarded by the Germans. However, Rype was intended to be a much larger force than Woodlark, with strength enough to defeat a large guard force, while the Norwegians were dependent on attacking an almost undefended target. The problem of timing and moon periods were still haunting the operation. Weather became so bad that they could not exploit the favorable moon phases until the end of March. Then, the Air Force put pressure on the timetable, insisting that the entire group be inserted in a single drop at the next opportunity.[16] This is quite understandable, given the prospect of an air supply operation stretching far into the spring when longer days would make their machines more vulnerable to German air defenses en route to and from the target area.

Colby checked the equipment and made a list of who would go in. Farnsworth, who knew that his own skiing skills were below par, wanted his name removed from the first list. But his wishes were not granted. Farnsworth's demolition skills were essential for the success of their mission so it was paramount that he should go. Farnsworth's recommendation for the Bronze Star mentioned especially how he had just a couple of months of ski training in Scotland prior to being sent to Norway, and that he had been able to overcome his disadvantages through "determination and high courage."[17] The men also got their last leave before they would be sent into Norway. In addition to the inherent technical issues with flying into Norway due to topography and atmospheric conditions, there also seem to have been some administrative challenges. In the recommendation for the British Award Certificate of Recommendation to Major Arne W. Brøgger, Major General Gubbins wrote that after his visit to Stockholm in March 1945 a "better cooperation was secured from the OSS Mission out there and more satisfactory distribution of stores from the UK was arranged."[18] Brøgger had been Vetlesen's assistant when he joined SFHQ in April 1944, and would play a prominent role in dealing with the Swedes and allowing for the establishment of the *Sepals* bases along the border, and from Gubbins's statement we can only guess that there had been some conflicting views regarding the supplies for *Rype*. In August 1944, the OSS SO branch began setting up the first of a total of six supply bases for the Norwegian Resistance inside Sweden along the Norwegian border, but these were all located too far north to be of any use to NORSO.

Colby got the message from SOE to get ready for a drop on March 24, but as with the previous attempt at inserting the advance party, the Air Section of the OSS coordinated their part of the operation poorly. Nine aircraft were requested for the mission, each to carry four men. However, due to a lack of planes, only eight were available. Lieutenant Saether and the rest of the original reception party were loaded with the reception and communications equipment. But they discovered that their allotted plane lacked a Rebecca set and they had to switch to another. In his 1975 account, Langeland stated that they had to switch planes because he had a Eureka that was to be used to guide the remaining planes to the target.[19] That sounds a bit far-fetched since the Eureka set was portable and the Norwegian reception party already had one. The packages were changed to the new plane too, but not the containers. In Colby's progress report, dated April 1, he noted that the group still did not know if the radios, batteries, and hand generators had been dropped at all, and the confusion meant that they were searching for equipment that might not even have been dropped. Only after four more days of searching did they find the generator, but concluded that the B-2 radio had not been reloaded onto the next plane with Lieutenant Saether. This plane also lacked proper equipment to hook up the static lines and these had to be installed at the last minute. To add to problem of last-minute changes, the machine guns on the sides of the plane were still in place, but they had to be removed to make space for men and equipment.[20]

They arranged for the commanding officer of the 858th Bombardment Squadron, Major Ernest Holtzworth, to accompany them to Scotland in his aircraft so it could act as a spare in case any of the other planes experienced technical difficulties. On March 24, the force took off from Harrington in eight B-24s from the 492nd Bomber Group. This time they were landing at Kinloss in Scotland for refueling. There, the last briefing and reshuffling of men and equipment was made before continuing towards Norway. Onboard sat 36 men from NORSO in white camouflage suits over their American uniforms. There were four to six men in each aircraft. Colby described them in that moment in the following manner:

> These men made up an unusual group of Americans, and a casual observer would have picked almost any other nation to describe their origin. Yet when they removed the great white packs and parkas they wore; underneath was the traditional khaki of the American fighting man. However, their names read like heroes from some Norse saga, Paulsen, Johansen, Iversen, Eliasen, Oistad, as indeed they were, for the bulk of them had been stranded off Norwegian ships in the early war days and one way or another found their way into the US Army.
>
> Lieutenant [L]angeland had been a ship's radio man. Sergeant Listeid had been a seaman. Raivio, a Lapp, had fought the Russians in Finland and escaped to America as a ship's crew member. Sergeant Andreasen had been a first mate and talked of nothing but the sea. Myrland was a former ship engineer, all mature men, competent, born skiers, violently anti-German, lovers of another foreign country, that whose uniform they wore. Among this group were men who could do anything from butchering a cow to fixing a motor with a piece of wire or operating on a casualty with a jackknife. All these skills were used in the cold, hard work they were doing, and the success of our operation can be attributed almost solely to their high caliber and devotion to the mission.
>
> Through the years they had been combed from the millions in the Army and had volunteered to be dropped from a plane to sever the railway. They had been training and waiting since late in 1943, but, on their way at last, there was no excitement, no griping. They looked ahead reflectively, or blankly.[21]

Drop containers full of weapons and other equipment rested in the converted bomb rack. The loads on each plane were measured out to be enough to sustain the men onboard for 40 days in the wilderness without resupply—that is, while they operated in the field on skis in sub-zero temperatures without outside assistance. As extra water is needed to keep the body hydrated in a desert, extra calories are needed in an Arctic climate to sustain a normal body temperature, and without a proper diet the risk of hyperthermia would increase dramatically. A supply base was to be established on the Swedish side of the border. Bolland stated in his report that emergency supplies were to be dropped by air by Colonel Bernt Balchen, and resupply from the United Kingdom "was to be tried and used if found practical."[22] However, it is unclear which alternative was the preferred one. Resupply from Sweden for an active ongoing sabotage mission of the magnitude of which *Rype* was planned would still be difficult to handle for political reasons, even at this late stage of the war when the Swedish government grew more and more cooperative with the Allies each day. Colby's request for "large daylight drops from UK" could be arranged, probably pointing to a prospect for a situation when this would be allowed "if the area was secured."[23]

For security reasons, the flight crews were not allowed to talk to the NORSO personnel they carried, so they were barely talking to each other. If the crew was taken prisoner, they would be able to divulge as little as possible about the mission. The aircraft took off again from Kinloss in six-minute intervals just before sunset, on course for Gjevsjø. They used the GEE navigation system to find a point where they would cross the coastline. From there, they were dependent on landmarks to navigate. After a fatal accident in France, when a personnel parachute had collapsed after being hit by a container, it was usual for crews to jump in the first run over the target, with the containers released on the next overflight. The reception committee waited down on the surface of Gjevsjø Lake. The "official" group consisted of resistance fighters Agnar Andersen, Thoralf Lian, Jon Moan, and Kjell Sørli, but others may also have been present or watching the spectacle from the Swedish side of the border.

One of the more conspicuous members of the Norwegian reception party was a woman named Thale Prytz from the capital Oslo. She had trained as a jewelry designer before the war but had to flee to Sweden in the fall of 1942 after being warned that the Gestapo were looking for her. Though she was not engaged in the resistance herself at the time, her brother and many of her friends were. After a short stint as a maid, she started to work as a clerk at the Norwegian Diplomatic Legation in Stockholm. There, she received agents arriving from the field. She also made fake IDs, something her civilian profession made her more than qualified to do. She also worked at the cipher office, which was mostly staffed by women. One day, Odd Sørli asked her if she wanted to go with him to Norway and receive a drop. Prytz was more than happy to. Although without formal military training, she was a former member of a pistol club and had had plenty of training at the shooting range while in Stockholm. Prytz was also a very skilled skier, and Sørli gave her a crash course in close combat.

The reception party traveled by train and bus, and then by ski for 50 kilometers to Gjevsjø.[24] They stayed in a cabin on an island on the Swedish side, from where they would organize the reception party. According to Helgesen's report, a Norwegian signaler, Trond Trondsen, also took part in the reception and operated the Eureka. Both Odd Sørli and Trondsen left the area as soon as the drop was accomplished.[25] Hans Leirmo and several others joined too. Erik Gaundal had been given the task of being a courier.

Just before midnight, after hearing the coded message on the BBC, the Norwegians gathered on the frozen surface of Gjevsjø Lake and heard the sound of aircraft engines in the distance to the east as the course of the B-24s took them slightly into Swedish airspace. According to Helgesen, the advance party started out one hour before the rest because of uncertain weather and heavy air traffic due to Easter, but the four planes that made it to the target arrived at about the same time. Out on the ice, logs were arranged to form an inverted "L," soaked in kerosene to mark the DZ. Hans Leirmo stood by the logs and saw a black dot over the mountains in the south grow larger, along with the increasing sound of the four-engine bomber. He lit the logs and sent the agreed Morse code signal for "F" with a flashlight. The same signal was also sent from the Eureka device. The first plane broke off, a sign that they had found DZ. However, only four of the eight planes reached the DZ. They circled around, leveled out at approximately 600 feet on a northern course and made the drop, spreading their cargo over an 8-kilometer-long area.

As mentioned above, the initial plane for the advance party was discovered to have no Rebecca, so they switched to plane *Trygve* (named for the senior NORSO man aboard) before taking off from Kinloss. *Trygve*'s original complement was thus stranded and would later crash on the Orkneys on March 31. The plane codenamed *Ed* had to turn around and head back for Scotland before it reached the Norwegian coast also due to lack of a Rebecca. The sixth plane reported that all compasses were off by 50 degrees and turned around, and with mist reaching up to 100 meters above ground, finding the DZ had become too difficult. A total of 14 men had been on board the three planes that had to turn back or never took off from Kinloss. They returned to Harrington, expecting to be dispatched later. The eighth and last plane went off course but dropped the men and equipment on the frozen Landösjöen in Jämtland, 80 kilometers inside Swedish territory.

Colby's flight almost dropped into Sweden too. Around midnight, the pilot announced that they were 40 kilometers off course and over Sweden but that the course was being adjusted. As they approached the DZ, Colby gave the men orders to buckle on the equipment, while the pilot swung to port and descended. The last thing they did was to check that the static line was attached to the plane and readied their personal weapons. Some wore cold masks as protection against the shock that would hit them when they jumped out into the icy night air. Paulsen and Sverre Aanonsen tore up the hatch in the floor, exposing the "Joe Hole." From one of the other planes, Langeland also observed the landscape below and later gave the following description:

> In the bright moonlight, they could see the snow-covered landscape below with rugged mountains and bare rock walls gleaming steel blue in places where the snow had been blown away. In the deep valleys between the mountains, there were forests of birch trees and fir, their branches covered with snow. Here and there they could see a bare area indicating a frozen fresh water lake. From the air, it looked like a wild inhospitable country in which survival would be difficult. Bathed in the bluish light from the full moon, and millions of stars, it appeared like a picture from a fairy tale.[26]

Before they reached the DZ, they could feel the planes making a turn in a north-westerly direction. They crossed the barren border zone back into Norway and as they did, the mist came rolling down and engulfed the valley floor. Somewhere below them, hopefully, the Norwegian Resistance movement was waiting. The jump master, a sergeant from the USAAF, went over the hooks that attached the static line to the airframe to check that they were properly hooked up. The red light in the ceiling was lit and jump master commanded "Action stations." On "Ready number one" Colby sat down on the edge of the hole with his legs down through it. The green light was lit, and the jump master screamed "Go!" Colby addressed the pilot and said, "This is it," before he disappeared down the hole in the floor out into the darkness. The rest would follow at five-second intervals. About 9 meters below the plane, the static line snapped, and with a slight jerk, the chute opened.

The planes reaching the DZ were codenamed *Bill*, *Glenn*, *Einar*, and *Trygve*, after the senior ranking NORSO officer or non-commissioned officer (NCO) on board. The last had its original complement exchanged for the advance party and was originally carrying the men who would later crash on the Orkneys on March 31. According to Colby's progress report dated April 1, the drop was scattered across the surface of the large lake, and into the forest to the northeast. He partially blamed the reception party, as "it pointed towards shore," but did not explain how they should have been pointing. Consequently, according to him, some of the late packages went into the trees. *Einar* failed to spot the sign on the ground as the mist came in, but still managed to make two passes on Eureka alone and dropped perfectly in both. *Bill* had a perfect starting point on both runs, but the aircrew were slow to dispatch the packages, and they were spread up to 4 kilometers to the northeast of the lake. *Glenn* dropped about a kilometer from the reception party, but all packages and containers were eventually found. The first men and equipment dropped from *Trygve* landed only 800 yards from the reception party, but some of the last ones ended up in the woods. There, Helgesen supposedly landed in a birch tree, not far away from Gjefsjø Farm. On the second run, some containers ended up about 3 kilometers away to the northwest corner of the lake. A total of 54 containers and 45 packages were dropped with the men.[27]

As the roar of the engines died in the distance, it turned oddly quiet. Colby could see the rest of those who jumped from the same plane come out, one, two, three. The formation was perfect. But he wondered if there would be a friendly reception waiting for them on the ground. Then the canopies opened about 10 meters below the plane. From 150 meters Colby could spot the burning logs, and he felt safe knowing that they were in the right place. Everyone who got as far as to jump over Gjevsjø landed safely in the soft snow. But the following link-up with the men from the Norwegian Resistance could have gone very wrong.

There are at least three different versions of what happened. According to Colby's later account, the Americans were to ask in Norwegian: "er fiske godt i denne sjøen?" ("Is fishing good in this lake?"), and the Norwegians on the ground would answer "ja, spesielt om vinteren" ("Yes, especially in the winter"). Instead, Hans Leirmo answered "for å være helt ærlig, er det ikke noe bra i det hele tatt" ("To be honest, it's not good at all"), either because he was trying to be funny or had forgotten what the answer was supposed to be. The Americans reached for their guns, but Helgesen recognized resistance people and was able to confirm that they were not agents for the Germans.

Borge Langeland, the telegraphist, said that the confusion arose because Farnsworth was unable to pronounce the question well enough in Norwegian. Farnsworth, however, remembered that one of the resistance people was named Hans, and when Farnsworth asked for Hans, one of them replied that he was—it was probably Hans Leirmo. In the November issue of *National Geographic* in 1945, a third version of the story was given. One of the Norwegians was said to have forgotten the answer in the excitement to see the Americans and remembered when he had a gun pressed against his back. It is possible that all three versions could be true since the Americans would have hit the ground spread out in both time and space, and that several "first encounters" like this might have occurred.

As there are no mentions of intrusions into Norwegian airspace in the German daily reports, it is fair to assume that the transports were not detected. The 16 who were dropped from *Glenn*, *Bill*, *Einar*, and *Trygve* and managed to land on the Gjevsjø on the night of March 25 were:

Major William Colby
Lieutenant Tom Saether
Lieutenant Glenn Farnsworth
First Sergeant Einar Eliassen
Technical Sergeant Borge Langeland
Staff Sergeant Arne Listeid
Staff Sergeant Alf Paulsen
Staff Sergeant Marinus Myrland
Staff Sergeant Odd Anderson
Staff Sergeant Fred Johansen
Corporal Kai Johansen
Technician Fifth Grade Sverre Aanonsen
Technician Fifth Grade Matti Raivio
Technician Fifth Grade Asmund Gravdal
Technician Fifth Grade Odd Stiansen
Technician Fifth Grade Halvor Nipe

The Norwegians listed on the roster for March 25 were Lieutenant Hoel (Helgesen), (Thoralf) Lian, a name that is hard to read but could be (Alfred) Anderson, Leksvik (aka Jon Moan), (Kjell) Sørlie, and (Hans) Leirmo.

The drops from all four planes were executed between 01:00 and 01:30. Now that the risky business of getting men and equipment into Norway was accomplished, the laborious task of collecting all the items began. The farmer at Gjefsjø, Alfred Anderson, with Hans Leirmo and the Sámi reindeer herder Jonar Jåma, helped to gather everything together using horse and sledge. Fitted with snowshoes, the farmer's horse, probably of the Fjord type judged by postwar footage, moved through the snow with ease. The Fjord horse has a particularly powerful torso which enhances its mobility in deep snow. The paths of the drops are not documented, but Colby's report of April 1 included map references of where the content was gathered, stating that the containers were dragged from the ice to the nearby woods. The cargo from *Einar* and *Bill* were gathered at the northern end of the lake, about 1 kilometer southwest of Gjefsjø Farm. The men also visited the farm where they had an opportunity to rest and cook a meal and placed a guard post. The gathering of the containers from *Glenn* began at dawn on the marshes on the northeast side, just south of where Bjørkvasselv Creek drained into Gjevsjø. It had begun to snow, making the gathering more urgent.

The cargo from *Trygve* was discovered late in the afternoon, but the ice in the area was treacherous so they waited until 04:00 so that the cold had made the ice safe for the horse. By then some of the containers had already burrowed deep into the crust and were beginning to be covered by snow. In addition, the trees on the banks cast long shadows over the ice as the sun set in the west, adding to the difficulties of spotting the containers, which were later piled up on the western shore, on the north side of Angletjønn Bay. The daytime melt hid their tracks on the ice, making the surface look smooth and untouched. Later, the equipment was dragged even further inland to better hiding places. They used the horse and sledge to collect the most-needed items as a priority, but it took several days to collect it all.

In his report dated April 1, Colby said he and his men were still missing three packages of rucksacks, three packages of skis, and all the radio equipment originally packed in plane *Ed*. In addition, Colby and Fred Johansen, who flew in on plane *Ed*, were missing their rucksacks. Also noted as missing was one package of stemming rods, presumably for use if needed to place explosives into drainage pipes. A package of "H-1" broke up in midair, its contents scattered around, and one container loaded with Bren guns was believed to have gone through the ice. The latter items had to be searched for later.

Four days later, all equipment was retrieved, except two ski packages and one or two H-1 containers that burst open in midair. Another issue was the complaints from several of the men of personal items missing from their rucksacks, such as cigarettes, candy, and soap. Quite bluntly, Colby saw no other explanation than thievery at the packing station.[28]

Despite a thorough evaluation of the routines after the operations in France, some of the equipment was destroyed upon landing and Colby was worried that a German patrol would surprise them before they had control of everything and had only light hand weapons to defend themselves with so Colby later recommended that the reinforcements and follow-up forces to be dropped should be equipped with M1 Garand rifles, and every third rifle should have a (M7) grenade launcher. The equipment could also be detected from the air if the Germans had observation aircraft in the area. According to Randal B. Wood's biography on Colby, the NORSO guys regretted that they had not packed their own equipment for the drop. Traphagen and Solhjel claimed, however, that it was the crew onboard one of the planes who had failed to attach the static lines to the plane and that Colby in retrospect had petitioned disciplinary actions against them.

A guard post was placed on the Litlfjellet, from where it had almost a complete overview of all the surrounding swamps that drained into Gjevsjø Lake on the Norwegian side of the border. On each side of Litlfjellet there are two valleys with a lot of dense vegetation, the western broken up by Lake Grønningen and the eastern by Lake Langvatnet. Through these corridors, Rype had a good chance to get back and forth to Snåsa and the Nordland Railway undetected.

Being on guard could keep a man on alert even without Germans. Once when Nipe was on duty at Litlfjellet, he heard a strange howling from the outback. Sometime later, he saw an exceptionally large dog emerge out onto the field, followed by two smaller ones. When Alfred Anderson saw the tracks afterwards, he cursed badly and said those were the biggest damned wolf tracks he had ever seen. The crust on the snow could not carry a grown man, but the wolf had gone through.[29]

Colby was particularly worried about German patrols approaching from Holden Farm, Lake Langvatnet, Seisjøen Lake, and Sørli. The latter is a settlement north of Snåsa. A guard was also posted near Gjefsjø Farm. Colby's report mentions "a system of signaling was devised," but gave no details on how it worked, other than the guard at the camp was on the watch for the signals.

The courier, presumably Kjell Sørli, was dispatched to Stockholm to deliver a situation report. He was interrogated by George Brewer, who reported back to London on March 28. This tells us something about the lines of communications, alternative to the W/T. From the drop site to the nearest settlement in Sweden, Björkede, there is a cross-country trek of about 10 kilometers. Gjevsjø Lake makes up a third of it, but the rest traverses rough terrain. We know they had a telephone at Björkede in 1945 but, for security reasons, it is highly unlikely that the courier would have been interrogated in detail over a civilian telephone line. However, he could have gotten a lift by horse or even car from there to the nearest railhead. This would be in Åre, some 110–120 kilometers to the south. The courier could have reached Björkede in the afternoon on March 26, and perhaps had a car waiting for him. Even with modern cars and roads, the trip to Åre takes about 2 hours and 20 minutes. A modern train from Åre to Stockholm takes about seven hours. It is difficult to recreate the journey today, but it is fair to assume that even with the use of mechanized transport as far as it would go, written communication between Gjevsjø and Stockholm would at least take three days. It was quite a feat that Kjell Sørli somehow reached Stockholm in only three days. However, Erichsen's following report to London suggests that he would not be back until "Tuesday," which means April 3—a six-day return journey.[30]

The Norwegian reception party had just recently reconnoitered the area to ensure there was no enemy movement nearby. The resistance had held Gjefsjø and the surrounding area under surveillance over several weeks, but the Germans had so far made themselves scarce. A six-man patrol had been observed that morning at Holden Farm, some 10 kilometers as the crow flies to the southwest. But they had left in a southerly direction. Rype agreed with Jåma that he would alert them as soon as he observed that the Germans were on the way towards them, or of anything else that might be of interest. As a reindeer-herding Sámi, he had permission to move near the border and was able to roam the area without arousing suspicion. Nor was it expected that the German occupation troops stationed in the closest settlements would patrol the area with zeal now that the war was nearing its end. But although the farm was isolated and far from the nearest all-year road link, they could not be sure that they would not be discovered. They also had to watch out for the guards that accompanied the groups of Russian POWs who were sent into the forest to chop wood. It was also rumored that a Nazi-friendly sheriff in the nearby Sørli district had plans to inspect the area. Colby was afraid that the Germans had heard the B-24s and that they had drawn the conclusion that since no bombs were dropped, something or someone had to have been parachuted down nearby. There was also a Norwegian border police post, subject to the Hirden, but they numbered at most only 183 men nationwide in 1943 and they were not very effective.

The Americans had more reason to worry about Norwegian Easter tourists (Easter Day in 1945 fell on April 1) because at the time it was not uncommon for ski tourists in the mountains to seek out cottages and farms to ask for accommodation. It seems that NORSO did stay at the farm until March 27, then, so as not to take unnecessary risks, they vacated Gjefsjø to set up a concealed camp in the nearby wood, about 1.5 kilometers southeast of Gjefsjø, not far from where the equipment from plane *Glenn* was stashed. They reported to London that they would be back at the farm on Monday. Around the camp they made a circuitous ski track, so that if anyone followed it, they would be easily spotted from the camp. A guard post was placed at the entrance, and a system of warnings was arranged with the farmer at Gjefsjø. The camp consisted of four tents with a white outside, and parachutes were used for further camouflage. For flooring inside the tent, they used ponchos. Some accounts also mention shelters made of branches. Colby was quite satisfied, reporting that the camp was "comparatively comfortable and very well hidden."[31] A tight security regime was kept, and the men were only allowed to leave the camp on orders to rebury containers or fetch equipment or food. On March 30, Good Friday, they became aware of a group of adolescents approaching the farm, seven boys and four girls. They came all the way up to the farm and could not possibly have avoided seeing all the ski tracks and other signs of unusually high activity around a remote mountain farm. Helgesen decided to contact the group before they left to tell anyone what they had seen. He was wearing the British battledress, thus leaving little doubt who he was. However, the Americans kept out of sight, so they were left to believe that they had only blundered into a Norwegian Resistance camp. Helgesen questioned them and having ascertained that they were not Quislings (Norwegian Nazis), he made them understand that the farm was not a prospective place for Easter.[32] Helgesen dictated a letter to their families, explaining that they had escaped to Sweden, then they were escorted across the border by Kjell Sørlie. Their parents down in Snåsa were naturally concerned. The deputy sheriff of Snåsa—who as a member of the resistance knew what really had happened—sent two men into the mountain for show to ask Hans Leirmo about what had happened. Leirmo played along and told them that he had met the kids and that they had asked about directions to cross the border.

Another security concern was the forester in the area. He was appointed by the Germans and was suspected of being an informer. He resided on a farm some 10 kilometers away and "kept an open house" for the Germans and was known in the border area for his Nazi sympathies. This may also be the Quisling east of Snåsa referred to in the Field Order No. 2. Helgesen wrote in a report dated April 19 that on an unknown date, the forester had gone to visit Gjefsjø "out of curiosity." Helgesen was obviously concerned about having this man in the area, so "M.8" was asked to take him back upon his return to Sweden. M.8 was a codename for an unknown operative or courier. "I hope you will put him in a concentration camp for the duration," was Helgesen's final remark on the matter, however, there are no further mentions of this man's fate or details in any of Colby's own reports.[33]

Colby soon became frustrated at how much time and energy was spent by the group in sorting through the equipment and preparing food. This began a series of requests for the insertion of Sergeant Kyllo, Sergeant Ausen, and Technician Fifth Grade Anderson to take care of such matters. The former had intentionally been left behind in the UK to handle supplies from that end, but Colby was now evidently having second thoughts about that decision.

Odd Sørli was mentioned as present at the reception of the group. He would soon take charge of the necessary transports across the border from Stockholm. The importance of these transports from Sweden would grow proportionately with the difficulties of getting supplies air dropped. Of the group, Moan, Lian, Andreas Andersen, and Kjell Sørli were mentioned as being occupied with getting these transports into Norway, together with Bjarne Alhus. The latter individual's full name was Bertil Vestgöte Alhus. He was of mixed Norwegian-Swedish background, and had done his military service in Sweden, but was a native of Namsos in Norway. At the age of 21, he had to choose either Norwegian or Swedish citizenship, and he chose the former, according to Helgesen, in order to take part in resistance work. Helgesen described him as an idealist and well-liked by the Americans. He was even said to have wanted to go to the Far East with the OSS.[34] These men would all be engaged in transporting messages and supplies from Sweden and the nearest road connection up to Gjefsjø. They were invaluable to Rype, not just because of their local knowledge, but also because they had the necessary documents to travel in Sweden.

An attempt was made to contact London just after they had landed; their message was received, but they could not hear London in return. The day after, two-way communication was established and they sent a situation report and could confirm that only planes with codenames *Bill, Trygve, Glenn* and *Einar* had made successful drops at Gjevsjø. At the other end in London, women from the Female Auxiliary Nursing Yeomanry (FANY) received and dispatched messages. According to Langeland, they had insufficient training, and yet the fate of hundreds of Allied agents and special forces operators was put into their hands. SFHQ in London could confirm that three planes had returned fully loaded, and one had dropped men and cargo into Sweden. A report given by Kjell Sørli revealed that radio contact could not be made at first because one radio set could not be found, and the Nichols set (an American modified version of the Mark II B) was damaged after hitting the ground, but the damage proved only superficial. However, Odd dispatched Kjell to pick up a spare set at a base some 40 kilometers away (presumably the Woodlark base at Burvatnet). The radio was said to have weighed 18 kilograms (the Mark II B only weighs 2.3 kilograms), and when he got to the shore of Gjevsjø Lake on the Swedish side, Kjell was exhausted. He looked for food in the backpack, and finally found some crispbread in one of the side pouches. This gave him renewed energy to continue the trip. The damaged radio set was sent for repairs in Stockholm and was expected back on March 29 or the day after. Batteries were another problem, but a generator brought in from Sweden on March 30 solved that problem. A replacement set was also requested by Erichsen, specifying that it had to be powered by a hand generator. According to the initial packing plan, Rype was supposed to have a gasoline generator, but it is uncertain if it arrived, and Erichsen must also have realized at some point that gasoline supply was uncertain. Part of a British Mark II B radio is still kept at Gjefsjø Farm, but whether it was dropped with Rype or came from the Norwegians is hard to tell. Most likely it is the later replacement ordered by Erichsen since it was supplied with a hand generator.

During the first week Langeland operated their radio under the open sky, but sometimes he had to work inside a small tent to be able to use the light so that he could write down the messages. Their field order specified that the radio would have to be used as little as possible, probably not just to conserve power but also to avoid detection by German radio direction finding units that were constantly searching for resistance transmitters. Langeland noted an immediate interference when he came on the air, and he recommended that transmissions be kept as short as possible and limited to the strictly necessary,[35] but there are no indications that the Germans were onto them. The antenna was arranged by attaching a wire to a rock, thrown up into a spruce tree. The radio had a six-volt wet battery and was easy to carry in a briefcase. There were five or six frequencies to alternate between but establishing radio communications was challenging, and Colby praised Langeland for his ability to maintain contact.[36] Langeland elaborated on these challenges in his comments when he later published the transcripts of the telegraph messages between SFHQ in London and *Rype*. They had to be transmitted during allotted time slots during each 24-hour period. Sometimes contact could only be made during the day, sometimes only by night, depending on frequencies and scheduling, or the atmospheric conditions.

NORSO reported that the conditions for sending and receiving radio messages at Gjevsjø were unstable because of the varying atmospheric conditions but they were probably no worse off than what the SOE or the home front experienced in general—on the contrary, Langeland estimated that their set-up was the most reliable in Norway during the war, and Rype was therefore used as a relay station for messages that were going to and from other resistance and sabotage groups.[37] But even when conditions were good, sending and receiving messages was a tedious process. All the messages had to be encoded letter by letter before they were sent by morse signals, and when they were received, the whole process had to be done in reverse. In doing this, they had no machine to encode the messages. German radio detection devices of WWII were usually vehicle borne, and being far away from any road, meant accurate detection was unlikely, but interference of the broadcasts they experienced was interpreted as German attempts of just that. Being aware of the challenges of the weather, Rype would send daily reports, which were forwarded to the OSS Air Center.

According to the first message sent by *Rype* back to London on March 26, they needed at least two plane loads before attacking the target.[38] Field Order No. 2 stated that resupply would be flown in on the call of the NORSO Group Commander in the field, Major Colby. These flights would also be guided in by Eureka. Codenames for 12 DZs were picked out. Named after Greek and Roman gods, each had a letter code, and a coded message to be read over the BBC would signal in what zone Rype could expect the drop. The message would be preceded with the phrase "From Henrik to *Rype*." For instance, Area 2 had codename "Mars," code letter "C" and the BBC message would be "Full av sol" ("Full of sunshine"). The zones were to be chosen later.[39] However, it is not known whether this procedure was followed in the supply attempts that were to be made; it seems all missions were aimed at dropping over Gjevsjø. Messages from London about attempts to send reinforcements or supplies often came as coded messages over the BBC. Longer report-backs were sent to Sweden by courier. One obvious problem with this form of communication was that there was no feedback on whether these had been received in London.[40]

Langeland reported that they needed at least two additional aircraft loaded with supplies before they could be operational. London promised to send three as soon as possible. On March 27, they had already sent a request for additional equipment, to replace what they feared had either been left behind in Scotland or which they would be unable to recover. Bren guns, Garands, Springfield rifles, a generator, radio, batteries, a medical kit, 12 pair of skis, sleeping bags, and clothes were the items requested, along with a repeated request to send Kyllo, Ausen, and Harold Andersen to run the base. By then, they had realized that they needed more men to execute the planned attack.[41] Rype would also communicate by W/T with Erichsen in Stockholm. However, a report dated May 3 includes one puzzling passage: "Our radio man refuses to stay on the air because of possible difficulties with the Legation." Which legation is not specified (Norwegian or American), but it might suggest that radio communication from OSS personnel in Sweden directly to US operators in the field could have been regarded as conflicting with Swedish neutrality.[42]

NORSO's presence put the people at Gjefsjø in danger. The owner, Alfred Andersson, put himself and his farm at their disposal but his family soon evacuated to Sweden, where they would be cared for "by the Norwegian authorities, or failing that, by us [the Americans]."[43] Recognizing that this would be the responsibility of Norwegian authorities in exile, but feeling obliged to step into their place, Colby put a high value on Andersson's expertise as he was one of the most famous hunters in the region. Alfred himself said he would return after he had taken his family to safety. In Stockholm, they were lodged in a hotel in the center of the city. However well-meaning this luxurious arrangement was, the family were used to the remote and secluded Gjefsjøen and were scared to even cross the road—cars and trams seemed more terrifying than wolves and Nazis to these country folk. Colby and his men had moved back to the farm by April 5, and in return for the hospitality they agreed they would tend to the animals. This duty probably fell mostly on the indigenous Norwegians, as none of the Americans had any known experience in farm work. They spent a full day and night installing themselves on the farm. As mentioned, the plan was to have planeloads made up in "self-contained units," meaning that the men would be dropped with supplies and equipment needed to operate for 40 days. However, as resistance fighters were added to the group, and as Oistad's group were united with their comrades in arms, this would prove insufficient. The airdrop contained the US Army's K- and C-rations, which constituted the main part of the diet at the start. In addition, they received the British-produced pemmican, a mixture of dried meat, fat, and berries traditionally used as provisions by indigenous people across large parts of North America. The word comes from the Cree language, and pemmican was quickly adopted by European fur traders and explorers. It was also used by Norwegian explorers such as Nansen and Amundsen. It is rich in energy, but not always easy to digest. They also had some food brought in from Sweden. Though no quantities are given, Colby's progress report dated April 5 stated that Erichsen had provided them with additional 2,500 Swedish kroner and that food was arriving at Gjefsjø with the Norwegian auxiliaries.[44]

In early April, there was still optimism regarding the logistics of the operation. In 1945, Norwegian variety artist Arve Opsahl had a hit song called "There is a Boat with Bananas Coming." Of course, the song was not about a yearning for tropical fruit, but a metaphor for the end of the war and its tribulation. About the same time, some Norwegians sat on a mountain farm up in Snåsa in Nord-Trøndelag and dreamed of another southern glory—pineapple!

> A special request—enough canned pineapple for one meal for all men present—some 30 now. Lt. Saeter was talking when he really should have been listening and made a bet with Lt. Hoel [Herbert Helgesen] stating that we could have pineapple up here within two months. Lt. Hoel spread it around among the Norwegians as a joke since pineapples have not been seen here for years. It would be a tremendous shot for US prestige if the pineapples could be produced, and tremendous supply power of the US demonstrated. I think it would be a very worthwhile package to drop.[45]

As far as we know, this delivery never arrived. Pineapple certainly had the same symbolic value for these guys as bananas had for Arve Opsahl.

In addition to helping themselves to vegetables and potatoes from the farm, the NORSO men also slaughtered a couple of cows. Here, Helgesen's experience as a butcher came in handy as he knew how to process the meat. They also bought reindeer from the local reindeer-herding Sámi, or they shot them and compensated the owners later. This supply of provisions may sound sufficient, but wires back to SFHQ in London tell of the lack of food, especially towards the end. Supplements coming in from Sweden were erratic, and the men could sometimes experience shortages. Nils Albin Gjefsjø, Alfred Andersson's son, who was nine years old at the time, stated later that there was plenty of food there and that he could not understand that there could have been any kind of shortage. However, the NORSO guys may have been reluctant to deprive the Anderssons of the food supplies they would sorely need after the war. In addition, as the need for calories was extreme in this sub-Arctic environment, the OSS might have miscalculated the requirements. Replacements for the cigarettes, sweets, and soap, which Colby suspected was missing due to thefts during the packaging in the United Kingdom, were also requested. NORSO's preferred outfit appears to have been US Army Rangers wool uniforms and Ike jackets—lightweight warm parkas with fur-lined hoods.

But before they could fulfill their mission, they had to get reinforcements. Sixteen men was far too few according to Colby. On April 1 he sent a lengthy situation report—they knew at this point that the group on board the plane *Leif* had been dropped over Sweden, but not where. With the report, which was submitted in writing by courier, was attached a Swedish newspaper that was obtained via the Norwegian Resistance fighters, which read that US paratroopers had ended up on the Swedish side of the border. This news was also featured in the American newspaper *Stars and Stripes*.

Back in England, the OSS were also trying to find the causes of the failures thus far. As a summary of the air support of the mission, Skabo and Bolland stated in a joint report on April 10 that:

> a) We believe that our OSS Air Liaison Office has failed in performance of its duties in connection with this operation.
> b) The evidence seems to indicate that certain of the ships flown on these sorties were not up to the standard required for such an operation.
> c) The experience seems to show that the crews employed for this operation were not sufficiently experienced for flights in northern latitudes.[46]

To rectify these deficiencies, they recommended the allocation of aircraft in first-class condition, probably referring to the aircraft having been retired from anti-submarine warfare duty over the North Atlantic,[47] which meant that the airframes had been subjected to stress and could not be expected to perform optimally. They also recommended that they had to be equipped with the proper operational devices, especially homing devices. Likewise, competent aircrews were needed, according to Bolland and Skabo, preferably from the Royal Norwegian Air Force, assigned to American aircraft. If these requirements were not met, further attempts at reinforcements were not recommended.[48] It must be noted that while Norwegian aircrews had extensive experience in flying Mosquitos and PBY Catalinas along the coast, none had ever flown four-engine bombers, let alone B-24s, deep into the interior of the country. However, the OSS had already requested back in October 1944 that Colonel Balchen be put in charge of the air support of the resistance and Allied special operations in Norway.[49]

CHAPTER TEN

Swedish Escapades

By March 26, 1945, the men at Gjevsjø Farm were informed that one of the planes had made a drop in Sweden. Three days later, they were also notified that the plane was Leif Oistad's plane. The five on the plane *Leif* that landed on the Swedish side of the border were:

Technical Sergeant Leif Oistad
Corporal Knut Andreasen
Technician Fifth Grade Tom Rusdal
Technician Fifth Grade Sivert Windh
Technician Fifth Grade Eddie Hovland

In later debriefings, these NORSO men stated that the pilot had ordered them to jump, allegedly after having contacted the reception party's Eureka and receiving the letter "F," but that the equipment had malfunctioned. The NORSO men could not see the ground from their position inside the plane and had no reason to question the pilot. However, the pilot's report stated that "Joes dropped out knowing they were not at exact target position, knew they were in area and wanted to be dropped. Were cast of[f] target pinpoint."[1] So, there were two contradictory versions of who was responsible for the jump that was about 66 kilometers off target.

The men hit the ground around 02:00. Since there were no burning logs on the ice and no one was waiting for them, they realized that they had ended up on the wrong lake. At first, that was all they knew for certain, so they had no reason to suspect anything other than that they were in Norway, but simply at the wrong place. According to Sivert Windh, they had also been informed that there would be snow on the surface of Gjevsjø, which there was not on this lake—something that Windh learned the hard way as he hit his head hard on the ice upon landing. Oistad later recalled that they cursed the pilot's ancestors for the misery, and reckoned that the issue of fuel may have been part of the reason why they were dropped into an uncertain location.[2] After acquiring a pilot's license himself after the war, Oistad then understood why it had been better to have been dropped in an unknown location over land, rather than later in the North Sea when they would have been perilous low on fuel if it had been decided to try to take them back to the UK.

On the other side of the lake, they saw lights emanating from a house. These might have come from the house of Sigrid and John Palm, who were awoken by the engine noise, got dressed, and turned on the lights. John took a kick sledge down to the lake and saw several dark objects spread out on the lake surface. The equipment dropped with Oistad and his men was spread out in a half-moon pattern over some 5 kilometers. They realized they would not be able to collect all of it and get away before daylight, when their presence would be revealed. They assumed the site would soon be swarming with Germans, as they still believed they were somewhere in Norway. Although Field Order No. 1 claimed that they would be treated as POWs if caught in uniform, Command Order mentioned above must have been well known to Oistad and his men. Therefore, the men dug in and prepared to fight to the death.

From here, there are at least three versions on what happened next, all of which end up with the Americans being apprehended by Swedish authorities and later released to join their comrades at Gjefsjø. For the locals in the small community of Lien on the banks of the lake, it sounded as if the aircraft went straight over their houses. On March 26, both national and local Swedish newspapers featured the story of these stranded Americans. Their source was the *landsfiskal*, a public official—a mixture between a sheriff and a district attorney—named Herje Skuncke. According to the newspapers, the Americans were approached by Skuncke and his *fjärdingsmann* (deputy) who managed to explain that they had ended up in a neutral country, and the NORSO men surrendered with no shots fired. The explosives picked up from their supplies consisted of dynamite, trotyl (TNT), precharges, and fuses, and were said to have made up an entire truckload.

Skuncke told the national newspaper *Expressen* that he had heard engine noise at his home in Offerdal but was scrambled by telephone by some civilians telling him of objects spread out over the surface of a lake. He and his assistant skied across the lake in the direction of the site when they spotted five men moving about cautiously along the tree line that ran along the opposite shore. Skuncke hailed the men, telling them that they were in Sweden. Civilians who had followed were instructed to keep their distance in case something unfortunate happened.

The local newspaper, *Östersundsposten*, only reported drily in a short note that American soldiers were apprehended by military personnel after they and their equipment had been dropped on the wrong side of the border.[3] But according to what Skuncke told *Expressen*, the encounter was far more dramatic. The Americans were manning their weapons, ready to fire, when he and his assistant approached. He also described them as well-trained and armed to the teeth. But they handed over their weapons and helped in gathering the equipment that was still littering the lake surface, as well as some that they had managed to hide away amongst the trees. Skuncke found them easy-going and friendly. All of them had skis, and they skiied with Skuncke away from the site, revealing further details of who they were. There was one sergeant (Oistad) and four corporals aged 21–27, from places such as New York, Chicago, and Long Island.[4]

In 1953, Skuncke published his memoirs and provided further details on his version of the story. In addition to what Skuncke told the Swedish press in 1945, his memoirs describe even more drama.[5] The backdrop to the story is a train ride after the war, when Skuncke was approached by an air warden officer, who had received Skuncke's phone call back in 1945 when he reported the incident with the Americans. The officer, referred to as "Mr. Z," more or less dragged the story out of Skuncke. The engine noise that awoke him at his home in Offerdal that night at the end of World War II, was not unusual in those days. However, this time it was louder and more sustained. He realized right away that it was a foreign aircraft, crossing from Norway. But despite the moonshine, he could not get a visual on it. When Skuncke said that he called the air warning central in the town of Östersund, Mr. Z commented that they had already received reports of 10 (*sic*) aircraft entering Swedish airspace from Norway. After a sleepless night, Skuncke was preparing to go skiing with his sons the following morning, when he received a message from a man called Lind from the small community of Lien on Lake Landösjöen who had spotted some "suitcases" out on the ice that must have appeared during the night. He took along his assistant and two sons to meet Lind in Lien. Once at the shore, Skuncke could see the objects for himself.

Skuncke, his two sons, and the assistant approached the lake on skis. The snow was deep but covered by a crust. Lind followed on a kick sledge. Once they reached the lake's surface, they spotted people about 1.5 kilometers away on the opposite shore. Through binoculars, Skuncke observed five men facing towards them without moving, partially hidden behind some timber. He initially assumed they were timber cruising, but then realized it was a Sunday. From the way in which the objects were spread out in a semicircle, Skuncke assumed they had been dropped from an airplane. When they closed in further, the men got very busy and headed quickly for some dark objects placed at a point covered by trees. They picked up these objects and carried them away into the thick fir forest. Skuncke halted and ordered Lind and his sons to return to the opposite shore and seek cover in the woods. As a public official in the Norwegian–Swedish border areas in wartime, this would not have been the first time Skuncke had been in contact with airmen, the resistance, deserters, or whoever these men were.

Skuncke was dressed in uniform covered by a white anorak, over which he had a belt and shoulder belt. He also wore a blue cap and was armed with a pistol, but this he kept in his backpack. Skuncke's assistant was in civilian clothing. When they were 100 meters away, Skuncke spotted two of the men hunkered down between the trees, some distance from the shore, in what he assumed was a firing position.

As he closed in further, he could see that they were manning machine guns. Standing behind the branches of a fir tree, he spotted a third man. All of them wore civilian clothing, sportswear, but they looked quite menacing at this point.[6]

This sounds odd, as NORSO was always instructed to wear uniform while on operations. However, Field Order No. 1 had one provision for donning civilian clothes—if they were forced to abandon the mission or ordered to do so by SFHQ, they would retreat to Sweden. In that case, they would contact Woodlark and try to obtain civilian clothes through them, and leave uniforms, equipment, identification cards, and money behind. It was "of the greatest importance" to avoid the Swedes realizing that they had come from the UK. However, if at this point they believed they were in Norway, the order stated that they had to be in uniform at all times.[7] Although it is therefore hardly likely that they would have worn civilian clothes on the first encounter before they realized they were in the wrong country, it is possible they could have put them on after they had realized they were in Sweden before the *landsfiskal* caught up with them.

Skuncke himself was exposed on the lake without any cover, and he still had no clue about who or what these men were, but he understood that he had to approach them with caution. At about 70 meters he hailed them in Swedish: "This is Sweden, we are Swedish police!" Nobody moved. Skuncke repeated his words in English, then in German. As he closed in further, he spotted yet two more men. All were pointing their weapons at him, looking back at him with serious faces. Skuncke composed himself amidst the tense situation. He was now only 3–4 meters away as he stopped and repeated that they were in Sweden. He addressed the machine gunner to his right and asked their nationality, upon which the answer was "American." Skuncke repeated that they were well into Sweden, and that it was his duty to take care of them. There was some commotion and discussion amongst the Americans. Were they to be interned? Before Skuncke answered these questions, he requested that they handed over their weapons. Two of them complied immediately and handed over their pistols. One of the machine gunners pulled violently on the belt, lifted the gun above his head and threw it into the snow so that the muzzle pointed straight up against Skuncke's torso, to his indignant protest.[8]

Again, Field Order No. 1 provided some guidelines for conduct. If they were forced to flee into Sweden, NORSO would claim they were ordinary Norwegian refugees fleeing the German occupation. They would not disclose having taken part in any "secret work" and were to appear as unimportant as possible in every respect so as to not provoke the interest of the Swedish secret service. In case these measures were required, they were also discouraged from carrying documents or any other items that might contradict this story. However, if they could not obtain civilian clothes, they would surrender themselves as American paratroop soldiers who had escaped from operations in Norway and be ready to be interned. If so, it was believed that they would also keep their identity cards, dog tags, and money.[9]

The American standing farthest away from Skuncke, started to wade through the snow towards him, with his pistol drawn. He seemed agitated, and the Swede felt uneasy about his approach as he feared the weapon might be accidentally discharged as he stumbled through the deep snow with his finger on his trigger. The American protested against any talk of internment, although Skuncke had not yet mentioned it. He presented himself as the sergeant and leader of the group, which identifies him as Leif Oistad. Oistad continued that they were certain that they had landed in Norway and that it was only luck that Skuncke had not been shot, which might have happened if he had addressed them in German first, and not English. Oistad explained that they initially believed him to be a German officer, with what Skuncke perceived as hatred. Still agitated, and with the finger on the trigger, he tore off his cap, tossed it into the snow, and jumped on it several times, almost losing his balance and sometimes with the muzzle pointing straight at the Swede. However, Skuncke could not help but be a bit amused since the American had a snowshoe on one foot. Oistad then took off and disappeared between the trees, but soon returned of his own free will. Apparently, he had now calmed down and handed over his pistol, but not without kissing it first.[10]

By now, Skuncke's two sons and Lind had caught up with them. Skuncke described the American warriors as:

> … lively, and keen lads, maybe more of a genuine cowboy type than the more alert kind we are used to here in our country. But without a doubt suited for their mission, that of the saboteur. Their equipment also seemed to be state of the art. That their dress was civilian—sportswear of a type and color that would also be familiar to us [in Sweden] (aut. trans.).[11]

According to Skuncke, the Americans told him how they had jumped at approximately 02:00 that night, believing they had landed on Gjevsjø. Two of the planes circled Landösjöen, and one dropped its cargo there. If this is correct, the other plane might have been the one carrying Colby, which also went off course before finding its way back to the correct bearings. Further, they continued to reveal that their destination was Gjevsjø, their mission to blow up the Nordland Line, and that there had been 10 aircraft in total. Here, several details of Skuncke's account do not match what is generally known about OGs and OSS operations, nor the information given independently by other eyewitnesses. It is not known that NORSO deployed with any belt-fed machine guns, as Skuncke claims. It also seems unlikely that they wore leisure suits, as OGs operated in uniform and not civilian clothes as OSS's special intelligence agents would.[12] It is also unlikely that the Americans would divulge such details as the intended drop site and their target.

However, Skuncke's account does reveal detailed knowledge of the operation, irrefutable facts, and that he knew what their mission was, their destination, and how many planes there were in total, which suggests he had some source of information of what went down. This is most peculiar since the book was published back in

1953, before much had been published on NORSO and *Rype*. Also, in an undated letter to Arne Sandness, Oistad seems to confirm some of the details in Skuncke's account that are not reconcilable with those given by the locals, and indeed Windh and Oistad themselves upon their 1999 visit to Lien:

> Oh, what a circus that ensued when we thought we were in Norway and was about to shoot the sheriff when he came to arrest us. I think it was a bit strange that they all spoke Swedish so well; I was a bit insulted when they took away my pistol and binoculars.[13]

"A bit insulted" of course being quite an understatement if we are to believe Skuncke's observations. In the 30th anniversary book, Oistad explicitly states that they gave name, rank and number only.[14] It seems unlikely, and certainly not according to their instructions, for NORSO to reveal such details on their mission as Skuncke implies. However, it is entirely possible that Skuncke got the story from some of the Norwegians who were involved in the operation immediately after the war. This assumption is supported by what he misses out on. Skuncke stated that none of the men understood Swedish. If Skuncke had picked up the story from the media, one might expect him to know that they were Scandinavians, and that one of them was even born in Sweden.

The end of Skuncke's tale has a twist that really questions his credibility as an eyewitness of the first encounter with the Americans. One of the passengers listening in on the story in the train car is none other than Kjell Sørli! He is supposed to have been in the same coach on his way home for the Easter holidays while studying medicine in Copenhagen. Kjell Sørli did study medicine in the Danish capital after the war, and served as a GP in the community of Oppdal—but what are the odds of him being in the same train carriage as Skuncke and Mr Z? Given Skuncke's position, it is not unlikely that he had contact with the Norwegian Resistance members, and that he had heard the story being told after the war and knew of Kjell Sørli's future career. That he had heard the story orally is supported by the misconception that the crash at Plukkutjønnfjellet (see below) is misdated to March 24, something that is not known to have been put into print anywhere. In Skuncke's defense, the style his memoir is written in is more that of an adventure story with a dash of crime novel, and it does not appear to claim to be an accurate historical account.

In the short version in Bruce Heimark's book, there are no references given for sources of these events but it there is reason to believe that Leif Oistad was his main source, given his frequent interviews with him. It corresponds with the account given by Oistad, Windh, and locals from Lind in a news story published in 1999 at the unveiling of a memorial to their encounter. In both versions, the first encounter between the NORSO men and the Swedes was with a man approaching them on a bicycle, something that was bound to stick in the minds of those present. Just before dawn, they spotted him approaching, according to Heimark, across the ice. They feared he was from the Gestapo and stopped him. According to Heimark:

> Sivert Windh greeted him as he approached. Windh asked him, where in Norway were they? The man chuckled and told them they were in Sweden, Norway being sixty kilometers west![15]

This corresponds with Langeland's account in his 1975 publication: Sivert Windh went after the man on the bicycle to bring him in for questioning. The Swede could inform them that they were in Sweden. "Shortly thereafter" the *lensmann* (sheriff, or *landsfiskal* in Swedish) arrived together with Swedish ski troopers. Although disappointed, there was some comfort in that the "200 ski troopers" that approached them were Swedes, rather than Germans. It must be noted that Langeland's account is not part of the telegrams, but rather in comments he later added, based on secondary information.[16] Oistad and Windh expressed uncertainty in 1999 about who they encountered first wearing what appeared to be a dark uniform and thought it might have been *Landsfiskal* Skuncke. The locals have since adamantly claimed that a man called Nils Persson from Lien was the first to meet them and also that he had arrived on a bike, but along a dirt road, not across the lake. Both the locals and the Americans agreed that the person approaching them came on a bicycle, not on skis. Oistad remembered the man coming across with a throng of kids behind him. When he came closer, the man shouted "skjut inte, skjut inte, ni är i Sverige!" ("Don't shoot, don't shoot, you're in Sweden!"). Windh, himself originally from Sweden, heard what the man said and reasoned that no German spoke Swedish that well. This probably prevented the situation from escalating if one is to believe this version.

One of the locals was John Palm, who took them back to his house and treated them to coffee and sandwiches. Their Swedish hosts believed that their guests were Englishmen, a belief the Americans did not attempt to alter. The locals also claim that Magnus Lien, who owned the nearest farm on the opposite shore of the lake from the DZ, was the one who phoned Skuncke upon discovering the objects on the lake.[17] When Skuncke arrived, the tone got less amicable and more formal. The NORSO men gave their names, ranks, and service numbers and the Swedes found neither plans nor codes on them, and they were commended afterwards by their superiors for having kept their mouths shut. Even hiding that Norwegian (and Swedish in Windh's case) was their first language would have been a challenge. There is no reason to question Skuncke's version on what followed the first encounter. The locals gathered their horses and began to collect and transport the equipment and supplies that were scattered around the surface of the lake into a pile on the shore. From there, they carted it away. Skuncke counted a total of 24 parachutes. One of the containers with explosives had gone straight through the thawing ice but was later salvaged. The total amount of explosives collected amounted to 1,200 kilograms. But not everything was found; in 1960 a fisherman caught a mine in his nets. Other items recovered much later included a radio transmitter, clothes, white painted steel-edged skis, poles, snowshoes, cigarettes, contraceptives, and provisions.

Not long after the Americans were taken to Palm's home, 200 Swedish soldiers arrived at the scene to investigate what the engine noise heard the previous night was all about. The Americans were taken in for questioning, much to the dismay of the locals, including the kids who got to taste chewing gum for the first time. The Americans did not get going until dusk and were driven away in a taxi cab to Skuncke's home in Ekeberg. The Swedes, of course, wondered what they were doing in Sweden and if they were the start of a larger invasion force. They asked what was in the boxes that contained plastic explosives, and Oistad answered "hamburgers." Then they were taken to Östersund. They were stripped of their clothes and led to a brick building. Inside there were five tubs filled with hot water. Behind each stood a woman from Svenska Låttakåren (Swedish Women's Voluntary Defense Organization) with a brush. Rusdal protested at the humiliation, but Oistad remembered later that he had never seen anyone who "fought so bravely, yet surrendered so gracefully."[18] After this brutal debugging, they were interned in a camp outside Falun in Dalarne. There they were lodged together with other Allied internees. Their quarters were comfortable, and they enjoyed a time of leisure with relatively great freedom of movement. Many would probably have been happy to wait it out in safety, but not Oistad and the rest of the group. In Knut Andreasen's words: "This damned war isn't going to last much longer. We have got to get our asses out of here because I should hate to sit here when the war ends."[19]

The OSS office in Stockholm got wind of the rumor that US paratroopers had landed in Sweden. Again, according to the contingency instructions in case they were forced to flee across into Sweden, they would have been expected to arrive at a refugee reception camp at Kjäsäter. There they would seek out Norwegian intelligence in Sweden (*Rettskontoret*—the Legal Office) and give the password "Holmenkollrennet er avlyst i år" ("The Holmenkollen ski race is canceled this year") and expect the response "ja det var det i fjor også" ("Yes, so it was last year too"). This procedure would convince the Norwegians that they were not Nazi infiltrators. When reporting to the Norwegian Legation in Stockholm, they would ask to speak with Major Axel Baumann, leader of the MilOrg office at the legation (MI IV) and give the password "vi er globetrottere" ("We are globetrotters"). This would trigger a message to Erichsen who then would know that members of Rype had arrived in Sweden.[20] Although events did not play out as provided for in the contingency arrangements, it gave Oistad and his men some clue as to how to get in touch with Erichsen, although it is not stated in the sources how it really happened.

According to the report sent by *Westfield* commander George Brewer, Erichsen returned from interrogating Oistad and the others in captivity on March 28, so there could not have been much delay from the time the Swedes had identified them until the OSS were notified of their presence and realized they had to act quickly, but the only thing they could do at that time was to pay five dollars per day as an allowance and to buy them $300 worth of civilian clothes. The NORSO men had carried plans, codes, and crystals to enable radio contact between Rype and Waxwing and between Rype and London. Luckily, Oistad and the rest managed to hide them from the Swedes and then handed them over to Erichsen, who took them safely back to Stockholm.[21] That late in the war, the Swedes might also have been quite lenient, not pressing body searches or interrogations too hard. At the same time, there was a danger that German spies could pick up that they had ended up in Sweden and that the Germans would send out patrols and start to look for the rest of the group on the Norwegian side. SFHQ in London not only wanted their release but also that they be infiltrated directly into Norway to join the rest of Rype. According to the official war report of the OSS, the Americans struck a deal with the Swedish secret police.[22] Skis, fake Norwegian passports, civilian clothes, and weapons had been provided through the OSS Office in Stockholm. With the help of a border guide, the men made the four-day ski march to Gjevsjø, where they arrived on April 12. There was no diplomatic aftermath, and the Swedes did not even send a formal protest about what was technically an American invasion of Sweden.

On March 29, Rype was warned over the radio that the event had created "extensive publicity" and that the Germans might send out patrols.[23] When the courier returned, he brought Swedish newspapers in which they could read for themselves the unwanted publicity that the mis-drop had caused. The initial report sent from Stockholm to London even revealed that the "fifth plane landed in Sweden," which of course would have meant even more trouble. When Erichsen interrogated them, they were already in Falun. He reported that the men were "[a]ll well and unhappy" and under tight security; the latter appeared to have been relaxed after a while. Further, he found their conduct impeccable. Neither were they to blame for the unhappy situation as the drop had all been the pilot's decision. One might suspect that pilots were inclined to drop their cargo blind to ease their own passage home. But even more strange is the fact that Erichsen did not dwell in his report on the pilot's claim that they had received the letter "F." Either this was a flat lie, or was there somebody on the ground nearby who managed to trick the pilot to make the drop in the wrong place? All the equipment of the Oistad group was confiscated, and even if they managed to rejoin Colby and the others, this would have to be replaced. Erichsen asked for this to be dropped with the remainder of the NORSO group, but that would not happen, and replacement supplies and material would eventually have to be sent through Sweden.[24]

In his report dated April 19, Colby expressed gratitude for Erichsen's effort to release Leif Oistad and his men, and they in turn felt that it was he who had "raised enough hell" to get them out so soon.[25] However, according to Norwegian historian Tore Pryser, it was Chris Randal at the US embassy in Stockholm who achieved their release.[26] The surviving rosters list Oistad and his men as reporting for duty on April 15, 1945. A much under-appreciated aspect of *Rype* was that the men had several civilians to deal with in between going out on sabotage missions.

It was a huge security hazard when civilians first arrived, however, the risk would only be aggravated by turning them away. After all, Gjefsjø was known to have accommodated several refugees and ever-present in these matters were the ghosts of Vercors. The same day Oistad arrived with his men, a family of one man, a woman, and a child arrived at Gjefsjø farm. They stayed until April 29, when they proceeded to Sweden.[27] According to a report sent by Helgesen to Stockholm, this was a husband, a wife, and a three-year-old daughter from Snåsa, who had arrived at Gjefsjø "a couple of days ago" (the report was dated April 19) to help Alfred Andersson out on his farm in the absence of his own family.[28] He might not have been present at Gjefsjø himself, as Helgesen further down the report urged that Andersson be sent up as soon as possible. But the place was practically crawling with "Anderson/Andersen"—two Norwegians and one American in addition to Alfred—so it is hard to be certain it meant him.

Windh's recommendation for the Bronze Star contained a special mention of the "Swedish incident," lauding him for keeping his cool and not doing anything to compromise the security of the operation, which might have jeopardized the safety of his comrades in Rype. However, the following is a testimony to how imaginative these recommendations could be: "Early that morning, the Unit, after hearing continuous machine-gun fire, watched the approach of troops. Preparing to defend themselves and their stores, they withheld their fire, when it was established that the oncoming troops were Swedish."[29] Although the content of recommendations for awards is notorious for inaccuracies, this one adds another version to the events that unfolded. During World War II, the Swedish military activity along the border was high and the sound of machine guns might have come from an exercise or a firing range. However, it does suggest that Swedish troops, and neither Skuncke nor the locals, arrived first.

CHAPTER ELEVEN

The Walliwall Tragedy

On March 27, the Rype group reported that the weather in the mountains was wonderful and recommended that future drops be made on the northeastern corner of the lake.[1] Later that evening, London reported that there would be no drops that night but urged them to keep sending weather reports, and that four planes would be sent as soon as possible.[2] The next day there followed a detailed weather report with the barometer reading at 2725 bar, temperature at plus six degrees Celsius, visibility 10 kilometers, cloud cover at 4,500 feet, and no wind or precipitation in the last 24 hours. But the response was disheartening—no drop on the evening of March 29, and further, skis, sleeping bags, medical kit, and food could be expected from Sweden, but the generator would be dropped with the men. On March 30, Rype got the message: "Four planes coming tonight (Stop). Northeast corner of lake "P" for Peter (Stop). Listen for BBC (Stop)".[3]

On the evening of March 30, five B-24s were prepared for an attempt to insert the remaining NORSO personnel and resupply the rest of the group. The men had finished their briefing and climbed onboard the trucks that would take them to the awaiting Liberators. The NORSO groups were the same as those who had been unsuccessful in the planned drop on March 25. One plane would fly six NORSO men, two planes would go in with four each, and one plane was loaded with supplies only. The fifth plane was empty and would follow them up to Scotland as a spare. Only one of these planes carried a Rebecca, which is puzzling given their experiences thus far. They followed the same flight plan as the initial mission six days before, refueling at Kinloss, and then the course was set for the mountains of Snåsa. The German daily situation reports (*Lagemeldung*) reported that at 21:53–03:47, four aircraft believed to be flying in support of the resistance had been observed in the Trondheim area (*Einflug sur Versorgung der Wiederstandbewegung: 4 Flugzeuge im Raum Drontheim…*).[4] It is highly likely that this was the *Carpetbagger* mission attempting to drop reinforcements to Rype.

Rype set up a reception committee on the northeastern corner of the lake, close to the Swedish border, and this time they made sure that the sign laid out pointed away from the shore. They could hear three aircraft but were only able to establish contact with one over the Eureka, not surprising since only one of them carried Rebecca in the first place. The returning crews reported that the weather was clear right up to the last 15 minutes before target.[5] According to Colby's progress report, a local sleet storm kept them from making the drop after it had been clear up to the last 10 minutes before the first plane could be heard. They then decided to keep the reception committee at the ready for the reminder of the moon period, in case there would be a drop. One of the aircraft carried the four men who were the original NORSO complement of the aircraft codenamed *Trygve* from the March 24 sortie, but who had changed places with the advance party. First Lieutenant Pulrang, in the soon ill-fated B-24 designated "Army 331," assumed they had reached the DZ, but the ground was under thick cloud cover. Rype reported that three planes were heard overhead, but that "momentary clouds" prevented the drop. The clouds suddenly dropped to a few hundred feet just moments before they arrived. They were very disappointed when nobody came tumbling out of the aircraft. Added to this, the clouds lifted again after half an hour, as if the operation was cursed by the elements. Again, a detailed weather report followed.[6]

The aircraft departed due west, changing to due south, but must have gone too far west and struggled to find the course to their refueling station in Scotland. They dropped equipment to make the aircraft lighter, but they soon lost No. 3 and 4 engines due to icing. The engines were restarted, but No. 4 soon quit for good. After a while, the dark silhouette of the B-24 could be observed in the night sky over Kirkwall in the Orkneys. The observation was duly noted by Royal Navy personnel at Hatston Airfield at 04:45, March 31, 1945. It followed a south-southwesterly course at a height of 1,000 feet. By now, the crew was uncertain of their exact position, but knew they were somewhere over Scotland. They tried to send out radio messages, but their calls went unanswered.

According to information given by witnesses, the aircraft's engines were already on fire as it came in from the North Isles and crossed Shapinsay, the closest major island north of Kirkwall. The Liberator overflew the town, and then came back from the south, trying to find the blacked-out airfield at Hatston. Then the No. 3-engine quit again. The height was 800 feet when the bail out order was given. They were on the right course but hit the ground about 1.6 kilometers from the airfield. Mrs. Margaret Harold, who was awakened by the roar of the incoming plane, stated in an interview given in 1989 that she thought it was an air raid. The aircraft almost hit her house where she, her husband, five-year-old daughter, and nephew had been asleep a few seconds earlier. For five minutes, she was too scared to move. When she and her family made it out into the street, they could feel the heat from the flames of the aviation fuel that burned with a roar as it flowed down the road. One of the wings had buried itself into their garden wall, the other lay in a field. Other witnesses were convinced that the plane was going to hit their house, but said that it had veered off seconds before, most likely because a telegraph pole had altered its course just enough for it to go clear of it.

The B-24 crashed at 04:50, five minutes after it first passed Kirkwall, in a field at Walliwall Farm, outside Kirkwall. Two men had managed to jump out of the aircraft; one was found dead on a stone wall. Witnesses assumed his parachute had failed to open. The co-pilot, First Lieutenant Peter C. Pulrang, managed to parachute out of the doomed plane at the last second. He broke his ankle as he hit the ground but managed to drag himself clear of the burning fuel and was able to get help. From a letter since lost, written by a local farmer to the brother of the navigator on the B-24, there was a thump on the roof of their house just after the plane had passed. The man of the house rushed out with his shotgun at the ready, fearing it was German, only to find a man standing outside that he soon found out was American. He notified the authorities, who picked him up and rushed him to the hospital. From this testimony, it sounds as if Pulrang landed on the roof then fell to the ground and perhaps broke his ankle in the fall.

There are several, and at times conflicting, testimonies on the details of the accident. Some said the plane was already on fire when it passed Shapinsay, others when it came in over Kirkwall. Perhaps it had been hit by friendly anti-aircraft fire? There is also diverging information on the course. No photographs have since been made public of the crash site, and most likely none were taken. With a dramatic incident happening out of the blue and witnessed by so many, there were many witnesses but given the lack of daylight and that most of them had been abruptly awoken, it is no wonder that accounts are inconsistent. Also, the surviving co-pilot must have been in a state of shock. Thus, any historian trying to reconstruct the event, must approach the facts with a humble state of mind.

The flight crew were:

Second Lieutenant Henry L. Polansky
First Lieutenant Peter C. Pulrang (survived)
Second Lieutenant Charles J. Alessio
Second Lieutenant Frederick W. Smickle
Staff Sergeant William E. Lewis
Sergeant William K. Stevens
Gunnery Sergeant Edward W. Kussman
Sergeant Eugene Graff Jr

NORSO personnel who died in the crash were:

Technical Sergeant Trygve Berge
Technician Fifth Grade Edward O. Søndenø
Technician Fifth Grade Leif E. Meland
Technician Fifth Grade Gjerulf Ottersland

Technician Fifth Grade Johannes S. Rørvik
Sergeant Edward E. Kjelness

Although all six NORSO members on board were killed, Langeland noted in a later comment to his telegrams that "for some reason known only to themselves, the Home Office had not wanted to inform us about the accident by radio."[7] According to the telegrams he published after the war, the plane had crashed on the Orkney Islands on the night of the original insertion.[8] Helgesen's report also implies that the crash happened on March 25. It is also worth noting that the error has since multiplied in several accounts of Operation *Rype*.[9] However, the log from Harrington, Bolland's report, and all other primary sources leave no doubt that the crash occurred on March 31. The message about the accident reached the men at Gjefsjø by courier on April 6, and either then or later, Langeland must have mixed up the two dates. According to the statement given by the surviving co-pilot, two of the Liberator's four engines had failed, causing the accident.

The fate of the B-24 that crashed on the Orkneys on March 31 has been documented in great detail in David W. Earl's book, *Almost Home*, from 2011. Earl's work is also an excellent source for the *Carpetbagger* operations in general. The number of men who went down were identical to the group that flew on *Ed* on March 24 and had to turn back because of engine failure then too. This might also have contributed to Langeland's mix-up, believing that the fatal crash happened on March 25. Helgesen's report on the matter also replicated this error.[10] Another twist to the mix-up was added in a newspaper article on *Rype* in 1989, which claims that the plane crash on March 31 happened at Plukkutjønn.[11] Earl's book also offers biographies of the men in the group who were lost.[12]

Earl did not manage to dig up the origin of Technical Sergeant Trygve Berge, but he noted that he arrived in the US some time in the 1930s, settling in Alameda, Kern County, California. Further, Berge is believed to have been one of the original members of the 99th Battalion, enlisting in December 1942 together with Kjelness, Sondeno, Ottersland, Rorvick, and Meland. They had also been parachuted into France for Operation *Percy Pink* on the night between August 11 and 12, 1944.

Staff Sergeant Kjelness was born on July 5, 1909, in Vestness, close to Molde, in Norway. He emigrated to America in 1925 to join his father, but when he returned to Norway in 1930, Edward stayed behind. He joined the Army in 1940 and was destined to be sent to the Philippines but it is obvious that he was not there to be overrun by the Japanese and marched into captivity. Instead, he joined the 99th Battalion.

Another of the fallen due to the crash was Technician Fifth Grade (Corporal) Leif E. Meland, born in 1914 in Lista on the southern tip of Norway. Meland had been a sailor before the war and happened to be in Narvik to watch the carnage there when the Germans attacked on April 9, 1940 and was himself shipwrecked.

He arrived in Britain later that same year, fleeing the occupation with his brothers and sisters. He was at sea until the Japanese attack on Pearl Harbor. With America in the war, he was given the choice between joining the Norwegian Merchant Navy or joining the US armed forces. He chose the latter. After he had joined NORSO, Meland's brother, Nils (himself in exile in Britain) tried to track him down but with little luck initially, a testimony to the secrecy surrounding the OSS group. A letter from SHAEF did mention Inverness, and he was lucky enough to meet with his brother there. They briefly met again in July, but that was the last time any in his family heard from him. Leif E. Meland was posthumously awarded the Bronze Star.

Born in 1909, at Sunde in Sundhordaland, Norway, Johannes Rorvick emigrated to the United States in October 1939. Rorvick lived in Polk County, Wisconsin, and joined the Army and the 99th Battalion in October 1942. The circumstances seem a bit unclear, but it looks as if Rorvick joined NORSO after deploying to UK with the 99th. He was dropped into Dordogne, France, on the night between August 11 and 12 to take part in Operation *Percy Pink*. A memorial service for Rorvick was held on July 22, 1945, at Atlas Methodist Church in Luck, Wisconsin.

Technician Fifth Grade Gjerulf Ottersland was born on January 28, 1920, and grew up on a family farm outside Arendal on the southern tip of Norway. He was the eldest of 10 children. He earned a reputation as a strong and hardworking youngster, but he left the farm to go to sea in September 1939. Sometime in 1941 he sailed on a ship that was torpedoed and sunk by a German U-boat in the Atlantic. Ottersland was rescued but refused to return to sea, despite being urged to do so by the Norwegian authorities in exile. Instead, he got US citizenship and joined the US Army and the 99th Battalion. He would become especially close to Halvor Nipe, who managed to land safely at Gjevsjø on March 25, 1945. Ottersland did not take part in *Percy Pink* but was with Nipe when he dropped into the Poitiers region for the similar Operation *Christopher* mission on the night between September 3 and 4, 1944. *Christopher* was highly successful in assisting the French delaying the German withdrawal, but the commanding officer, First Lieutenant Erling Salvesen, was killed. Ottersland was posthumously awarded the Bronze Star.

Unlike the other NORSO men who met their fate at Walliwall on March 31, Technician Fifth Grade Eddie O. Sondenå was born in the US, to parents Ola T. Sondenå and Jorunn Herem, on January 3, 1911. Eddie Sondenå's parents had immigrated in 1904 to Meageher County, Montana. However, they returned to Norway the year after he was born. Eddie grew up with four siblings but moved back to the United States on his own at the age of 16 and worked as a carpenter in Montana until he again returned to Norway in 1936. After the German attack, he moved to the United States for the third time, and eventually joined the 99th Battalion. There, Sondenå was recruited to NORSO, and went on to become a member of the *Percy Pink* operation.

Upon being notified of the crash, Skabo flew up to the Orkneys in a C-47 together with Air Force officers to investigate. They brought the bodies back to Harrington on April 3. On April 6, they were buried at the American Military Cemetery in Cambridge. Besides Skabo, Vetlesen's assistant, Major Brøgger, and several other OSS men attended the funeral. Then began the solemn work of sorting out their belongings and notifying their next of kin. All five of the NORSO members killed at Walliwall were later reburied on Norwegian soil.

CHAPTER TWELVE

Attack on the Tangen Bridge

After the failed drop attempt of March 31, London promised to send two radios from Sweden, and notified NORSO that carbines, Browning Automatic Rifles (BARs), Sten guns, pistols, Marlins, and one Bren gun were available through Twinkle stores. These Twinkle stores were weapons smuggled into Sweden by diplomatic pouch and stored at the US embassy in Stockholm before being transported to the depots of the Norwegian Resistance in the border areas. It may also be assumed that these stores were well known to Rype from the way they were mentioned in the cables.[1] The Marlins (UD-42) were sub-machine guns produced by United Defense and intended to replace the Thompson. Although that never happened, because it fired German 9mm parabellum rounds, it was handed over to the OSS for use by OGs and resistance movements. In a photograph left by Kjell Sørli, one of the Norwegian Resistance members, Bertil Västgöte, is seen posing with a Marlin at Woodlark's Burvatnet base. The NORSO Springfields would also be sent to the Twinkle stores "soonest."

For 12 days after NORSO had been dropped over Gjevsjø, they had been idle. In his progress report, dated April 1, Colby wrote that he would attempt to blow up the Grana Bridge with the NOROSO men he had at his disposal, plus any Norwegians he could muster. But that would mean they were unable to receive drops. Blowing up the bridge was deemed urgent, as "rumors" suggested that the transports were coming to an end.[2] The Grana Bridge was initially reconnoitered by Norwegian Resistance members Gunnar Steen and Alf Bromstad on October 12, 1944. They delivered the following report:

> Left from summer barn at 06:00 to the railway bridge over GRANA 4 ½ km south from Snaasa Station. The bridge is 100 meters long, 18–22 high, 7 spans, pillars of iron construction. There are barbed wire entanglements on both sides of the track down towards the river and alongside the river to the bridge. There is a good approach road from all sides. About 1 ½ km south from SNAASA station is a tunnel about 150 meters long. The road goes over a bridge which is over a railway about 300 meters from the station building at SNAASA. On the east side of the bridge is located a German installation. The guard walks close by the bridge.[3]

Harald Larsen, the new leader of Woodlark, was present during the planning to share his experience from the attack on Jørstad Bridge on January 13 and their previous planning of an aborted attack on Grana Bridge. Hans Leirmo also made a reconnaissance of the bridge—the exact date is unknown, but Colby mentioned it as a preparation for an attack.[4] Presumably, it was therefore made after the arrival of the Americans. Leirmo had approached the target in civilian clothes and asked one of the Germans for a cigarette. While chatting, Leirmo made a detailed mental note of the German guard postings. The total guard force around the bridge was estimated at 20 men—12 of them were billeted in a guardhouse on the south end, with four at the north end (this would of course leave four men without shelter, but Colby did not dwell on that in his report). There were three men on duty at all times—one on each side and one at the bottom below the bridge span, and "barbed wire is there in abundance."[5] Colby was worried that the noise that skiing made on crusted snow would alert the guards, although that was a factor which could change within a few hours in both ways. According to Helgesen, the noise from the skis and the poles could be loud enough to wake the dead during a sabotage mission.[6]

Colby therefore considered the following plan: they would stop an empty train by using a red lantern at a considerable distance south of the target area, then ride on the train and stop it on the bridge so that an attack group would be adjacent to each guardhouse. This probably meant they would defeat the German guards in Wild West style with small arms and grenades. After placing the charges, they would reverse the train, blow up the bridge, and then continue to a safe distance from where they could escape. Before vacating the train, they would set it in motion so it would crash into the bridge site. In order to execute this plan, Colby would depend on the Norwegian Resistance fighter Agnar Andersen and his skills as a former engineer on that line. In the reports, his alias was Andreas.

Colby also notes that: "Our maps are wrong—the bridge is actually at (299153), and the railroad goes almost straight to Jørstad." At first, one might think that he had simply picked the wrong bridge on the map. However, when the original War Office maps used by *Rype* are compared with a modern map based on satellite imagery, we can see how the railway follows a wholly different path, and the actual bridge lies 750 meters northeast from where it seems to be located on the map Colby used. Firstly, it is always frustrating to go to war with faulty intelligence. Secondly, it is quite puzzling how Allied intelligence managed to gather all those details about hundreds of kilometers of railway with stations, bridges, and tunnels, yet nobody noticed that the railway was not actually where the map said it was. But Colby's Norwegian helpers could probably tell him right away that the map was wrong the moment they started pouring over it. Remember that Leirmo knew the area like the back of his hand, as did Helgesen too, he was an experienced orienteerer, and Andersen knew the railway.

The NORSO I Group posing for the photographer in Trondheim after the war. Top row, from left: Kjell Sørli; Sverre Stiansen; Fred Johansen; Kai Johansen; Odd Arneson; Robert Anderson; Jon Moan; Ron Windh; Leif Oistad; Matti Raivio; Middle row, from left: Sverre Aanonsen; Eddie Hovland; Tom Rusdal; Marinus Myrland; Knut Andreson; Asmund Gravdal; Alf Paulson; Bertil Vestgöte; Halvor Nipe; Bottom row, from left: Einar Eliassen; Herbert Helgesen; Tom Sæther; William Colby; Glenn Farnsworth; Borge Langeland. (Schrøder)

Resistance leader Odd Sørli communicating by radio somewhere on the Swedish side of the border, awaiting the insertion of NORSO on March 24. (FMU RKT)

The enigmatic Thale Prytz who assisted during the reception of Rype. (FMU RKT)

The Andersson family evacuates to Sweden after the Rype group established their base at Gjefsjø. (FMU RKT)

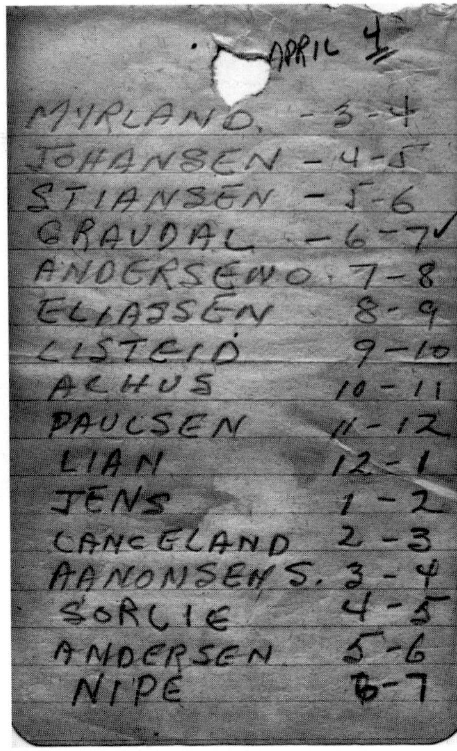

APRIL 4

MYRLAND. - 3-4
JOHANSEN - 4-5
STIANSEN - 5-6
GRAUDAL - 6-7 ✓
ANDERSEN O. 7-8
ELIASSEN 8-9
LISTEID 9-10
ACHUS 10-11
PAULSEN 11-12
LIAN 12-1
JENS 1-2
LANGELAND 2-3
AANONSEN S. 3-4
SORLIE 4-5
ANDERSEN 5-6
NIPE 6-7

Duty roster for April 4 found at Gjefsjø Farm. Five of the names are those of Norwegian Resistance fighters, a welcomed augment to the force. (FMU RKT)

Aerial photography of Gjefsjø farm from 1945. (FMU RKT)

Grana Railway Bridge, the target that eluded two sabotage groups. (FMU RKT)

Hans Leirmo, the trail blazer and mountain guide standing outside his goathie cabin. (FMU RKT)

Halvor Nipe manning the observation post at Litjfjellet Mountain northwest of the base. (FMU RKT)

NORSO saluting their fallen comrades on top of Plukkutjønn Mountain. (FMU RKT)

Einar Eliassen at Gjefsjø, one of the few men with prewar American military experience. (FMU RKT)

Lieutenant Tom Sæther, a native of Tromsø, Norway, was Maj. Colby's second in command. (FMU RKT)

Resting at the cabin at Brønstadsæter. (FMU RKT)

The cabin at Gomolia where Rype almost ran into a German patrol after attacking the Tangen Bridge. (FMU RKT)

Aerial photography of Woodlark base at Burvatnet on the Swedish side. Norwegian resistance fighters standing outside. (FMU RKT)

Starting off from Gjefsjø for the attack in Lurudal. (FMU RKT)

Resting in the mountains, probably en route to Lurudal. (FMU RKT)

As the snow was melting, rivers and creeks swelled and could only be crossed with great difficulties. (FMU RKT)

Basking in the sun on the barn bridge at Gjefsjø in between missions and guard duty. (FMU RKT)

The makeshift graves of the Germans killed on May 2. (FMU RKT)

On parade. Rype group standing at attention as the Norwegian National Anthem is played at Levanger. (FMU RKT)

The Americans and local Norwegian resistance fighters gathered at Gjefsjø at war's end. (FMU RKT)

Kjell Sørli, the young courier who scouted the landing zone and made several trips to Sweden with messages. (FMU RKT)

Rype group takes part in the May 17 parade in Trondheim. (FMU RKT)

Reviewing the May 17 parade in Trondheim, Lt. Col. Gerhard Bolland second from right, Rype's nominal commanding officer who reached the operational area only after the German surrender. (FMU RKT)

The men arriving at Namsos felt they were being excluded from the celebrations that were ongoing in Trondheim, but their skills came in handy in defusing German mines and boobytraps at bridges, harbors and coastal fortresses in the district. (FMU RKT)

While exiled in Namsos, NORSO I was visited by Col. Hans E. Skabo, the overall commander of the Norwegian Operations Groups. From left, Lt. Farnsworth, Lt. Sæther; Maj. Colby and Col. Skabo. (FMU RKT)

Herbert Helgesen (left) and Lt. Col. Wilson, head of SOE Scandinavian Section who did much to defuse the initial animosity between the OSS and the SOE, enabling Operation *Rype*. (FMU RKT)

In his progress report of April 1, Colby noted that they were getting along fine, but he hoped that the rest of the group would arrive before the end of the moon period so they could attack the bridge in full force. Though not stating it explicitly, he probably believed that the number of men at his disposal were too few for an attack on Grana Bridge, and when the moon period ended without the successful insertion of any reinforcements, he had to change the plans yet again. And again, almost all the planning and reconnaissance thus far proved useless. His frustration also grew from watching more and more German troop transports making their way past on the Nordland Railway. When the snow melted, it would be easier for the Germans to transport by means other than the railway. NORSO felt that the United States's credibility as an ally was at stake in all of Scandinavia. The shortage of men would make the job "extremely difficult," he wrote, but "still within the limits of probability of success."[7] Colby noted that a further reconnaissance mission was in progress by Hans Leirmo of the Jørstad Station area, and that the charges for the attack were almost complete. To remedy the lack of men, the group was augmented by six Norwegian Resistance fighters—four of them came from Woodlark, including Helgesen and Moan. Thus, only five men were left in the Woodlark group, where Harald Larsen was now the leader. In practice, the collaboration between the two groups was so close that it was difficult to distinguish them from each other. In a note after the war, Norwegian Lieutenant General Reidar Kvaal, who himself was part of the SOE group Lapwing, described Larsen as a tough and strong man, but no leader.[8] This might explain why Woodlark largely ceased to function as a separate unit. However, in contrast to the Americans, the Norwegian Resistance members had papers that enabled them to move freely into Sweden, which came in handy when they went to get supplies or needed to take a necessary detour for other reasons.

On April 5, Colby reported that six Norwegians were attached to NORSO, distributed as members of the squads. He also felt that an additional eight could be added. The Norwegians were trained at a camp for the Norwegian Police Troops in Sweden that officially was a holding camp for those who were selected for transfer to Scotland. In reality, it was a camp run by the SOE and *Kompani Linge*. The camp was located at Ählby Farm on Ekerö Island, in the Mälaren Basin outside Stockholm. Training there started in the summer of 1944; the students were given a crash course in sabotage, guerilla warfare, and courier work. Colby was keenly aware of the danger that too many Norwegian fillers would harm unit cohesion and possibly also discipline. But in limited numbers, he felt, they would "add considerably to the damage we could cause to the Germans but would not flood out the members of the NORSO Group. The unit would retain its military character and its discipline would not be impaired so that it became an irregular force."[9] The prospect of the reinforcement of the expected second NORSO Group would further add to the number of Norwegians who could be included.

Woodlark had only consisted of five men when they attacked Jørstad Bridge, so why did NORSO have too few with its 16 men? It must be noted that the Grana Bridge was a much larger target and more heavily guarded. On the latter, Colby also reckoned that the risk of losses would be so great that the subsequent work the group could accomplish would be greatly limited.[10] However, the shortage of men forced Farnsworth to rethink the system of placing the charges. Colby did not elaborate on this, but it might be that the amount of explosive that could be taken with them would be smaller. Also—or—that the number of individual charges had to be cut since placing them would take too long with fewer men. The damage was not expected to be to the same extent, but it would deprive the Germans of the use of the bridge for many weeks.[11] Farnsworth's recommendation for the Bronze Star mentioned the Tangen attack specifically and his "responsibility of preparing and placing the demolition charges at crucial points, which, by his acute calculations and careful planning, would assure the destruction of the bridge."[12]

Over the next couple of days, Colby must have had second thoughts about the Grana Bridge attack. On April 8, he telegraphed London, stating the present force was insufficient, and that unless there was a successful drop of reinforcements within the next six days, the target would be shifted to bridges between Jørstad and Valøy. The uncertainty had been sufficient for a long enough time to send Leirmo on a reconnaissance towards this area. If a drop was due soon, a reception party would be left behind to receive it.[13] The reply from SFHQ informed him that there would not be a drop until the next moon period, and that this would be the final chance for resupply by airdrop directly from England. The conclusion was then that Grana was off the table and Colby's change of target was accepted. However, if reinforcement by air was canceled, supply drops still seemed to be on since SFHQ asked for requests for skis, weapons, and rations.[14] But it appears that atmospheric interference prevented further communication that day. At SFHQ in London there was now concern about Rype's fate and whether they would be able to execute any of their plans. Colby's father, Colonel Elridge Colby, visited headquarters and asked for news of his son. Even though he had high security clearance, he was initially told that he did not have "need to know" status, but the staff gave in after Elridge Colby reminded them that he had a need to know since William was his son.

On April 9, 1945, Erichsen cabled London to announce that planning of the "bridge action" was complete and would take place with the force at hand, if necessary. Obviously, he was unaware of the last-minute decision to cancel the Grana Bridge attack. Erichsen also requested the drop of one officer and seven enlisted men as soon as possible. Colby even wanted the Second NORSO Group, originally commanded by Major Olmsted, to be dropped in and assured HQ that although they were not believed to be the best skiers, his existing force would be able to ensure security until they had installed themselves at the base. When the Second NORSO Group arrived, he reckoned that they could incorporate a further 15 resistance members without losing unit cohesion. Colby even had a request for their equipment to be one M1 Rifle per man, one Thompson sub-machine gun for every three men, and one M/1903A4 sniper rifle and one BREN gun per squad. In addition, every third M1 should be equipped to fire rifle grenades, and two mortars (unspecified) per unit. Colby also had a specific request for ammunition supplies.[15] This firepower would far exceed what was usually carried by sabotage groups and could be calculated for defeating the guard detail at Grana Bridge.

Colby's supply requests are also quite telling of his mindset. In addition to what might be expected such as coffee, food, cigarettes, etc., his progress report of April 5 also included uniforms and boots for the Norwegians who wanted to join the unit, and also Norwegian flag patches for these. Further, tire busters and antitank mines suggested he was planning for a lengthy campaign closer to populated areas. He also requested mosquito repellant.[16] Colby might have heard from the Norwegians how intense these critters could be in the Norwegian mountains, however, they do not become active until mid-June, another indicator that he was preparing for a long campaign. These supply requests were repeated in essence in a cable that was coded before they set off for Tangen, but it was not sent until April 18 because of atmospheric conditions during the allotted time, and frequencies for transmission did not allow it. Included in the message was a notification, upon London's request, that the radio station would remain closed until "next Monday" (April 15). This might be regarded as essential information, since no reply might imply that they had been captured or had to flee the base leaving the radio behind.

The following men started out from Gjefsjø:

Odd Anderson *
William Colby *
Einar Eliassen *
Glenn Farnsworth *
Asmund Gravdal *
Kai Johansen *
Borge Langeland *
Arne Listeid *
Tom Saether *
Marinus Myrland *
Halvor Nipe *
Matti Raivio *
Herbert Helgesen * (*)
Agnar Andersen **
Robert Andersen **
Harald Larsen **
Kjell Sørlie **

Jon Moan **
Hans Leirmo **
Thoralf Lian **
Bertil Vestgöte**
(* = Original Rype; ** = Woodlark, SOE controlled group)

Three Americans were left behind to guard the base.

There are some discrepancies about who of the Norwegian auxiliaries took part in which attack between Colby's reports and those of Helgesen. Since the latter knew these men better, it is fair to assume Helgesen is more reliable on this point. On the Tangen attack, Vestgöte, a Swedish volunteer, is noted as a participant by Helgesen, but is not mentioned by Colby. Technician Third Grade Fred Johansen had twisted his ankle and remained back at Gjefsjø, while Stiansen would be sent to Stockholm. Stiansen was reported to have sprained his knee or torn a tendon. The rosters seem sporadic, but he is not listed as "duty to hospital" until April 17. In his progress report, Colby asked if he could get a Purple Heart. Jørgen Havig is not mentioned in official reports, however, there is a man simply referred to as "Gaer," without any first name given. It is therefore possible that this is Havig; he was also transferred from Woodlark.[17] An indication that Havig indeed served with Rype is that he was decorated with a medal of unknown valor, by the US ambassador to Norway, Ulrich Bay, in 1948. This mystery person Gaer was also listed as having stayed behind at Gjefsjø. The roster for April 8 listed a Norwegian named Sverre Larsen reporting for duty—this was a cover name for Robert Andersen. Andersen had joined NORSO on April 8, according to Colby's later certificate regarding his service. This document stated that he had made valuable contributions, despite lacking previous military training.[18]

The rest departed on Monday April 9, five years to the day since the German invasion of Norway, and thus they missed the greetings on that occasion sent by the Norwegian commander in chief, who was now Crown Prince Olav. Each of the men carried a pack of 25 kilograms which contained a sleeping bag, ammunition, explosives, and rations for six days. For every third man, they had packed a *pulka* (sledge) weighing 30 kilograms that contained explosives among other things, which they pulled alternately. The attack and return marches were estimated to take a total of six days. During the day, the snow was thawing and the going was heavy, while it became a little firmer as temperatures fell and the snow froze at night. In his memoirs, Colby described it as a "brutal journey, often through blinding snowstorms with temperatures below zero."[19] He was concerned that someone would be injured, as the chances for getting assistance were slim. On the first day, they started out in the afternoon; this was a short leg since the next stop was an estimated day's march from the first one. They were hit by rain and strong winds that made everything both on their bodies and in their packs soaking wet. They stopped at Schulzhytta on the shores of Lake Grønningen, at a cabin allegedly owned by an infamous local Nazi. They emptied it of liquor and wreaked havoc. This, however, was not mentioned in the contemporary dispatches, and in Helgesen's later report, the delay was said to be due to bad weather.[20] Staying at the cabin gave them an opportunity to rest and dry out and, as a result, no casualties were suffered from frostbite or trench foot. When they were about to light a blaze in the fireplace, the whole cabin seemed it was about to catch alight, something that abruptly ended the party. The saboteurs were quickly sobered up and refocused on the mission.

For the next two days, a strong westerly wind raged with wet snow drifts, and on the advice of their Norwegian helpers, Colby and his men chose to wait it out as the next leg would take them over the naked mountains where they would be even more exposed to the weather. The wind was blowing humid air in from the North Atlantic and this was known to produce strong winds and heavy precipitation when hitting the cold mountains of the interior. The going was slow, and some men were sent back to Gjefsjø to replenish their food supply while others began to pull the *pulkas* up into the mountain. On Thursday, the storm had abated somewhat and Colby's patience was growing thin so he decided to start off again. But it was still blowing a slight westerly snowstorm as they climbed past Imsdalfjell Mountain. To avoid the German observation post mentioned in Field Order No. 1, they went south of the Flatfjellet Mountain and, according to Colby's report, they halted for the night at a shieling called Brønstadseteren at about 19:00. They would now have traveled across big lakes and mountains with quite gentle slopes but had reached the highest point of their journey west of Imsdalfjell Mountain at 872 MAMSL.

However, the pencil mark on the map used shows they must have stopped at another shieling called Kleivseteren, some 4 kilometers southwest of Brønstadseteren. The mix-up might have its roots in the planning. Looking at the topography and how the valleys run, Brønstadseteren would make perfect sense as a stopping point if they were heading for Jørstad or Grana to the north, but as they changed their target to Valøy and Tangen Bridge, Kleivseteren would be more in line with their route. One can imagine how confusing it must have been for Colby to be bombarded by unfamiliar place names as his Norwegian assistants would have been discussing the possible routes to the target in their own language.

In the morning, they descended into the Roktdalen Valley at about 300 MAMSL. The Rokta River meanders through the flat valley floor, running west by southwest, which sounds like easy going. However, this would mean that the chances for wet snow and possibly going through the ice on lakes, marshes, and the river itself would be great. However, the local guides probably did know how to read the terrain and avoid accidents that could put the whole operation in jeopardy if one or more of the *pulkas* went through the ice and men got their clothes soaked. The flat terrain lasted for only 5–6 kilometers before they broke straight up the northern slopes of the valley and reached Raudbeinseteren at about 460 MAMSL on the northern slopes of the Raudbeinklumpen Mountain. There they rested for lunch.

At some unknown point during the Friday, Colby, Helgesen, and three others made a detour north around Bjørnhifjellet. The purpose was to do a long-distance reconnaissance of Jørstad Bridge. According to Helgesen's report, it was still Colby's intention to attack Jørstad Bridge. Their route is not noted on the maps. However, if they left the main party that morning as they all went out from Kleivseteren, it makes more sense that they passed Brønstadseteren which lies along a more logical course towards Jørstad. There is a course marked on the maps towards Jørstad, and though it crosses the route described for the Tangen Mission, it does so back at the Schultz Cabin and continues south towards Holderen Lake into Sweden and proceeds via Björkede to end up at Gjefsjø from the south. Whether or not this path has anything to do with the mission discussed in Colby's progress report remains a mystery. More likely, this was one of the routes used by Hans Leirmo on an earlier reconnaissance. Helgesen's report also confirms that they left the main force after spending the night at a shieling in Roktdalen.[21]

Colby, Helgesen, and the others kept their distance from the bridge itself out of fear of being detected. According to the report, the area around the bridge was almost clear of snow as the banks of the Jørstad River only lie at 50 meters MAMSL. They were able to get some idea of the layout of the new makeshift bridge, which was described as a straight plate girder span from abutment to abutment. The guard detail always consisted of three to four men on duty, with the reminder billeted nearby. With a similar number of men on duty, they could reckon that the total guard force would be 12–15 men, the same as for Grana. There was also a machine-gun position southwest of the bridge, and according to Helgesen a bunker at either end of the bridge. While they were making their observations, a train went past—according to Colby the one they were planning on hijacking. It was a freight train with empty boxcars, but with a caboose in the middle. It slowed down to a near stop before it continued.[22] This reduction of speed might have been due to the poor quality of the makeshift bridge. On their way back, they continued southwest, climbed Korsmæren, and slept under open skies in a cleft on the south side. They then probably left for Øyingen to be rejoined with the main force the next day.

The group established a forward base at Valøyhytta, a hunting cabin not far from Tangen Bridge, and began reconnaissance of the target area. Two patrols left on Saturday morning for Valøy Station and Tangen Bridge respectively. The party that moved towards Tangen Bridge soon ran into difficult terrain that does not necessary appear that difficult according to the contours on the maps that Colby carried, as the differences in MAMSL is not all that great. However, on a low scale map, the contours reveal steep drops that could not be negotiated on skis, even by stepping sideways downhill (the safest way to descale a very steep slope on skis). The party had to return in order to get back in time for H-hour.

The party heading for Valøy Station, led by Lieutenant Saether, had a more pleasant journey to their target, but when they reached their lookout point some 300 meters from the station, they saw about 10 Germans running to their positions, putting on their gear, and preparing to fight. After their scramble, the Germans moved up into the mountains, but in another direction from the position of Saether and his men. What had alerted the Germans was impossible to tell. A lookout might have observed the Americans in the distance, it might simply have been a false alarm for some other reason, or they had accidentally run into a drill. One possible trigger for the emergency was a party of woodcutters working nearby. After the attack on the Jørstad Bridge in January, German forces in the area had been nervous and on high alert, which might have caused them to rush out at the slightest sign of anything suspicious. Rumors had it that those who had been manning the closest guard post on January 13 were promptly dispatched to the Eastern Front because they must have heard the explosion yet failed to investigate or even report an incident. Saether and his men withdrew to avoid detection, and the Germans soon returned to their quarters, the probable cause for this was that they had made contact with the woodcutters and felt comfortable that they were the real cause for the alarm.

A third Rype patrol was made towards the bridge at Strindmoen, about 10 kilometers up the line from Tangen. This patrol consisted of Colby, Jon Moan, and Helgesen. According to Helgesen, their target was named Strandløkka Bridge, however, this site is not on any present map, but there is a site with a similar name (Strandvika) some 5 kilometers closer to Valøy with a bridge called Heggesbekkbrua. Langeland too writes about "a large bridge further to the south," but it is only negligibly larger than the Tangen Bridge.[23] The going was so rough (they were probably heading down the ravine that Heggesbekken runs through) that Colby decided to return to the main force, now positioned at Øyingen, while Helgesen and Moan continued to the target. Enemy positions had been reported in the area, and their mission was to map these and meet with the northbound evening train south of this bridge. What this meant, the sources do not reveal, but they seem to have expected to have seen a white flag waving from the right side of the train so it is possible that a secret rendezvous had been agreed upon with the driver, perhaps to use the train as a vehicle of attack as was the original plan for the Grana Bridge. However, the train came along and passed by without any signal, so the patrol remained in hiding. Also, the train contained three passenger cars full of people and whether they were Germans or Norwegians they could not tell, according to Colby.[24] The rest of the train carried coke and coal. However, Helgesen stated that the train was unexpectedly full of German soldiers, which prompted them to abandon the hijacking and settle for the Tangen Bridge instead.[25] The book later written by Jarle Skjei and Arne Sandness also gives the impression that Grana Bridge was the real target, right up to the final moment.[26] According to Langeland's account, the train hijacking was abandoned after the episode at Valøy Station, but that is revealed in his later comments, not in the telegrams.[27]

The enemy forces most directly in position to interfere with the attack were 11 Germans lodged at the Vikran School, just south of Valøy Station. A similar number were positioned at the station itself. The main mission for the Germans there was to patrol the railway line from Snåsa to a location south of Tangen Bridge, a distance of about 40 kilometers. Above the station, there was a POW slave labor camp with 20 to 30 guards. The local station and the stationmaster were held under close observation after the Woodlark attack in January. In addition, the Germans had cleared a 60-meter wide and several-kilometer-long strip of vegetation along both sides of the railway line. This gave the German patrols good overview of anything that approached from the sides.

Local historian Mr Skjei lived on the second floor of the schoolhouse as a child. He was 12 years old in the winter of 1944/45 and got to know several of these German soldiers. There was a certain turnover through the winter, but the force of about 11 consisted of a core of three or four Germans, two to three Austrians, a few Czechs, and a pair of Poles, as well as a man from Alsace. However, it seems that these men were so-called "Volksdeutsche," ethnic Germans from settlements outside the Reich. Skjei writes that the group was led by a 19-year-old "Polish Übergefreiter" (sic),[28] which strengthens the assumption that they were *Volksdeutsche* as it seems doubtful that the Germans were going to set so-called "Osttruppen," mainly Slavs, to lead their own.

One of the keys to American success was to use better men and better skiers than the Germans could field against them in the AO.[29] And the bar was not that high. The young Skjei was not impressed by the quality of the German soldiers, whom he described as "either old or very young." Two of them were only 17 years old, and one of them "ignorant."[30] They appeared to the young Norwegian observer as second- or third-tier soldiers who were neither good skiers nor good shots. Although a 12-year-old boy might not be able to assess the soldiery qualities of troops, a Norwegian growing up in the countryside surely would be able to separate good shots and good skiers from those who were not. Morale was also low among the German troops, quite naturally this late in the war, and after the attack against the Tangen Bridge, the Obergefreiter in charge at Vikran did not take searching the surrounding farms very seriously.

There was the 12-man detachment from the *702. Panzerjäger Abteilung* at Sandnes. Although they had heavy weapons, probably at least a 37mm PAK gun and machine guns, they were some 25-minutes' drive away. Still, they could have intervened if Rype were delayed, pinned down, or attempted their planned train hijacking stunt, which would have taken longer to execute and created far more commotion.

The Strindmoen patrol, now reduced to Moan and Helgesen, returned to a rendezvous point at Åsvasseteren, according to Colby's progress report.[31]

The position given with a map reference lies more than 20 kilometers as the crow flies southeast of Strindmoen and much further across the rugged terrain. Helgesen and Moan thus were heading in a very different direction from that of Tangen, but they were close enough to hear the coming explosion. Colby arrived at Øyingen at 16:30 to meet with the men and consider the intelligence that had resulted from the reconnaissance. The time for the trip between Øyingen and Valøy had been estimated by Colby to 1½ hours. The rugged terrain and slushy snow proved this to be insufficient. Together with the alarm at Valøy, this led to the conclusion to attack Tangen Bridge alone, despite this being a rather insufficient target. The report put together by the Inter-Service Topographic Service did not even mention the Tangen Bridge, and they went for the attack without much other knowledge about the target apart from what a last-minute reconnaissance and local guides could tell them.

Sudden change of plans due to unforeseen elements during preparations are not uncommon in war, and for the OSS it was a kind of trademark, thus Operation *Rype* proved no exception.[32] The unit moved out at 21:00. Rucksacks were left in the woods, and they continued southwest, climbing up a narrow gorge from the Øyingen Lake. Several times along the route, they would have to take off their skis to climb up or down or cut through thick brush. The march was, according to Colby, unimaginably difficult, but taken along the best possible route from Øyingen down to Tangen. They crossed the moors and climbed down again to Åsvatnet and went onward to Raudsjøen. To their right, there were areas whose names in Norwegian meant "Hell," "Little Hell," and "Big Hell," which gives an impression of the topography even without looking at the contour lines on the map. In addition to the steep slopes and cliffs, the area was littered with boulders left by glaciers retreating at the end of the last Ice Age. At Åsvatnet they took off their skis and continued on foot. An advance party went ahead to reconnoiter the target. It was now 04:30. As they got down to Raudsjøen, the going was easy for a few kilometers, but 2 kilometers from the target, they started downwards again. The reconnaissance party signaled that the area was clear, and the rest followed closely.

At Kvernatjønna they turned straight northward and began their descent towards Lake Snåsa and the railway line. A crust had formed on the snow, and it was a clear, quiet winter morning. Their footsteps could be heard from hundreds of meters away. Close to the target, they came upon a house that stood on a hill overlooking the railway. It looked empty as there were no tracks in the snow around the house. However, they spotted movement inside and Colby and Langeland went to investigate. They forced entry and discovered that a family who had been evacuated from Finnmark was living in the house. As the Germans were forced out of Finland and Finnmark by the Soviet advance, they forcibly evacuated the civilian population southwards and resettled them all over the rest of Norway, and these poor people had been placed almost on the target for *Rype*'s first attack. The family informed them that the Tangen Bridge was unguarded, but also that it was frequently patrolled by the Germans. While Langeland stayed in the house and did the talking, Colby went out to examine the bridge in more detail. Soon the rest of the group showed up. Sure enough, there was not a German in sight near the bridge. (In Tom Saether's personnel files, probably originating from his recommendation for the Silver Star, it is stated repeatedly that the Tangen Bridge was guarded,[33] however, there is nothing in the field reports to substantiate this claim.) As they approached the bridge, they divided into four teams.

One group, led by First Sergeant Eliassen armed with an M-1, Staff Sergeant Listeid with grenades and a Bren, Technician Fifth Grade Ravio with a BAR, Vestgöte with a Thompson sub-machine gun, and Kjell Sørli with his carbine, covered the sector north of the target. The other covering group, led by Staff Sergeant Paulsen with a rifle (possibly a Springfield) and grenades, Technician Third Grade Myrland with a BAR, and Technician Fifth Grade Aanonsen armed with a Bren, covered the southern sector.

As the covering parties found their positions, the demolition team led by Lieutenant Farnsworth and consisting of Technician Third Grade Odd Anderson, Corporal Kai O. C. Johansen, Technician Fifth Grade Nipe, and Technician Fifth Grade Gravdal moved in to place the charges. The bridge was 12-meters-long and carried by four I-beams with a thickness of 2.5 centimeters. In total, 40 kilograms of explosives were placed. The amount was in excess of what was needed for a target of that size and composition, but it had been brought along with a much larger bridge in mind.[34] This again brings up the question about when Colby changed his plans and decided against attacking Grana Bridge. The bridge at Strindmoen was only one meter longer and of similar construction to the Tangen Bridge. There was also a third bridge, the 15-meter-long span crossing Svartelva between Tangen and Jørstad. This one also had supporting pillars, but it does not show up in the sources. Alternatively, the amount would make sense if they were planning on hitting more bridges, but Colby specifies "a larger bridge." For whatever reason, having brought the explosives along, all of them were used. The group was not particularly interested in taking any surplus with them back to Gjefsjø or having to hide it away, so must have decided to use it all.

A group led by Lieutenant Saether and consisting of Harald Larsen, Hans Leirmo, Toralf Lian, and Robert Andersen was kept as a reserve and possible assault party should the enemy interfere with their work. Major Colby and Langeland constituted the HQ group. This was Colby's allocation of his men, according to his progress report.[35] However, it must be noted that not all the men who left Gjefsjø are accounted for, disregarding Helgesen and Moan who were on their way back after reconnoitering the Strindmoen Bridge.

When they were about to finish laying out the charges, a train whistle could be heard in the distance. This might have been the same train that was observed by Helgesen and Moan further up the line. A scout was sent up a hill so that they could make sure whether it was a German troop or freight train, or a regular Norwegian passenger train with civilians on board. A group (probably the reserve group) was deployed along the height overlooking the bridge. Lieutenant Sather, on Colby's instructions, had entered a nearby house and broken the phone to delay any early warning the Germans might otherwise have got about them.

It might be easy to think that they also hoped to capture the train in the explosion. The explosives manual developed for the British Home Guard, and evidently used also by the SOE as one copy was found among Helgesen's belongings after the war, recommend this.[36] But the group might also have recalled how close the Germans came to lashing out against the local civilians after the attack on Jørstad Bridge. The head of the civilian German administration in Norway, Reichskommissar Joseph Terboven, had demanded that 10,000 people be rounded up and executed in retaliation for the 78 Germans who were killed in the following accident, before Berlin blocked this. Perhaps in every other German-occupied country, the resistance would rejoice at such a bonus, however, in interviews after the war, at least one of the Woodlark men expressed horror that so many ordinary soldiers were killed.[37] The presence among Rype of many of these men might also have influenced the mood of this group.

As Rype heard nothing more of the train and finally gave up waiting, they blew up the bridge at about 06:30 (Helgesen writes 08:00 hours). The quiet and clear Sunday morning was ripped apart by a powerful explosion that must have been heard several kilometers away.

At the Tangen smallholding, only about 100 meters from the bridge, Arne Lagesen, his wife Ingrid, and their two children were sitting drinking their morning coffee. They could see some men working on the bridge but, believing they were Germans, they did not take much notice. Then there was a loud explosion. One of the kids who sat on the father's lap was thrown to the floor. The coffee cup was ripped from the hands of the mother and landed in a corner but, miraculously, no one was hurt.

A girder was blown clear off the bridge and flew right through the window of a cabin on the other side of the track; luckily, it was vacant. Before they withdrew, the men left an American flag to identify this as the work of Allied soldiers and not the local resistance to ensure the civilian population would be exempt from suspicion by the Germans.[38] The men were already exhausted, and although they were now relieved of the weight of the explosives, the climb up the slopes to Øyingen must have been tiring. They stopped at the same hut on the western shore of the lake for a good rest and a meal. During the late afternoon a single-engine aircraft was heard above, possibly a reconnaissance plane, but no visual observation was made. At midnight they started up again, heading on a more southern course than that of the approach march. Venturing out at night in treacherous terrain might sound like a recipe for accidents, however, looking at the map and assuming that the weather was still clear, the going was, if not easy, at least without many dangerous slopes to negotiate. Also, the snow-covered ground would reflect whatever atmospheric light there was, giving the men some visual impression of the terrain. Ascending the slopes on the southern banks of Øyingen, they traveled from 261 MAMSL to 386 MAMSL before reaching open marshland. After a couple of kilometers, they began climbing up the slopes to Brandheia, reaching 550 MAMSL before having to negotiate a gorge and going back up and leveling out at 511 MAMSL. After 4 kilometers, they descended into Roktdalen Valley where they ate breakfast at Flåtjønna from around 09:00 until 12:00.

The Germans did not arrive at the site of the attack until several hours after the explosion, and it took 24 hours before they managed to organize a search operation from Valøy which, in the end, was not carried out with much zeal. At the nearby smallholding, the yard was suddenly full of Germans and Norwegian Nazis with the sheriff of Stod in the lead. Arne Lagesen was arrested and interrogated but set free after a couple of hours. A German search party followed the tracks of Rype but made slow progress. To delay any followers, Rype had laid out explosives with tripwires across their ski tracks. Later, they learned that a six-man patrol had taken up pursuit from the railway line, and that one had broken his leg and one was badly hurt by one of their booby traps and lost a leg. In later statements, Colby noted that the explosive charges were not deadly so as not to take the life of any civilian Norwegian skiers that followed the same track later. German troops in Ogndalen to the south were also alarmed, and a 24-man patrol headed north towards Skjekerfjella to intercept Rype.[39]

Heading up the far side of the Roktdalen Valley, Rype ascended to the 510 MAMSL Grønberget before turning straight south to Daltjønna Lake and further to Åsvatnet and Gomolia, where they arrived on Monday, April 15, at 22:00. This was the intended base area for Woodlark when they arrived in the fall of 1944 but later decided to move into Sweden. Here, Colby had intended to give the men "substantial rest," but then they met Helgesen who had spotted a German patrol of 23–25 men on Tjokklia, a hillside some 2–3 kilometers away on the far side of Skjækervatnet Lake. These were the men who had set out from Ogndal. In other words, there would not be any rest for the tired men from Rype who had not had a decent night sleep in almost a week and had all but run out of food. Colby did not feel like taking on an enemy patrol, so they started up again at 06:00. In addition, it was moonlight, with no wind and crusted snow, which made it extra hard to shake off pursuers under the cover of darkness, but the going was by now not particularly difficult. If they were to have any hope of putting any distance between themselves and the pursuers, Rype had no time to lose. They ate pemmican at dawn, which was undoubtedly very nourishing, but it was foul-tasting, and it took a lot of willpower to eat. Only the knowledge that they needed the nourishment to be able to keep going forced the men to eat it.[40] Colby could not allow his men breaks of more than a maximum of five minutes, and yet one of them managed to fall asleep while he hung in his ski poles and tumbled into the snow.

In the late afternoon, they continued up the steep Grønnhaugen Hill and into Storskardet Gorge between Sukkertoppen (Samí: Gihpersgaejsie) to the north and Skjækerfjella to the south. This meant a climb of almost 200 meters in height over a distance of 500 meters. Each time they seemed to reach the summit, there was another ridge ahead. The men dubbed this climb "Benzedrine Hill," as they had to break out their pep pills to get through it. Benzedrine sulfate was a drug introduced onto the open market in the US in 1937. It contained amphetamine and was prescribed to prevent narcolepsy and chronic fatigue. But it was not nearly as potent as the German equivalent, Pervitin, which contained methamphetamine. By the time Colby and his men took the pills, the Germans had broken off their pursuit, probably assuming that the saboteurs had exited to Sweden.[41] According to Helgesen, Hans Leirmo led the way. At this point it is also worth noting that Sergeant Langeland, in his published and much-read account, including transcripts of the telegrams sent and received, misplaced the Benzedrine Hill event as occurring after the later attack in Lurudal–Agle.[42] This is also repeated in Skjei. However, the contemporary reports leave no doubt about the date. Colby and his men, having managed to avoid contact with the Germans, soon emerged on a flat plain that went almost all the way to the Swedish border. They went around Snjåamentjakerøysa Mountain on the border and arrived safely at the Woodlark base at Burvatnet. Later, they learned that another 11-man German patrol set out the day after they passed Gomolia. They tracked Rype to the foothills of Sukkertoppen Mountain, but then gave up the chase.[43]

In his report, Colby gave the men credit for having endured in high spirits despite being wet, cold, tired, and hungry, and have not eaten anything but K-rations and other dried food for a long time. If such meals do not get properly prepared, they can cause constipation, and it is very likely that Rype did not take the time to prepare it properly. The differences in skiing abilities also became more and more apparent, as Colby wrote:

> Of a limited skiing ability (due only to lack of months and years of training) in comparison with the native Norwegians, they have gained the unrestrained admiration of these Norwegians by the spirit of determination which carries them through obstacles which lesser men would declare impossible.[44]

Helgesen put it more poetically:

> If you looked along the line, you would soon discover that they were not all skiing experts: but what can you do, if you have not seen bigger hills than those in Dakota? The Norwegians stood out, first and foremost Hans [Leirmo] who was casually strolling at point with a mountain man's flex in his knees and a loose body. The Americans had it more in terms of energy, and what effort they put into it was impressive.[45]

If all the Americans were equally poor skiers, all it took was just one to slow the rest down. The group's best skier in addition to Leirmo seems to have been Harald Larsen, and the two appear to have taken turns at skiing at point and making the trip easier for the rest. They crossed the border and arrived at the Woodlark base, where fish and elk were on the menu. There they also could rest and they learned, for the first time, that US President Franklin D. Roosevelt was dead. But to share in a brotherly way with their brothers in arms would prove to be problematic for Woodlark, who were reprimanded for having shared their rations with the Americans, allegedly since it was not easy to keep them resupplied.[46] It was also risky for Colby and his men to cross the border since they did not have any Swedish papers and risked internment if they came into contact with the Swedish police. Colby, Langeland, and Larsen soon headed back to Gjefsjø to establish radio contact and report back to London that the attack against the Tangen Bridge had been successful, while the others followed somewhat later. Within a week, however, the Germans had built a makeshift bridge across the break, and traffic was resumed by the evening,[47] although the repairs must have entailed some reduced capacity.

When Colby and his men returned from the attack on Tangen Bridge, they found that Leif Oistad and his group had finally arrived at Gjefsjø from Sweden. Officially, Swedish intelligence had been helpful in sending them back to the United Kingdom, while in reality, they helped them out of the internment camp in Falun and into Norway. Colby noted in his report to Skabo, that the lost sons of the OSS were full of high praise for how the OSS in Stockholm had taken care of them. However, they only had one uniform each and no military equipment, so Colby requested this should be dropped soon.[48] After the Tangen attack, Colby was also full of praise for the Woodlark crew, and fought tooth and nail to keep them under his command while London began to demand they be released. He referred to "conditions" for their work with the Americans that he suspected were imposed by the SOE. Colby did not specify, but continued with poorly hidden indignation:

> It seems a strange way for allies to prosecute a war, lending men on "conditions" that they do not do too much against the common enemy. My aim is to do the maximum of damage to the Germans in this region, and in order to carry out this mission I wish to be able to use the men available as I see fit. The mountains of Norway is no place for the existence of petty political maneuverings. I should like to keep the men and also, I should like to have Lt. Hoel [Helgesen] with me, as his knowledge of the region and the people in it is vital to the proper fulfillment of my mission. [49]

From London, Skabo congratulated Colby on the successful demolition, particularly that there had been no contact with the Germans and no casualties. However, London was puzzled to learn that Colby had moved on the target with a total of 24 men. As far as was known, Colby only commanded three officers and 13 men, of whom Stiansen was injured and remained at Gjefsjø. (Stiansen would soon leave for Stockholm for medical care.) Adding Helgesen and two men from Woodlark still did not bring the total up to that number. Skabo requested that Colby, in the future, would be franker about the number of volunteers he had accumulated and whether they were in uniform or operated as "guerillas." He was clear that recruiting Norwegian Resistance fighters to the group, or inciting a revolt, violated the instructions given by the joint Allied SFHQ that the OSS "must" (Skabo's underlining) abide by.

SHAEF had already begun to issue instructions to downscale sabotage pending a German surrender, however, Skabo emphasized that there was still "plenty of operations for both your group and Olmsted's group to perform in Norway." They were to continue operations that would force the enemy to transport troops still in northern Norway by sea. Thus, sabotage against the Nordland Railway, bridges, and roads were still on. Skabo also visualized the NORSO group acting jointly with MilOrg or separately as Jedburgh teams.[50] That sounded cryptic and contradictive to his emphasis to refrain from interacting with the resistance, but considering the nature of the *Jedburgh* operations, this would only make sense if he was thinking about a forceful Allied dismantlement of the German occupation.

CHAPTER THIRTEEN

Plukkutjønn Crash

On April 2, 1945, Rype sent a telegram to Harrington, recommending future drops be made over Litlefjellet, some 3.5 kilometers west by northwest from Gjefsjø Farm, as the ice on the lake had begun to soften up. This was confirmed; in addition, headquarters wanted drops to be made at dawn when the outline of the ground could be seen to minimize the risk of accidents. It was a difficult decision. For the flight crew, they had to weigh up the hazards of flying in darkness against the prospect of being shot down by enemy air defenses. The Operation *Rype* group accepted this only reluctantly, as they were afraid the chutes would be visible over a long distance and disclose the location of the DZ.

On April 6, yet another attempt to fly in reinforcements was made. According to the telegrams to Rype, two planes loaded with equipment only and two carrying eight NORSO personnel took off from Harrington. Rype obviously expected more, as well as 12 containers.[1] A later dispatch to Colby indicated that only three planes took off, two with personnel and one with supplies.[2]

The day before, the weather report from Rype sounded promising—barometer at 2729, temperature plus one degree Celsius, visibility 30 kilometers, 10 percent cloud cover, no wind or precipitation in the last 24 hours.[3] However, the weather in the mountains was notoriously unstable and unpredictable. Maybe, if Rype did not purposely manipulate the reports, they perhaps unconsciously reported the best condition in order to receive the much-needed reinforcements and supplies. Then, only hours before the arrival of the new flight, the courier notified them of the tragedy at Walliwall.

Over Gjevsjø, one of the planes succeeded in establishing radio contact with the men on the ground, but the signal was poor because of the weather and all contact was soon lost. A strong northwest wind was blowing, and there were heavy snow squalls in the area. Halvor Nipe, who had been sent as a lookout to the west of Litlfjell, reported that he had heard an explosion about 24 kilometers west of Gjevsjø. (It later tuned out that real distance to the crash site from Gjefsjø was 10 kilometers, direction north by northwest.) According to an interview Halvor gave when he revisited the site in 1977, they heard the planes overhead but could not see them through the blizzard.[4] The weather report after the failed attempt revealed that there had been cloud cover and sleet.[5] Only two planes returned, the supply plane and the one carrying Technical Sergeant Jøa and his group. The last B-24 had probably hit a higher peak with a wing tip as it circled to find the DZ, and then crashed on top of the Plukkutjønnfjellet and exploded so that wreckage was scattered down the mountainside to the west.

The NORSO men killed were:

First Lieutenant Blaine E. Jones (namesake of the flight)
Corporal Knut J. Falck
Technician Fifth Grade Bernard N. Iverson
Technician Third Grade Robert N. Anderson (not to be confused with the resistance fighter Robert Andersen).

The aircrew members were:

First Lieutenant William H. Hudson
First Lieutenant Leon G. Dibble Jr.
Second Lieutenant Richard A. Bosch
Flying Officer Arthur H. Bardknecht
Sergeant Gilbert L. Magruder
Sergeant Fayette Shelledy
Sergeant Jack H. Spyker
Sergeant Angelo Santini

It took some time before it became clear what had happened and where the crash had taken place. A compass bearing based on the sound was attempted and it was estimated that the plane went down on Imsdalsfjell Mountain. Rype was quick to send out patrols but would not risk going too far from the base out of fear of running into the Germans, and nothing was found. They got as far west as Raudfjell, some 8.5 kilometers as the crow flies, less than half the distance to the assumed crash site. Besides, their course had been 45 degrees out, bringing them to a point 10 kilometers from the real crash site. How their estimates could be that wrong is hard to explain but in the mountains, echoes and wind might make it difficult to estimate the direction and distance to the source of a sound. From Nipe's post to the real crash site, there would be only 5–6 kilometers, and the wind would have been blowing the sound straight to him without many obstacles, except for the summit of Plukkutjønn Mountain itself. That leaves the snow squalls as the most probable cause for him misjudging the direction. For some time before they found the wreck site, there was still hope that the missing NORSO men and the air crew had managed to jump out somewhere over Norway and were possibly being held prisoner.

On April 26, Bengt Jåma, the younger brother of Jonar, happened upon the real crash site from the northwest. He passed over a ridge and then spotted something that looked like glittering stones in the distance. At first, Bengt believed it was lumps of ice and tied up his dog before going closer to investigate. It turned out to be twisted aluminum gleaming in the sun. A gruesome sight awaited the young reindeer herder. Around the burnt-out plane parts, he saw the bloody remains of at least four people, scattered throughout the site. Bengt went straight to Gjefsjø to notify Rype. They, however, had only just returned from the Lurudal attack, so decided to rest before sending a party to investigate. The next day, Colby and eight others went up to the site to pay their respects to the dead. From the initial investigation, they assumed that the plane had held a course due west when it crashed and bounced down the slope, and from the condition of the bodies, they also assumed they had all died instantly. The plane had broken up into hundreds of pieces that were scattered over a large area. Containers had broken open and their contents were strewn around.

Some bodies that were found were identified by their dog tags, and the NORSO men by the close acquaintance of their comrades in the search party. From the number of bodies found, they could assume that the full complement was accounted for, but four of the airmen were not identified initially. Rype sent the dog tags they found, Second Lieutenant Bosch's bracelet, badge of rank and bombardier's wings, as well as two medallions belonging to Santini, back through Sweden. One of the men was recognized by his ring by Fred Johansen, who was a childhood friend, and he ensured it was taken care of and mailed to his mother. Another item retrieved from the wreck was Helgesen's hip flask, evidence that his personal belongings, originally to have been carried by *Ed*, were on the doomed flight. The flask would later be placed on the mantelpiece in Helgesen's home.

Before Rype could reach the crash site, snow had fallen, and it was not possible to salvage any usable equipment. They did find a Rebecca, but it was smashed to pieces. However, it was nonetheless important to retrieve it so it would not fall into German hands.

The dead were wrapped in parachutes and put in a makeshift grave in a depression near the summit overlooking Lake Langvatnet. The bodies were covered with rocks and an American flag. The order in which they were buried, from south to north, was included in the report Colby sent to Skabo. A short ceremony was held, followed by a three-volley salute. They took a picture of the event for the families of the deceased. Among the wreckage a mailbag was found containing personal letters to the crews, which should have been encouraging, but the loss of their comrades snuffed out that joy. In addition, the wisdom of sending mail to a special forces group out on a mission, was questionable. If the letters had fallen into German hands, they would have been able to extract much information about the group, such as their identities, numbers, and perhaps would even have enabled the Germans to trace relatives still living in Norway, who could have been used as hostages.

On April 30, Rype reported back to London that they had found 12 bodies. Graves were also dug for the fallen from Plukkutjønnfjellet at Gjefsjø Farm, as they had planned to carry the bodies down there. But rivers between the mountain and the farm began flooding so the fallen were left in their makeshift grave for now.

Meanwhile, at SFHQ in London, Lieutenant Colonel Bolland and Colonel Hans Skabo worked feverishly to produce a status report and provide an explanation of why the problems with the deployment and insertion of reinforcements and supplies had occurred. They felt that their future careers in the US military hung in the balance. When Skabo and Bolland delivered the report on April 10, six NORSO men were known to have been killed and four were still missing. From a total of 16 flights, only four had been successful. The crews lacked experience in navigating that far north, which was extra challenging due to the weather conditions, topography, and the proximity to the magnetic north pole. Maintenance of the planes was also below par. And as summer was approaching, the hours of darkness would be too few for further flights to be made, so the two men recommended that the USAAF stopped the flights until the appropriate machines and personnel were supplied or they would have to find other means to get in supplies and reinforcements.

This left Technical Sergeant Knut Jøa, Technician Fifth Grade Otto Twingley, Corporal Vernon L. Austreng, and Technician Fifth Grade Wilton M. Rasmussen stranded in Britain. Another group was Technician Fourth Grade Einar M. Kristiansen, Technician Fourth Grade Otis L. Ausen, Technician Fifth Grade Harold Andersen, Corporal Arne M. Hoff, First Lieutenant John Kroona, and Lieutenant Colonel Bolland. The plan was to fly both groups to Sweden and try to infiltrate them by land across the border.[6] When they were to be infiltrated and in what order is not certain. The report also stated that they would have to be provided with Norwegian cover names and passports. But the risk of this approach to all but those most fluent in Norwegian would be high. Also, Kyllo had to remain in England at this point as he was responsible for getting the NORSO supplies, equipment, and personal effects from the staging area of the drop to make them ready for air transport into Sweden. However, we do know Bolland was in time for the tour from Snåsa to Trondheim and that he took some of them with him.[7]

The exact date of the extraction of the bodies is unknown, however, a notice in a Norwegian newspaper article, dated June 27, 1946, lists it as immediate. Arrangements were made with the Norwegian Air Force to transport the bodies from Snåsa and hand them over to the adjutant general of Task Force A, the United States Army detachment in Oslo. The initiative seemed to have been taken by Skabo who, in an undated report, probably written in early June 1945, called for "definite arrangements be made for proper disposal of the bodies of 4 members of the NORSO Group and also the members of the crew of the plane which crashed in Trøndelag."[8] Not much detail can be found to do with the actual extraction in written accounts, however, the operation is well documented in the photo collection left by Helgesen and which is now among the collections of the Norwegian Army Museum, The Armoury, in Trondheim. They show a Norwegian PBY Consolidated Catalina marked "J" landing at the former German floatplane base at Ila, Trondheim. Although it could be assumed from the newspaper article that the mission went ahead some time in late June, snow patches can still be seen in the mountains when they arrived at Snåsa. On board were four young American airmen who set up a tent camp on the shores of Lake Langvatnet. Both Hans Leirmo and Herbert Helgesen can be identified in the pictures. They probably stayed at Leirmo's cabin, not far from the site. They are seen approaching the Catalina in a dingy that appears to be about to sink. Several pictures show the American airmen in parkas, huddling from the cold; in other photos they are wearing T-shirts. In other words, the weather must have been just as shifting as it had been during Operation *Rype*. Pictures also show some unknown civilians and a horse heavily laden with what must have been equipment and supplies, and local helpers from Snåsa are seen ready to lend a hand in the gruesome task ahead. One of them is a woman, presumably in her twenties. Several of the pictures are taken on top of the mountain itself. Some show people and the scenery, others the makeshift tomb of the fallen and the excavation itself. In one picture, the woman and Helgesen are poring over a map, as if discussing the best route to negotiate when transporting the remains down to the floatplane.

The extraction itself appears to have been made as follows: they took the remains out of the tomb, still wrapped in parachutes, though some pictures show that some of the remains were exposed. The horse is seen dragging what could be three or four bodies on a sledge across the heather. They must have made at least two or more trips up to the site. At the shore of the lake, the bodies were put into simple wooden caskets, which straddled the dinghies and were then rowed out to the Catalina one by one. It seems they had two dinghies and a rowing boat at their disposal. A tech corporal seems to be in charge of the American group, and in one of the pictures he and another airman are bent over a Browning machine gun among the wreckage, making notes. Obviously, they had orders to document the crash site too, or what equipment was left behind.

The party also visited Gjefsjø, as one picture shows the grave of the Germans who fell on May 2. Five plaques made by their comrades who came looking for them are mounted on a cross of birch. The grave site is marked by a rectangle, made of birch logs.

After the extraction, the transport made a stop in Trondheim. This might sound illogical as they had decomposing bodies in their cargo hull. There are two pictures showing two of the airmen in Trondheim, probably taken at the Hornemann Mansion. The two men are sitting in a jeep, and it is possible that the photos were taken on the inbound journey, however, the men seem more tanned than in other pictures, and the hair of the aforementioned corporal looks bushier. Thus, it is likely they had already been to the crash site—and the thousand-yard-stare in the Corporal's eyes suggests he has seen and smelled death.

Besides the materiel and emotional losses, what human resources did *Rype* lose due to the tragedy in the mountains?

Technician Third Grade Robert N. Anderson was born in Jamestown, New York, by Lake Erie, to Swedish-born parents with American citizenship.

Technician Fifth Grade Bernard Iverson was born in Ferryville, Wisconsin, to parents of Norwegian origin. A small village in northwestern Wisconsin surrounded by undulating terrain, it should have had opportunities for skiing, but it is not known if the area had much of a tradition for it during Iverson's childhood and youth or if he enjoyed outdoor sports. Iverson was just 19 and listed as having "some high school education," and experience as a farmer and clerk.[9] He took part in *Percy Pink* in Dordogne, France.

Corporal Knut J. Falck was a native of metropolitan New York and married. He was part of the Jedburgh team *Christopher* and was dropped over Dordogne in France on the night 3/4 September together with 12 officers and 43 enlisted men. Their mission was to harass the Germans retreating through the Belfort Gap.

First Lieutenant Blaine Jones was 23 years old in 1945 and grew up in the small town of Lewistown, Pennsylvania. Both his parents were born in the United States. Jones was a trained W/T man, although not of Langeland's qualifications. He had been parachuted into Haute Vienne, France, on the night of 26/27 August as part of Operation *Percy Red*, together with one other officer and 16 enlisted men. Their orders were to strengthen the Maquis, attack the railway, and provide communications.

Although none of the deceased had any special skills within fieldcraft and winter survival, *Rype* lost an officer, a signaler, and significant combat experience with the demise of the four men who were killed at Plukkutjønnfjellet Mountain.

CHAPTER FOURTEEN

The Lierne Plan and Supply Issues

Even before full clarity about what had happened to the missing B-24 that crashed on April 6, 1945 had been obtained, the OSS in London decided to stop further attempts at resupply and reinforcement by air due to the poor result thus far. They decided that they would not risk any further lives. All further supplies to Rype would therefore have to be taken in through Sweden. Whatever it was not possible to procure in Sweden had to be flown there from the UK, and then infiltrated into Norway. Rype was notified of this in a message received on April 20.[1] However, in early May, the courier Erik Gaundal reported that it would not be possible to transport many goods across land either. In his dispatch to Colby, he did not specify why, however, it is likely that the spring thaw had already made the dirt roads to Björkede impassable. Further, what ice cover remained on lakes would be covered with surface water, and rivers and creeks flooded. Erichsen reckoned that Colby and his men had already received enough supplies to last through the worst isolation. One possible solution was to drop supplies just across the border near their base. This would of course require clearance of a lot of red tape, but Rype was asked to pick out a possible DZ.[2]

In London, Skabo also worked hard to infiltrate the remainder of the NORSO men supposed to have been dropped on March 25 by other means—now down to Technical Sergeant Jøa and three others. In a message dated April 21, and again on April 28, Colby urged several times to send both this group and Olmsted's men.[3] However, the OSS in Stockholm didn't think this should be done overtly. They recommended that the teams were flown into Sweden under regular military status, then proceed to Norway under false Norwegian identities. This could be done by sending all Norwegian-speaking personnel in groups of six. In Erichsen's dispatch to Colby, dated May 2, this seemed to be in progress and not pending any high-level clearance. However, despite Colby's recommendations, Skabo warned that they would keep Kyllo because he was needed to organize supplies at Areas P and H. However, the infiltration of non-Norwegian speaking men, including Olmsted and Hall, as well as the promised Greek contingent, would be more challenging.[4]

There was also work done in Stockholm to process materials for NORSO brought in from the UK, as well as procured in Sweden. The equipment for the Olmsted and Hall group would also need to be handled before they could be infiltrated. This was led by Captain Damman.

Colby and his men could in no way be certain when the war would end so they had to consider that it might drag on for much longer than we now know it did. With this prospect in mind, the plan to seize and hold the small community of Lierne, north of Snåsa, took form. The plan would cause much headache and friction between Rype's superiors in Stockholm and London. As its progress is intertwined in the progress of the operation in general, the analysis of it is embedded in the general chronological narrative, but to fully grasp its scope, it will be dealt with separately.

The first mention of the Lierne Plan was made by Colby in his progress report of April 5. Colby wanted to seize Lierne about May 1. He argued that the roads into Lierne would be blocked by snow during the winter and later by the spring thaw, so could easily be defended against German counterattacks if Rype and Waxwing joined forces. The mountains ensured that transport by means other than road were "prohibitively difficult."[5] Once the roads opened, however, they would need more men as the Germans could then pour in whatever reinforcements they had available. This could be countered, Colby believed, by recruiting local resistance fighters. How seizing Lierne could be combined with an anticipated loss of men after attacking Grana Bridge, Colby did not say. Towards the beginning of May, Rype and the Norwegians would seize control and establish a base for training and arming Norwegian patriots. Their numbers could be increased by bringing in Norwegian (police) troops from Sweden to defend the area when the roads opened again. This would require supplies brought in by air from England, as well as from Sweden. He also imagined daylight supply missions by Flying Fortresses, probably acknowledging the risk from enemy air defenses such a mission would entail due to the long hours of daylight in late spring or summer this far north.

From the Lierne base, a large force could then begin to clear central Norway of Germans. As a first step, Colby wanted to establish a communications plan with Waxwing for the necessary planning.[6] It is questionable whether Colby realized the security risk which this extensive communication would imply for both groups in terms of being detected and pinpointed by German signals intelligence. Colby even requested to pay a visit to their commander, Major Bangstad, whilst making a reconnaissance of the area to be occupied from a distance. For a more detailed recon, they would have to rely on the local population. Aware that this would be in breach of their field order, Colby requested that it be amended to fit his proposed operational objective.[7] In a message dated April 10, but not received by Rype until the 18th, Colby was ordered not to contact Waxwing at this point, and also notified that the group only numbered 12 men. Still, Colby asked if Waxwing were to be reinforced in a message dated April 21, sent by courier because there was no time to wait for the allotted timeslot for radio communication until they left for the Lurudal attack. A planned OSS reconnaissance of the border areas on the Swedish side was also dropped.

The above-mentioned letter from Major Nordli that spurred the insertion of Waxwing did mention establishing a bridgehead or a corridor in the area and having the government declaring it "liberated" with Swedish assistance, another lead suggesting that Colby's plan did not come out of his imagination alone but had substance in at least rumors and ideas held in higher echelons. The answer to Colby's request, however, was that it was a case for SHAEF to decide. The only thing Colby achieved was increased temperature in the debate about how the war should be waged in Norway. The snow was almost gone, and the thaw and flooding also hampered NORSO's own mobility, not just that of the Germans. Colby felt that they should get Jeeps dropped to solve this problem.[8] He also suggested they contact the British SAS who had some experience in dropping vehicles by parachute, but it does not seem that this was seriously considered in London. In his progress report dated April 5, he elaborates further on the Jeep issue. He wanted to harass German road communications, which makes sense given the strategic goal of the mission—to stop German troop transports. When the snow was gone, roads would open as alternative routes of transport when they blew up the railway. While visiting a Special Air Service base outside Leeds in October 1944, Colby had watched experiments of air dropping Jeeps for himself. He vowed in his telegrams while in the Snåsa Mountains that he knew how to dismount the vehicles from their dropping cradles, and that they could be dropped any time after the next moon period as soon as a proper reception area had been secured.

With Jeeps, they could ambush whatever transports the Germans organized to bypass the bridges and stretches of line that had been attacked. This would require relocating to a new base on a road network; again, Colby saw the opportunity to mention Lierne. That this would bring them closer to German forces, he did not mention in his requests. In his words, Colby also felt they lacked personnel to handle the supply and provision situation, specifically requesting the transfer of H. Andersen, Ausen, and Kyllo.[9] The request is restated in the April 5 progress report, where some unnamed Norwegians are also requested from Stockholm. In a roster, dating from after the German surrender, they are listed as a mess sergeant and S-4 respectively.[10] There was also some confusion about where Colby would place his requests—to Stockholm or London. Sometimes he would send it to Stockholm, sometimes to London, and sometimes to both. He suggested that all requests be sent first to Stockholm and they forward them to London when they were unable to comply.[11]

The snow being gone also increased the chance that the German patrols were coming after them in the mountains. Colby reported that they were making dispositions to defend themselves and to minimize the consequences if the Germans seized their base while they were out on a mission. They knew that Snåsa was rife with rumors of Allied paratroops being nearby, and Colby regarded the possibility of a German attack on Gjefsjø as a "likely possibility." On top of that, all the transport aircraft and the failed drops might have led the Germans to think that a substantial Allied force was hiding in the mountains, and Colby feared they would send a large expedition after them.[12] This might explain why he was so eager to get the Second NORSO Group in. He suggested they could stay on the Swedish side, ready to move in when the snow melted, which he feared would be soon. But he also hoped that by adding this force to their numbers, the attack on Grana Bridge would again be within reach. In hindsight, the rumors of a substantial force hiding in the mountains might also have deterred the Germans from mounting a search, as they probably did not have the resources for a big operation.

In his progress report of April 5, Colby argues for inserting the second group, pointing out that spring was just around the corner—snow would be gone by mid-May, if not sooner (the report is hard to read at this point). If they jumped in late April, they would have some time to get accustomed to the area and get organized in time for the ground becoming clear of snow. It might be true, as Colby writes, that they would be safe from the Germans who would not have the desire nor the means to mount a search-and-destroy mission against their combined forces. Also, the additional men would be needed to execute the Lierne Plan.[13] The question of the mobility and initial security of the second group (denominated "Olmstead" after the intended commander at this point) had also been an issue in the telegrams going back and forth on April 8. In a dispatch intended to be sent on April 8, Colby assured SFHQ that they would be able to protect them until the snow melted and that no German had been seen within 20 miles. After Oistad's team reached Gjefsjø, a suggestion posed in a telegram on April 18 was to dress Olmsted's men in civilian clothes (possibly brought by Oistad) and billet them in the cabin by the Swedish side of the lake.[14]

Colby also requested several drops of food and explosives. But his report of April 19 revealed that they were into the last moon period in which drops could be made. Any later, and the aircraft would not be able to exit Norwegian airspace under cover of darkness because they were so far north, almost on the border of the land of the midnight sun. Finally, he had the disheartening answer that additional supplies must come via Sweden. Colby feared early on that the oncoming thaw would prevent any movement of supplies, and in his progress report of April 1, he had suggested that the supplies be flown to Sweden, and then dropped on short flights over Norwegian territory.[15] Even after that, they would have to rely on boats and horses to get things moved around. He telegraphed London that he would meet George Brewer in Stockholm. The purpose was to discuss the plan to use the Lierne base to train Norwegian Resistance fighters, bring in supplies by air, and to discuss working with Waxwing to reconnoiter the area. They were also short on weapons.

They had yet to recover the Bren guns lost in the drop of March 25 and had too few M-1s. Colby stated that he felt silly running around in the mountains doing reconnaissance with only pistols. As the longer days would make the next moon period the last opportunity to get any supplies in from Britain, Colby wished that the operation would be directed from Stockholm from then on. He might also have realized that Erichsen in Stockholm was easier to convince of his own plans than Skabo in London. They also arranged for Jåma to provide them with one reindeer per week to alleviate the supply situation.[16]

By April 5, they had retrieved the Bren container, but Colby was still worried about the group's firepower and made some recommendations about the Second NORSO Group. All should have M-1 rifles, one out of three equipped to fire rifle grenades. The latter could launch a hand-grenade-size warhead. An M-1 Garand equipped with the M7 adapter and using an auxiliary grenade cartridge as a propellant had a maximum range of up to 200 meters but with dubious accuracy. Colby also felt that one in three men in the squads should carry a Thompson sub-machine gun "for special attacks," and one M-1903 A4 Springfield rifle per squad. The latter was the US Army's standard weapon until the introduction of the M-1. It was a powerful and accurate weapon that was still in use as a sniper weapon into the Vietnam War. Perhaps he had to actually go into the Norwegian mountains and meet the local hunters to appreciate the range and power of such a weapon for Operation *Rype*. Colby also requested two 60mm mortars, something that would be especially needed in case they made their stand in Lierne.[17] Colby temporarily backed down ("for now") on the Lierne Plan in message dated April 21 but urged that the work of planning it and providing supplies continue.[18] In addition, Colby reported they were beginning to run short of food. The first request for food to be sent to the Swedish side had already been made to London on March 27.[19] Colby now suggested that the supplies could be flown in from Sweden and pointed out the operations led by Bernt Balchen from Kallax in northern Sweden. According to Bolland's report, it had been a part of the initial plan to have Balchen organize the supplies.[20] Rype also asked when Balchen would get into the game in their messages.[21]

Colby's plan to free the Lierne area and entrench themselves in the village, which he sent to Vaudeville on April 9, doesn't seem that far-fetched when studying the topography. Lierne constitutes a salient in the border and has Sweden to the east, south, and north, and to the west there are several large lakes and rivers that would not be easy to cross for the Germans in the spring thaw. In other words, the area would be isolated, probably for weeks still, even after the snow was gone. Besides, it was believed only 25 Germans were in the village at this time—information that was revealed to Rype by London and could be interpreted as an encouragement.[22] Colby also shared his fear that the Germans and/or Norwegian Nazis would make a desperate last stand in Norway, which made the plan make more sense. Many of the NORSO men had also taken part in the *Jedburgh* operations in France, in which they would recruit and coordinate guerillas forces immediately behind the front, so the Lierne Plan was for a form of operation they were familiar with from earlier in the war and possibly a testimony to the human tendency to seek out of familiar types of action in times of uncertainty. Many probably also had happy memories from the festivities that often followed in France when they emerged as the first Allied soldiers the local populations would see. In the Snåsa area, they did not expect to be short of willing recruits. But London remained silent. It seemed as if at times they lost all radio contact with the SFHQ in London without apparent explanation, conveniently when some question was asked about supplies or proposals for actions that might be unpopular with London. They were given no instructions on what they should do when the Germans capitulated but were firmly put in their place when they presented their own plans for emerging from their mountain hideout. This was a recurring pattern in their contacts with London in the final days of the war.

Rype's message dated May 2 sheds more light on Colby's thinking about the Lierne Plan. There he revealed that he "thought collapse of Germany was the agreed time" for executing the plan.[23] As a timeframe this was highly ambiguous and open to interpretation. Was it when it was evident that capitulation was imminent, or when it was finalized? Colby seemed to lean towards the former interpretation. A foothold in Lierne would also solve the food problem, as it would connect them to the road network in Sweden. How much more passable these dirt roads would be compared to those leading to Björkede in the spring thaw he did not dwell on. Finally, he also revealed the reason for the urgency:

> We can help liberate Norway more by organizing and preparing a guerrilla force during this period for use in potential civil war by Quislings, stubborn German resistance or protective role if they surrender, that [*sic*] by highly laborious pin prick attacks on railway [.] Supplies are available in Stockholm, men in Norway and instructors and leaders [are] here [.] Lierne is easy to take and equally easy to defend [.] what are instruction in case of unconditional surrender including Norway [?].[24]

In other words, if Norway descended into civil war and a German force made a last stand, their position at Gjefsjø would be untenable. How realistic this prospect was is beyond the bounds of this account to assess, also whether this was a temporary motive for something else is hard to tell. The fact that movement would be difficult in the "next few weeks" due to the spring thaw also made the execution urgent (or at least to get approval to do it and prepare for it) and could prevent Colby and his men from getting to Lierne in the first place.

As the Lierne Plan required a drastic change in the field order, which the British most certainly would oppose, Erichsen chose to send the request through what he called "the US line." Whatever that might have been, it was obviously not a good idea to let the British in on the full extent of the discussion. However, the OSS in London still seemed entirely negative about the plan, and the existing field order remained in effect. Erichsen suspected that the project had been stopped "at such a high level that my puny efforts on your behalf seem stranded."[25] Exactly who or on what level this was, he did not speculate on further. However, it might have reached Eisenhower himself as any such project would challenge existing Allied policies and strategies of liberation, a fact to which Colby seems to have been oblivious. According to a cable sent to Colby by Erichsen, Major Bangstad from Waxwing had also visited Stockholm and presented a plan similar to Colby's.[26] Firstly, this seems so coordinated it may suggest that there had been unofficial contact between Rype and Waxwing in which the Lierne Plan was discussed. The field order had provisions for contacting the "other group" (Waxwing) to join forces in case of an emergency or even to take part in joint sabotage operations provided SFHQ gave permission. However, they were explicitly forbidden to seize and hold populated areas, except in "dire emergency." Risings of the local population were to be discouraged, but recruitment of volunteers would be allowed for guides and labor.[27] This was contradicted in Field Order No. 2, stating "avoid all civilian contact."[28] As could be guessed, Colby found plenty of loopholes if he selected those parts that would enable him to push the Lierne Plan and he interpreted them in the most favorable way. Secondly, it gave Erichsen hope that sufficient pressure could be built up over time favoring the project. However, he did not seem to question whether there would be sufficient time for this build-up to take place before the war ended. There was also some effort to get Skabo to Stockholm, which might have helped to solidify the section chief's support for the plan. This proved impossible due to Skabo's workload. He would also be further away from London when the necessary decisions would have had to be made, Erichsen concluded.

In London, Colby's Lierne Plan had been subject to extensive discussion, with the conclusion that it had to lie dormant for now. In a message dated April 20, Rype was notified that the plan was "not feasible at present" and that SHAEF approval was necessary.[29] Rype/Woodlark were too few in number if the Germans would counterattack, it was maintained. In Skabo's cable of April 25, it was assumed that there would be only 12–16 Norwegians available, perhaps referring to the Waxwing group. In addition, many more Allied operations were dependent on Swedish goodwill, and Colby ran a serious risk of jeopardizing these. The OSS in London simply feared that if the Germans acted, Rype would be forced to retreat into Sweden. This would not only result in an embarrassment for the Swedish government, but it was also likely that the Germans would move in, resulting in reprisals against the Norwegian population.

Erichsen, who visited Rype on April 23, seemed to support Colby's plans. He also pictured the liberation of a larger area, from Namsos in the north to Steinkjer in the south, anchored on the Swedish border in the east. The Lierne Plan was discussed between the two, and Colby must have been very convincing, according to his own later account. Taking Lierne and forming a guerrilla force among the men there and men from the surrounding valleys, was agreed upon as a good strategy by "all present."[30] One prerequisite of success, however, was the build-up of a weapons store on the Swedish side of the border that could be transported in once control was seized. Without it, they were vulnerable to being forced out by a German counter move. The operation depended on an allotment of arms for these stores, which in turn would require approval by higher headquarters. One could infer that Colby could have been inclined to go ahead with the plan regardless of approval, had he not required the additional weapons store.

Upon parting after their meeting on April 24, Erichsen and Colby set May 9 as the new date for the coup. According to Brewer, Westfield never received the field orders issued to Rype,[31] which might explain why the OSS in Stockholm was more sympathetic to the Lierne Plan than Skabo and London. When writing his book on the OSS in 1972, Harris Smith presented the following example of the relations between rear echelon planners and OSS operatives in the field:

> Mutual antipathy plagued all aspects of OSS operations. An OSS major working with the Norwegian resistance asked his London headquarters for permission to take and hold a town as a fort from which to waylay the Germans. Relaying a decision from the Supreme Command, OSS headquarters denied the request. But the major tried again. "I am here," he said. "I know what I am doing. I know I can do it; the resistance wants me to do it." That made OSS headquarters angry: "You have your orders. Disobedience will be subject to disciplinary actions upon your return." Was headquarters bluffing? Probably, but the incident suggests the flavor of "normal" relations with the men in the field.[32]

The usual conflict between the man in the field and an officer behind a desk was particularly strong within the OSS, the divide being almost consistent with the geographical distance between the two.[33] Drawing on the experience in France, Italy, and Yugoslavia, "the officer behind the desk" knew very well that the value of the resistance as a fighting force did not add up to much unless it corresponded with the invasion of regular forces.[34] General Donovan himself was known for taking the side of the "man on the ground," the agents and OG members in the field over that of office clerks and staff officers who were miles away, and in Rype's case in London.[35] But also:

> … the men in the field were often at fault because they didn't know the whole picture and blamed Headquarters for any and all shortcomings, a number of which were the direct result of policy making decisions made at Supreme Headquarters.[36]

As late as April 28, London signaled that the final word on the Lierne Plan was not yet said, as they promised a decision "next week." This, of course, made hope live on with Colby.[37] Skabo was also concerned about Swedish reactions, and with not embarrassing their government by Americans seeking refuge. He considered the plan to be rapidly growing redundant as the collapse of German resistance was growing imminent.[38] London also rejected Colby's plans to take Lierne for what they called "obvious reasons."[39] Hitler was now dead, and the war could end any day. But the plan caused some discussions in the SFHQ after all. Colby replied cheekily that he did not understand what was meant by "obvious reasons" and said that Rype had what it took to organize a guerrilla force. What he did not know (and what "obvious reasons" hinted at) was that the Allies negotiated in secret with the German High Command, and therefore that the Lierne Plan could put the execution of a peaceful settlement in danger locally.

CHAPTER FIFTEEN

Attack Against the Lurudal–Agle Railway

The trains soon rolled past the site of the attack at Tangen, but that did not seem to dampen Rype's morale. At least Colby reasoned that given the amount of resources the Germans spent repairing the damage, it just proved how important the mission was. Rype's next target was the railway line through Lurudal and the railway station at Landsem. Colby made this decision before they hit Tangen. According to Helgesen's report, the attack on Tangen had led to increased German security on all railway bridges, and London had informed them that the effect of blowing up tracks would be good as the Germans had a shortage of rails and could not produce enough for repairs without breaking up side tracks.[1] Colby had also requested supplies be dropped at given locations en route to their next target so they did not have to carry the entire load from Gjefsjø.[2] The content was specified in Colby's progress report dated April 5. The locations of these requested drops, however, seems mysterious. In Erichsen's dispatch dated April 9, the locations are roughly given as "East of Lurudal" and "South East of Snaasa [Lake]." The drops would be received by Rype with Rebeccas. A date was not yet set, and these made sense at the time, as Rype was then en route to Tangen, and had not yet set out for Lurudal. But these requests were repeated in message number 25, sent April 18, and specified to Sandstad at coordinates 2201 (codenamed "Ares") and Storåsen at 4614 (codenamed "Mars"). The first location is a bit puzzling. Sandstad is located on the northern slopes of Roktdalen, which the group had passed en route to Tangen. There is no mention of any new operations planned in this direction, and it would be far off any natural course to or from Lurudal. However, Langeland writes that message 24 was drafted before they left for Tangen, and it is therefore fair to assume that the first part of message 25 was also drafted at this point, and that Langeland simply did not edit out the redundant location when he sent it after they got back.[3] Storåsen makes more sense, as it is along a natural course to Lurudal, although there are four locations with that name in the area (Storåsen simply means "big hill"). Colby's request was that each drop contained two containers of railway charges (H-21), eight SNF

(Special Norwegian Food) containers, and two containers of K-rations. Of course, these drops would never materialize as no more supplies would be brought in by air.

Kjell Sørlie, Lieutenant Harald Larsen, Technician Fifth Grade Sverre Aanonsen, and Vestgöte did not go on the Lurudal mission because they were sick. But those who had been accidentally dropped over Sweden were now available for this next operation. Otherwise, it was the same group that had been on the Tangen Mission, divided into groups of three:

Group 1:
- Major Colby
- Technician Fifth Grade Windh
- Andreas Andersen

Group 2:
- Lieutenant Saether
- Technician Third Grade Myrland
- Technician Fifth Grade Hovland

Group 3:
- Lieutenant Farnsworth
- Corporal Knut Andreasen
- "Gaer"

Group 4:
- Lieutenant Hoel
- Technician Fifth Grade Gravdal
- Jon Moan

Group 5:
- First Sergeant Eliassen
- Staff Sergeant Listeid
- Technician Third Grade F. Johansen

Group 6:
- Technical Sergeant Langeland
- Technician Fifth Grade Rusdal
- Thoralf Lian

According to Helgesen, the Norwegians Ludvik Kruksve and Jørgen Havik also took part in the Lurudal attack, but they are not mentioned by Colby.[4] One of them could be the mysterious "Gaer," but not both.

They started out from Gjefsjø on April 23—the distance was less than what it had been during the attack against Tangen Bridge and their cargo was somewhat lighter. Helgesen later described them as:

> a white stripe that slid forth along a ridge, first two men, then a long line. At a distance, it would have looked strange, that is, we should not have been visible at a distance. We were camouflaged, but weeks in the field with campfires and close encounters with ski wax had put its mark on upon a winter camouflage suit.[5]

The maps used for the Lurudal attack are preserved, but unlike for their first attack on Tangen, the route taken towards the target area is not marked on them. But Colby's reports are very detailed on the route they followed. Helgesen's more colorful account in "Jernbanesabotasje" also picks up the story about this point. As before the Tangen attack, they first climbed Litlfjellet to the northwest of Gjefsjø, from where they could head directly north to Seisjøfiskløysa. The weather was clear, and they had a wonderful view all the way to Sweden. This meant that they would probably have had an easy going with firm and relatively dry snow.

The Lurusneisen Mountain towered in the distance with its sharp peak looking a bit like a New York skyscraper, according to the Americans. In the afternoon, they made good progress; Hans Leirmo was pulling them like a machine. They stayed at about 600 MAMSL before dipping down to just over 509 MAMSL as they descended towards Seisjøen and crossed reindeer tracks on their way down. This meant they would be traveling along the wood line. As they labored downhill with the *pulka*, some of the men were sent ahead on reconnaissance. They came upon some fresh ski tracks and wondered if a German patrol route went through the area. The evidence of spring was all too apparent, and some creeks and rivers were already breaking up from underneath their winter shroud. The danger of falling through a snow bridge and landing in the freezing melt water below was very real. The ice on Seisjøen was blue and rotten, but they had to get across. They managed to clear the open channel in the ice along the shore. According to Helgesen, nobody was wet further up than to their necks. They found the hut at Seisjøen abandoned and safe, referred to by Helgesen as the "Government Hut,"[6] most probably what is marked on modern maps as Seisjøen Skogstue, run by the public Norwegian forestry enterprise Statsskog. There they spent the night, but the cabin was a very tight spot where "you could force 30 people inside only with a dash of good will and a shoehorn".[7] As there were no room for them all inside, about half of the men had to spend the night outside.

While there were no signs of the Germans outside except for the tracks, on the inside, the Germans had made their presence visible. There were marks on the walls and on the ceiling, and empty liquor bottles lay everywhere. They got the coffee pot going, and the Americans impressed the Norwegians with the amount of coffee they were able to down, themselves having a reputation as the heaviest consumers of coffee in the world. One of the Norwegian contacts came to visit them during the night (name unknown) probably with latest news from the village and German movements. The contact too downed three to four cups before going to bed. He had a turbulent night, tossing and turning and making some awful noise. At 04:00, he put on his backpack, and they sent him on his way, probably tired of the disturbances.

The next day the party started out around 07:00. The weather had taken a turn for the worse with sleet, snow, and wind. "Sabotage weather," Colby called it, probably in an attempt at inducing a positive, light-hearted mood in the men before the trials ahead, but with limited success. The skis were icing badly, and many of the Americans struggled as they had poor skiing technique according to Helgesen. They continued north to Andorsjøen Lake, then turned northwest to Gaos Lake and now faced the Luru River. By now, they had gone around Andorfjellet Mountain on the north face. Then they went southwest and traveled down the valley between Andorfjellet in the south and Reinhornfjellet in the north. As they emerged onto the naked slopes, they were quite happy about the weather and the poor visibility as without it they would have been very exposed from down in the valley if the winter camouflage suits were as dirty as Helgesen claimed. Why they did not take the much shorter route from Andorsjøen Lake along the south face of Andorfjellet Mountain and follow the Storåselva River, the sources do not say. It might have been due to the going and terrain, as the snow tends to be slushier and melt quicker on the south face than on the north face of a mountain. It was a tough day; they rested every hour as they used to. The backpacks were getting heavy, and the water trickled down their backs. The *pulka* felt like small mountains when they tried to move them. Nothing was packed with more evil than a full *pulka*, Helgesen remembered in his account. Uphill they are heavier than a rock, and downhill they get entangled whenever there is a chance.[8] The men descended into the fields around Bomo Shieling and crossed the Geila River, which runs along the valley floor. The ice had broken up, but it did not matter much as they could not get wetter than they already were.

Down the hills, they had difficulty keeping up with Hans Leirmo as he skied around the bushes, stones, and trees. After a sharp descent through thick brush, they ended up at Skjørsjøen Shieling where they rested. This time it was the turn of those who had slept outside at Seisjøen to spend the night indoors, and inside Helgesen and Leirmo found what they described as the biggest bed in the whole of Snåsa. From the cabin they could see down into the valley where the railway ran, and through binoculars they saw cars driving on the roads. This also meant they themselves were exposed, and movement outside was restricted to the absolutely necessary, and under no circumstances without the white camo suits, although they were now so dirty that it hardly mattered. From Skjørsjøen there was only 5.5 kilometers to the railway track, but the terrain from the shieling further towards the target area was treacherous. After eating that night, Helgesen and Leirmo strolled outside to find a path through the difficult terrain ahead. They crawled on their hands and knees, having in mind how they could get down the next day in case they were followed, if they carried wounded comrades, or just had broken skis. "It usually works out well," Hans Leirmo commented on Helgesen's worries. They finally found a way through. On modern maps there is a trail ascending from the north shore of the Skjørsjøen Lake that cuts diagonally up the steep hillside and it was probably this path they finally discovered. Back at the shieling, they could watch as the lights came on all through the valley below, down towards the blackened blue surface of

Lake Snåsa. Leirmo and Helgesen went to bed after a few cups of coffee, not certain when they would get any sleep.

The next morning, they woke up to the smell of bacon, which brought a smile to the face of the old mountain man. They checked their equipment, waxed their skis, and checked the charges and the weapons. The charges were taken from the *pulkas* and distributed; each man took eight double charges in their packs. Each team carried 30 prepared charges joined in pairs, 240 charges of plastic explosives were used.[9] Each double charge consisted of two ¾lbs charges linked by 1 meter Cordex detonating fuse cord and pencil fuses with timers set to 8–10 seconds. Each man also carried a hand grenade. The procedure was to have two men work side by side, placing the charges on every other rail, while the third followed behind and placed the detonating devices, as it was known that carrying detonators together with the charges was not safe. They had to work fast and stay low in order not to be detected too soon. Then they had to run as fast they could while pulling the cords on the detonators. Under extreme cold temperatures, the fuse would burn slower, but that did not seem to have an effect during Rype's attack. Colby made it clear that if anyone got hurt and the Germans were on to them, they might have to be left behind to save the rest of the group. The grim realities seemed surreal as the sun came up and the sound of the black grouse could be heard in the distance. The final timing, passwords, rendezvous points, and secondary rendezvous points were given, every man knew his team and what his tasks were. The team leaders would go through every step once more before they approached the target. A couple of skis were laid out on the ground to mimic the rails, and Farnsworth went through the placing of the charges.

A reconnaissance party made up of Colby, Langeland, and Leirmo started out first—their mission was to scout for approach routes to the points selected to be blown up. Around noon, Colby and the recon group set out again. Saether took charge of the main group about 14:00 and led them to the first rendezvous point at Skartneset, a shieling about 1 kilometer from the railway line. There was no sign of people and the sunlight was reflected by the newly fallen snow. Despite the serene surroundings, according to Helgesen's informants, there were 112 Germans ahead of them guarding a stretch of 5 kilometers of railway—40 men were stationed at Lurudal. The latter could mean Luru Farm, some 5 kilometers north of the area of attack, as Langeland later reported that a "large farmhouse near the tracks was used by the Germans as headquarters of the farm."[10] In the railway warden's quarters, about 2 kilometers south of Lurudal Station, 8 men were located, probably responsible for guarding the nearby Plutten Tunnel. At Landsem to the south there were further 12, and at Agle, 40 men.

The main party were in no hurry according to the set timetable for the attack. They hid inside the barn at Skartneset, and they were so close to the target they could hear voices from people working on the rails. Skartneset would also be their rallying point after the attack. The password was of a call-and-response type. The call would be "Hoko Moko" and the answer were "Slowly I turn." Hoko Moko was from the name of the 1916 show tune "On the Hoko Moko Island," sung by Collins and Harlan about an Irishman who was stranded among the natives on a South Pacific Island and fantasized about marrying a girl on a crocodile. One cannot help but see the irony to it. Colby, himself being half Irish, was kind of stranded among natives, but the climate was not exactly of the Hawaiian kind. And neither were the natives. The response, "Slowly I turn," was a reference to a Vaudeville sketch. Meanwhile, Colby crawled out on a ledge on his stomach and saw Germans standing by the railway line. Some trains also went past. Worse still was that he became soaking wet from lying down flat. Back at the barn, Jon Moan was freezing his toes off—his feet had not been dry for two days. He snuck inside the farmhouse, came back with a pelt, and soon fell asleep in the barn. Colby and the reconnaissance party returned; it was now so dark that they dared not light a fire in the stove to make coffee without worrying that the smoke from the chimney would expose them. Detonations made by the Germans were heard in the distance, but that did not worry them—it would be nothing compared to what they had in store.

They listened to the Norwegian news on BBC which told them that peace was coming, out there in the world, but warned that the Germans might fight to the last bullet in Norway. At 21:00, they got ready. They checked the charges, fuses, and weapons one last time. A kettle was put on the stove so it would be ready to brew some coffee when they returned. The snow was gone from the area around the railway line, so they took off their camouflage suits. They set out at intervals in order to reach their targets simultaneously, as the groups had unequal distances to their objectives. It was getting colder, and a full moon hung over them. The two northernmost groups who had furthest to go, led by Lieutenant Saether (with Myrland and Hovland) and Sergeant Paulsen (with Kai Johansen and Nipe), left first, guided to their positions by Leirmo, who would then join Paulsen's group. Colby had gained some familiarity with the area from previous reconnaissance and found the way to the target area by himself. His group consisted of Technician Fifth Grade Windh and native Norwegian Agnar Andersen. Colby had reserved the most dangerous part of the job for himself, as his group would engage the target area closest to the guarded Plutten Tunnel. Lieutenant Farnsworth led the next group down the line (with Corporal Knut Andreasen and Gaer). First Sergeant Eliassen had Staff Sergeant Listeid and Technician Third Grade F. Johansen under his command on the next point of attack; then followed Sergeant Oistad with Technician Third Grade Odd Anderson and Technician Fifth Grade Raivio; then Sergeant Langeland with Technician Fifth Grade Rusdal and Norwegian native Thoralf Lian; and finally, Lieutenant Helgesen with Gravdal and Moan. The sound of a train whistle could be heard in the distance—it was the approaching night train. Helgesen and his group gambled that the noise from the train would drown out the sound from their skis and sped up across the snow.

Helgesen and his group reached a fence 150 meters away from the line, took off their skis, and then arranged them so they would be quick to put on in case a hasty retreat was necessary. Still, they sank to their knees in the snow. They reached their final cover, a spruce 15 meters from the tracks. At 23:15, all groups were in their starting positions. The three northernmost groups were the most exposed should the enemy counterattack. Saether and Paulsen's groups had the slopes of Reinhornfjellet Mountain at their backs, a force of 40 Germans on their right flank, and the guard post at the tunnel to the south (8 Germans). If the Germans deployed, they would be forced to either fight their way through or climb over the 400-meter high Krulhaugen to the east, presumably under fire. Colby's group was also perilously close to enemy forces but had a shorter way to a safe escape south of the hill. If any one of the groups came under attack while placing the charges, they would retreat along the line and the next group down would set off their charges immediately. Just before they went in to place their charges, a singing noise rose from the tracks and a man on a draisine went by. He was probably a warden, but luckily, he did not pass a couple of minutes later when he either would have run into the Rype men or even risked being blown to pieces. If he had surprised them, the history of *Rype* could have taken a very different turn.

The moon was on the rise when the groups began approaching their targets at 23:30. The temperature had dropped below freezing and a hard wind blew from the west. The snow was crusty and gave off a noise that must have sounded like crashing thunder through the tension, but there is no evidence that the Germans ever heard them even though the nearest guard post would have been only a couple of hundred meters away at most. The charges with the pencil fuses inserted were placed on every other fishplate (joint) on the rails to maximize the number of rails destroyed. The exact method of blowing up the tracks has been somewhat debated. The explosives manual mentioned above only recommended "close and intimate contact between the explosive and the material to be destroyed." This could be achieved by "firm lashing" or shaping the explosive to fit the profile of the target. The latter could be somewhat difficult in winter conditions as plastic explosives are hard to mold at low temperatures. Some sabotage groups are known to have pre-shaped the charges in a base area where normal room temperature could be maintained, but nothing is mentioned of Rype doing this. The manual continues, "to damage the maximum number of rails with the minimum of effort" the charges should be placed at alternate joints to maximize the number of rails destroyed. Modern trained military engineers are taught to lay "scissor charges" where one charge is placed on either side of the rail with distances a couple of centimeters apart so the blast will create a scissor effect by forcing the two parts in opposing directions. It is doubtful that Rype used this method; Helgesen's manual specifies that the charges should be placed on the inside of the tracks, thus implying they did not use scissor charges.[11]

Each of the railway rails were 12 meters long and each team was responsible for 200 meters. Contrary to procedure, Helgesen chose to attach the fuses to the charges before his group approached the target. Jon Moan covered the group with his machine gun, the phosphorous on his front sight giving off a slight glow. His family had been hit hard by the occupation, and in his later account, Helgesen imagined what was going through his mind as Moan was patting the gun as if to say this is for his father who was incarcerated at Grini prison camp outside Oslo and his brother Kristoffer at Vollan Prison in Trondheim. Åsmund, the American on the team, and Helgesen placed the charges in just 10 minutes, while Moan followed them, switching positions as they went along. As they finished, they took cover, but the American had to go back to check one of the charges that he felt was out of position. Over the railway that passed through a cut in the mountain, two shadows appeared on a bridge across the tracks (the place best fitting this description is 20–30 meters before the Lurudal road crosses the railway today at Setdalsbekken Creek). "I think somebody is coming to take a look at us," Moan whispered and lifted the backstock to his cheek. But the shadows turned around and disappeared.[12]

Colby was supposed to send up a green flare at 23:45 to signal that they should start lighting the fuses. If no flare was seen, they would all start at 23:50. Colby and his team were slowed down by the presence of the guardhouse near the entrance of the tunnel. Because of its proximity, Colby decided not to fire his flare for fear that they were going to be detected before the charges went off. Therefore, he and the rest of the group began pulling the strings of the fuses at 23:50. Ten seconds after, the explosions rang all along the line. But with such a short fuse, the operation was not completely risk free, even without German intervention. Rocks and iron fragments flew through the air and one of the Norwegians described later that he had never been so scared in all his life, even after what he had experienced through a long service with the resistance. Not all teams were finished placing their charges, and only about 190 double charges were detonated, the reminder being left behind as they withdrew.

At the southern end of the attack, Helgesen and his group saw a red flare, then heard the cracking from machine guns, and then began pulling the strings on the fuses. The explosions and the flashes never seemed to end. Helgesen reached one charge where the peg on the string of the detonator was gone, and suddenly realized he had come to the end of his charges and reached one that Åsmund had already pulled. He threw it away, took a big dive down the bank to get to safety, and suddenly, the whole world was engulfed in light. Rocks and iron fragments flew around his head, and then came the shockwave and the bang. The line turned into a trail of blackened rocks, twisted metal and gaping holes in the railway embankment. But, as if by a miracle, Helgesen was unharmed. In total, about 218 individual rails and 2.5 kilometers of railway track were destroyed during Rype's attack on Lurudal.[13]

The retreat would be almost as dramatic. At the northern end of the attack, the world seemed like an orgy of flares and machine-gun fire. The guards at the Plutten Tunnel fired in the direction of Colby's group and sent up several flares to mark the general direction they assumed the attackers were heading. But it seemed that they did not manage to locate Colby and his men as they appeared to be firing wildly around them. One of the bullets hit the ground near Colby and he was struck in the forehead by rock fragments. Helgesen would later comment on Colby remaining calm even under fire during this action.[14] Sergeant Windh on Colby's team was armed with a BAR, and asked if they should return fire, but Colby refused since they were not able to pinpoint where the shots came from, and they would only risk revealing their position. Lieutenant Saether also reported that he heard a machine gun being fired in his direction during the withdrawal. The Germans immediately began a pursuit, but soon gave up as they did not dare follow the saboteurs into the forest in the darkness.[15]

At the southern end, there was less drama. Helgesen's group retreated nice and gently, and soon ran into Eliassen's group. The correct call and response was given, and they could lower their weapons. The two southern groups arrived at Skartneset, placed guards outside and began to prepare coffee as the other groups began to arrive. Finally, Tom Saether's group also appeared and was able to ascertain that no one in the group was seriously wounded. Tom was just lifting the first cup of coffee to drink when one of the guards knocked on the window and said "Jerry!"—somebody was coming up from the railway towards them. Tom threw away the cup and everybody stormed out and put on their skis that were lined up outside. The guards followed, after having set up a couple of boobytraps with tripwires. A flare went up and landed by the shieling, and on the other side of a bank the Germans opened fire. Behind them, they could hear an explosion and then a scream. One of the Germans had set off a booby trap. Langeland later wrote that only "blank explosives were used mostly as a warning, hoping to slow the Germans down," and that "live ones were not used because of the danger of killing innocent Norwegian skiers."[16] What was meant by "blank" in this regard is unclear, but it could mean that there was no fragmentation involved. However, if so, the Germans showed that these were dangerous enough. Soon they came to the point where they had left the extra equipment and slowed down. Behind them, lights came on in the buildings and headlights of cars could be seen whirling about down in the valley. "Just like 4th of July," was Farnsworth's comment.[17] They followed the same route as on the approach march, except that they went east and not west of the Seisjøen. Downhill, they made sure to make some turns between trees and bushes, stringing tripwires between the tree trunks at neck height.

To London, they later reported "no casualties ... slight contact with the Germans."[18] As they reached the bare mountain they relaxed, feeling certain that the Germans were poorer skiers and probably would not follow them this far, even with the help of local Norwegian Nazis. They did not even try to cover their tracks, leaving them to show their enemies they had been there. This time, no aircraft were heard overhead, and the windy weather ensured that their tracks were soon obliterated, and they were confident that the guard post on Litlfjellet would alert them of any pursuing enemy once they were back at Gjefsjø. They arrived there at 16:00 hours on Thursday after having skied continuously without major breaks. Colby's report was full of praise for his men, how they had endured the long march through difficult terrain (although hardly comparable to that following Tangen), hitting the Germans by surprise despite the crusty snow, and he especially lauded the junior officers and NCOs. Colby also recommended that a special letter of commendation be written to Hans Leirmo for acting as a guide and for his choice of route and assistance during the reconnaissance.[19] The recommendations for Bronze Medal to Eliassen read:

> On April 25, 1946, Private Eliassen [then Sergeant] was detailed to lead a group of enlisted men in the action on the Nordland Railway at the Plutten Tunnel in Lurudal. This operation is reported to have been a complete success. A severe blow was dealt the enemy in the destruction of that part of the railway which was most heavily guarded. Approximately 2½ kilometers of rail were rendered useless. Private Eliassen conducted himself in a very superior manner and completely justified the responsibility placed on him as leader of his group. In the withdrawal he was called upon to make a 50-kilometer march without rest, even though he had already been subjected to 18 hours of extreme physical exertion, the natural strain of an attack, and the rigors attendant to the near arctic terrain. To quote a report of his Commanding Officer: "Special commendation is due the junior leaders and NCOs for the perfect way in which their teams reached the line, performed their tasks, and withdrew in perfect order."[20]

The aftermath of the Lurudal attack highlights some of the special challenges posed by special operations in an Arctic environment, soon to be discovered the hard way by some of Colby's men. Upon returning from Lurudal, Windh complained about pains in his abdomen, and he was transported to Sweden and hospital as it was feared that he had appendicitis. The roster also notes that Thoralf Lian and Jon Moan departed for Stockholm—perhaps they were accompanying Windh. Windh arrived in Stockholm on May 2. However, it turned out that his pains were due to drinking too much ice water in the mountain. This is known to make the intestines and surrounding blood vessels contract, a condition that could prevent food from being digested properly. Also, the body uses a lot of energy heating up the icy water, which could cause nausea, exhaustion, and possible erratic heartrate and loss of consciousness in extreme cases. As Erichsen got back to Stockholm, he received the news that Windh was ready to return to duty. Quite cryptically, he was to be returned with the courier together with "some men who are to serve with you as general assistants and bottle washers."[21] This points to the difficulties of maintaining good hygiene under these circumstances, especially while on missions. According to Langeland, who admittedly mixed up events at this point, on the return trip, they rested in a summer cabin where they ate crackers and pemican for supper. The only nutrients left the next morning was some cocoa that two of the men were assigned to prepare. But they were too tired to go out, get snow, and melt it, so they used the dirty water in which they had cleaned their mess kits the night before. This made the beverage undrinkable, although everybody tried to drink it.[22] Langeland's account is casual about this, but hygiene negligence in this situation was potentially fatal. If anyone had come down with diarrhea, they might not have been in a physical state to continue. Even without German interference, or accidents because of exhaustion, it could have led to serious dehydration and hypothermia if they were left incapacitated on the cold, naked mountains.

CHAPTER SIXTEEN

The German Patrol Incident

From the local population, Rype learned that a German force of 50 men was out looking for them. According to Helgesen, a 40-man patrol had headed south towards them from Sørli as a response to the Lurudal attack and were combing the border in search for any sign of the saboteurs.[1] According to Colby, his men were tired from a week of heavy guard duty when the German patrol found the camp.[2] From here, there are about as many different versions of what happened as there are reports and testimonies available. The following day, Langeland sent this message:

> Five-man German patrol from Seven Two Two Grenadier Regiment blundered in here last night … All killed, one Norwegian wounded in short fight … Our security must have been good … Now worthless …[3]

In the evening of May 2, Sergeant Marinus Myrland stood guard in the front yard when he suddenly faced a German patrol of five men armed with automatic weapons. They had rapidly slid down the hill above the farm, possibly at a moment when Myrland was not paying full attention. He told the Germans calmly that Gjefsjø Farm was full of American soldiers, and if they shot him, a firefight would develop that they would be doomed to lose. According to Colby's report, as Myrland was talking to the Germans "several men were around them with Thompson Sub-Machine Guns."[4]

In Helgesen's report, the Americans deployed in a semicircle out of sight of the Germans, as they "probably found everything to be in order when resistance fighter Karle Berre came out with a pistol."[5] In this version, Berre is the one who made first contact with the Germans, not Myrland. In both versions, the *Oberfeldwebel* leading the patrol agreed to surrender. According to Helgesen, upon hearing that, Berre lowered his pistol, after the German asked him to do so. Then, in both Colby's and Helgesen's, versions, the *Oberfeldwebel* shot Berre in the stomach, the German's sub-machine gun jammed after the first round and the five Germans were then gunned down "still armed and with weapons in hand."[6] This incident prompted London's order to avoid further confrontations at all costs and to move the camp to a cabin belonging to the Swedish Forestry Authority on the other side of Gjevsjø Lake. Admittedly, Helgesen was not present at Gjefsjø during the incident, however, his account makes more sense as it is likely the Germans would open fire if they too believed they were only facing one resistance fighter with a pistol who was bluffing about a farm full of American paratroopers.

In 1989, Berre gave a newspaper interview about the incident. Berre was a veteran of the fighting in 1940 and had later joined the resistance and had also been a guide for refugees. Before the war he had been a renowned competitive skier and marksman. After making his last trip as a refugee guide in March 1945, he and three others brought a radio back into Norway, to be delivered to Gjefsjø Farm. After the order came from London to suspend the attacks, a calm descended on the group at Gjefsjø, Berre said. A warm spring breeze was in the air, some of the men cleaned their weapons, other tended to the more domestic chores. According to Berre, Colby and Helgesen sat and talked in a corner but this is inaccurate since Helgesen and Leirmo were guiding the new reinforcements up from Snåsa at this point. Berre said Myrland stood guard alone because one man was enough, according to Colby. As Berre stood in the kitchen, looking out of the window, the blood froze in his veins when he saw five German soldiers approaching the farm. He grabbed his carbine and ran out as he knew Myrland was standing on the opposite side of the house.[7]

In a split second, Berre was faced with the dilemma to either hit the ground and open fire or to try to talk the Germans into surrendering. He chose the latter. Berre recognized *Oberfeldwebel* Alfred Witt because he had been stationed near his home at Bangsund, Namsos, and he knew that he spoke Norwegian. In this version, Berre spoke to Witt, warning him that there were 20–30 American and Norwegian soldiers inside. *Oberfeldwebel* Witt said something like they had no intention to fight, and that the war would soon be over. Berre lowered his gun but suddenly Witt lifted his sub-machine gun and Berre felt as if a hot bolt had shot through his body. Witt had discharged his weapon, either intentionally or by accident. Berre was hit in the abdomen/hip, and the bullet went straight through his body and lodged in the wall behind him. The projectile was later retrieved and handed over to Berre after the war. Berre was still conscious but admitted in interviews to having only vague memories of what happened next, which is unsurprising since Berre was bleeding heavily and was going into shock fast as he yelled to the others that they should "get the Germans!" In the newspaper article, *Oberfeldwebel* Witt claimed that the shot was fired by accident (supposedly as he was killed), but later examination of his weapon revealed that only a jam had prevented Berre from being riddled with bullets from a sub-machine gun set on full automatic fire.[8]

Technician Third Grade Fred Johansen patched Berre together and administered penicillin, making the resistance fighter one of the first Norwegians to receive this new wonder drug on Norwegian soil. Then he was warmly dressed and evacuated to Sweden on an improvised ski stretcher. On the first leg of the journey, he had to be hauled on a sledge for 40 kilometers, not an easy task through wet, melting snow that was broken up by creeks, lakes, and soaked marshes.

From Saether's letter of recommendation for the Silver Star, he and Fred Johansen also followed Berre across the border, probably to Björkede, together with three Norwegian Resistance fighters. Many of these recommendations exaggerate the number of enemy and some of the struggles. According to this, they donned civilian clothes for the first time and negotiated 30 kilometers across "hazardous terrain through enemy patrols" to reach the border.[9] In reality, it was only about 4 kilometers across the flat surface of Gjevsjø Lake until they were on the Swedish side. The hardship was real, but it only began once inside Sweden when the last kilometer or so must have been a struggle, with Berre bleeding on the *pulka*. It is not certain how far Johansen and Saether followed Berre as he was transported by horse and sledge from Björkede to Sandvika, and then by car to the hospital in Östersund.

The Germans were buried in the graves that were originally intended for the Americans who died in the plane crash at Plukkutjønnfjellet. They were:

Oberfeldwebel Alfred Witt (b. 1909)
Gefreiter Eugene Schor (b. 1926)
Gefreiter Alois Stadler (b. 1926)
Stabsgefreiter Gerhard Treichel (b. 1911)
Anton Schneider (b. 1926)

Their bodies remained there until 1950 when they were moved to the war cemetery at Havstein in Trondheim, except *Oberfeldwebel* Witt who is not listed in the grave records and was probably moved to Germany.[10] The plaques that stood on the original graves are still at Gjefsjø Farm; they were probably made by Germans who visited Gjefsjø in September 1945. Despite his outburst in the heat of the moment as he was shot, in later years Berre felt sorry for the Germans who lost their lives at Gjefsjø and he was plagued by post-traumatic stress which presented difficulties for him and his family.[11]

In hindsight there has been much speculation about what really happened on the farm on May 2, 1945, and ever since just after the end of war, there have been rumors that the German patrol laid down their arms and were then executed on Colby's order. Leif B. Lillegaard's 1978 novel *The Last Patrol*, builds its plot around an assumption. The preface states that:

> The first time I heard the account was in the fall of 1945. It was impossible to get rid of it. In the summer of 1955, two German cars came to Snåsa, I went over and got to hear the account for another time. Ten years later, I visited the mountain and border areas in Snåsa. I heard the narrative repeatedly and began to believe in it. But when I went to see the eye witnesses, their mouths were closed. The heroes were silent.
>
> Last summer I visited my friend Jens Bjarne Mohrsen in the mountains where the tragedy took place, not far from his home. We agreed that it *could* have happened as here described. We do not know. The three who know the story, know that. But they say nothing. I just got

> this response: war is made up of people. Every action has a motive. This report is printed from the simple motive to throw a small human light into the darkness of war.[12]

That a fiction writer can find inspiration in real events and would like to create a little extra excitement and intrigue is understandable, but it was unfortunate that his claims implied that named—and at the time still-living—people had committed war crimes. The danger is naturally also present that readers take the content of so-called historical novels as fact and fail to distinguish between what is historically accurate and what is the author's own writing.

In the 1997 book *Sjongløren*e by freelance journalist Ola Flyum, Berre confronted the Germans, not Myrland. After they had shot and wounded him, they were disarmed and were then executed on Colby's order—but only after they had dug their own graves in sheep's muck in the summer barn. This was according to "witnesses," without further reference being made by the author. Some of the American officers supposedly suggested that the men should urinate on the Germans' graves.[13] Flyum's version is problematic in several ways. It lacks source citations and statements are unverifiable.

A 2001 newspaper report by the Norwegian Kåre Olav Solhjell and German Friedrich Traphagen is perhaps the most trustworthy among those claiming that the Germans were first disarmed and then shot in cold blood because their version includes sources, is rich in detail, and dissects the events step by step. Here too, Berre is the one engaging in dialogue with the Germans. Another element shared by Flyum with Solhjell and Trapphagen's version, although it is not essential to the question of how the Germans were killed, is that they did not believe the house was full of Americans. According to Solhjell and Trapphagen, when one of the Germans pointed an MP-40 sub-machine gun at Berre, he is supposed to have hit the barrel so the shot went off by accident. Traphagen and Solhjell's version excludes the scandalous assertions found in Flyum's account of someone encouraging urination after the burial in a dung pit.

Traphagen and Solhjell's report mainly seems to be built on the interview with Berre. Firstly, it must be remembered that after being hit, Berre was going into shock and cannot be regarded as a reliable eyewitness. On top of that, he had been taken inside the house when the executions supposedly happened. In the 1989 interview, Berre stated that until recently he had believed the Germans were killed in a firefight. The newspaper then added "for a fact" that they were killed later that evening, but without any sources. In other words, the whole claim is built on a circular argument leading back to non-verifiable "facts." Traphagen and Solhjell also make vague reference to testimonies by the Germans who exhumed the bodies after the war, but the bodies were never examined by forensic experts, or even medical personnel in a post mortem, only German service personnel who had just lost a war who later testified their comrades were killed by a gunshot to the neck.[14]

The listings of the German War Graves Commission (*Deutsche Soldatenfriedhöfe*), states that they were killed in combat with Allied paratroopers (*Gefallen im Kampf mit Fallschirmjägeren*).[15]

Looking at the circumstances, there are several other factors that might have spurred these speculations. One recurring feature of the revisionist accounts is the claim that Colby had demanded that the men present at Gjefsjø on May 2 remained silent about what had happened. Firstly, this code of silence was a general instruction to both the OSS as well as the Norwegian Resistance. Everyone involved was under a code of confidentiality about their wartime service and the reports on *Rype* were classified until the mid- and late 1970s. Illegal killings or not, they were simply not allowed to talk about any of their wartime experiences, even though many did put their memories into print or gave interviews long before the moratorium expired. Another motive for demanding silence was they had let their guard down and allowed the German patrol to enter the farm. That did not reflect well either on Colby or on whoever was on duty.

When Langeland published his telegrams, he also left a comment on the incident that proved to be ambiguous:

> It was only a week before the German capitulation, but this was not known at the time. The first rule of guerrilla warfare is never to be burdened down with prisoners. In World War II this worked both ways, since it was common knowledge among guerrilla fighters that Hitler had ordered all American members of OSS caught behind German lines executed.[16]

Langeland refers here to the *kommandobefehl* of the Germans. This has led Jarle Skjei and others to conclude that the Germans were executed. Solhjell and Trapphagen refer to Reidar Kvaal, head of MilOrg in Norway at the end of the war, saying the Allied soldiers did not have the authority to "make use of Hitler's methods." Now, it is doubtful whether a district chief in the MilOrg had full insight into orders to US special forces, but Solhjell and Traphagen maintain that:

> Although the action can objectively be characterized as violations of international rules of warfare, and, moreover, might seem unnecessary at a sufficiently late point in the war, there is little reason to moralize. The American soldiers on Gjefsjø had experience from France. There they lived in danger of their lives from hour to hour. They experienced that their buddies fell victim to snipers. Between themselves, the soldiers said that if they were captured, they could expect no mercy.[17]

This could be a tacit justification of the killings through the principle of reciprocity, which states that if one is expected to be treated according to the rules of land warfare, one must abide by them. If a warring party does not have the capacity to maintain or provide adequate subsistence, prisoners of war should admittedly be released. But given the Germans' *kommandobefehl*, this of course would be suicide for Colby if the Germans were given the opportunity to report on their presence, either after they were escorted to Sweden or when they got back to Snåsa. However, this justification logically also implies guilt in the first place.

Statements from several witnesses could to some extent shed light on the course of events, but when they claim anonymity, using them as sources presents a difficulty due to lack of verifiability. The value of such testimonies decreases with time, and there are examples of inconsistencies between what people have written in their own reports on recent events, and what they remembered 50–60 years afterwards. A journalist or others who consciously or unconsciously have a predetermined "story," may very well contribute to distort the memories of a witness to past events.[18] The disagreement between Helgesen and parts of the Woodlark group may have reflected badly on Colby's image through his close relationship with Helgesen among those affiliated with Woodlark. The later events in Colby's career may have had a retroactive effect because the OSS was the precursor of the CIA, which during the Cold War was the subject of a series of scandals, such as the Bay of Pigs invasion in 1961, the coup in Chile in 1973, and the Iran–Contra scandal in the 1980s. Colby himself was involved in much of it, particularly as chief of station in the South Vietnamese capital of Saigon and as Director of the CIA during the tumultuous Nixon and Ford presidencies. It has also been revealed that he became involved in the buildup of Cold War stay-behind groups together with Helgesen. How history can devolve into a public whispering game also became evident in a 2012 interview with author Ola Flyum in *Dagbladet*, one of Norway's largest national newspapers. Colby's claim that the Americans urged the Norwegians to urinate on the dead Germans on Gjefsjø Farm turned into a claim that the Americans *did* urinate on the bodies.[19] Again, contemporary events suggest a cause for the retroactive perception of history, as the scandals of American soldiers who urinated on dead Taliban warriors in the same month as the interview was published, and the torture and degradation in the prison camps of Abu Ghraib in Iraq and Guantanamo had just recently reached the public.

One or more of the Germans could also just have been wounded and then put out of his misery because there was nothing they could do for him. Regardless of the legalities, the deaths of five enemies only days before the surrender in Langeland's statement could be interpreted as a post-rationalization of the tragedy. And if the Germans at first had pretended to be surrendering, then shot Berre, it seems highly unlikely that professional soldiers would have responded with anything other than lethal force. From a purely legal point of view, it could be argued that the Germans, by shooting Berre after first offering to surrender, were committing an act of perfidy thereby relinquishing their right to POW status too. Alternatively, if the discharge was an accident, the Americans were in no position to know that or to be expected to take it into account while facing a split-second life-or-death decision. Another question is whether they had any reason to omit revealing that the Germans were killed after being disarmed. A similar situation occurred at the *Waxwing* base, without further questions asked. On May 3, Rype reported the event to London. In a report probably written in June 1945, Skabo recommended that an investigation be launched into what really happened at Gjefsjø on May 2,[20] but no such investigation is known in the records of the OSS. And he was probably more concerned about how the Germans could ski straight into the base without being detected, as well as how the incident might affect a peaceful surrender of German forces in the area.

Colby's reports do not mention an active recruitment of resistance fighters, rather he claimed that they arrived on May 4, as they were taking to the hills, implying that they fled from something. Conveniently relieving "the tense feeling of worrying over the arrival of a larger follow-up German patrol, as we then had enough [men] to handle them." However, Helgesen's report reveals that at least the additional resistance fighters originating from Snåsa were actively sought by Colby. The new arrivals could also tell that a force of 30 Germans went out looking for the base after the Lurudal attack, but that they had lost track and given up after being led astray by the initial direction taken immediately after the attack.[21]

A German patrol was also sent out to look for their missing comrades (who were killed on May 2), at the same time as men from Rype were also out on patrol. The Germans wore white armbands to signal that they were not combatants, but it is doubtful whether it would have helped if they had suddenly encountered each other in the dense scrub forest in the lower valleys. However, Norwegian civilians intervened so that the two forces avoided each other.

To prevent any unnecessary confrontations with the Germans that could interfere locally with the surrender, it was decided to move the base temporarily to the Swedish side. The order from London was prompted by the clash with the German patrol. The group decided to relocate to a lodge on the Swedish side of the Gjevsjø Lake, where they stayed until May 7. But in the middle of the spring thaw, moving men and equipment was hard work in mud and snow slush. In addition, they slaughtered a big ox to have provisions for their stay. Trees were felled to bridge the gap in the ice close to shore, and the water on the ice reached half-way up their legs. Not all of them could all fit into the lodge they appropriated, so many had to sleep outside. Added to that, they had to make the trip three times before all their equipment and provisions were moved. The whole operation took nine hours. The transports were down to three to four trains a day, but they carried mostly freight and officers, while most soldiers who passed moved on foot.[22] The troops walking south were Austrian mountain troops, and they looked badly fed and in poor shape. These would have been the remnants of General Rendulic's Lapland Army. The *Volksgrenadiers* in Snåsa seemed to have high morale and good discipline, but obviously did not share their supplies with the troops in transit.[23] At the same time, Soviet POWs were in the area in great numbers, available for making repairs on the railway.

CHAPTER SEVENTEEN

Endgame

Once Rype were back at Gjefsjø Farm on April 26, they were able to wire the SFHQ in London that they had succeeded in blowing up the railway through to Lurudal. After the demolition, Russian POWs were sent to repair the line, but the traffic never again reached its previous level. The Rype group received a lengthy memorandum from the chief of the Norwegian Armed Forces High Command, General Wilhelm von Tangen Hansteen, who thanked Colby for his written reports, and Langeland for his excellent cables. Rype had also learnt that because of the plane crashes, the unit would be supplied via Sweden. The courier had already experienced difficulties in delivering this message due to the spring thaw, which did not bode well for this method of resupply. Colby felt that USAAF failed them.

Hansteen wanted to know if the Norwegians Rype had recruited were in uniform, and it was clear that MilOrg had their own plans for these men. Especially in the Trondheim area, MilOrg had been targeted by several successful raids by the Gestapo, and the Norwegians were concerned that they might lose control over the resistance groups to the British and Americans. At the same time, the Norwegian High Command was critical of Rype's recruitment of local Norwegians, due to fear of German reprisals against them and their families.

Nor was it a surprise that London disliked a large assembly of resistance fighters at Gjefsjø Farm. Helgesen himself had warned in October that it was "impossible to conceal any large assembly of people," in Norway, which in itself was an argument to move the base over the border. Also, he said he lamented the gossip by the local community and the activities of pro-Nazi informers.[1] On April 18, Rype had messaged concern about a suggestion that the Woodlark men and Helgesen were to be separated from them. Then, on April 25, Colby was ordered to release the men belonging to Operation *Woodlark*, because MilOrg had "other plans" for them, without these plans being revealed to Colby.[2] These plans happened to be protection of targets that the Germans might destroy if they employed scorched earth tactics. In addition to *Woodlark*, Operation *New Corsham*, including two former *Woodlark* men, was to be especially dedicated to the protection of the Follafoss Power Station and Folden Dam some 20 kilometers west of Steinkjer.[3] Woodlark was also to provide MilOrg with general support, such as training and organizing of fighters and W/T communications. Colonel Skabo urged that the wishes of MilOrg should not be interfered with. If this also included Helgesen, it was not specified.

Then message number 25 specified that Helgesen would remain, while the rest of the Woodlark men should return to Burvatnet "at once."[4] The names of the six Norwegians sent from Stockholm that Colby was allowed to keep were not disclosed.[5] Colby was promised additional men "as soon as possible" by his superiors.[6] On April 23, when Erichsen visited Colby, he noted that there were 20 Americans and 10 Norwegians at the base, "[a]ll first rate."[7] Discussions between the two centered around the supply situation and further operations. Another issue that arose was the question of payment for the Norwegian "irregulars" who had sought out Rype. Colby made a request for this. Erichsen answered that London had forbidden the recruitment of resistance fighters in the first place. Secondly, Norwegian Resistance fighters did not get paid by MilOrg either so no distinction could be made.[8] It is not hard to imagine that they foresaw the danger of every resistance fighter for miles around seeking to join Rype if payment was involved.

Brewer concluded that by the end of April, the Nordland Railway had lost its strategic importance and served only as a link between German troops in northern and southern Norway. He questioned whether continuation of Rype's original operations would be in line with SHAEF policy, understood by him to be swinging towards a passive organizational period in preparation for the final liberation of Norway. This he saw as an argument to alter Rype's field orders to include recruitment and training of Norwegian personnel for resistance, centered on Lierne but including a sector stretching from the Swedish border to Namsos in the west, and to Steinkjer in the south. However, he would refrain from offensive guerilla action unless specifically authorized by SFHQ. To choose reliable recruits, they would rely on Helgesen and the other Norwegians acting as guides for Rype.[9] They were, however, ordered by London "not to enlist MilOrg personnel, except those in trouble who are willing to join you as uniformed members of your party."[10] Again, this was a "no, but yes" phrasing. How would they know if Norwegians were already enlisted in the MilOrg if they were not frank about it? And "being in trouble" was also a relative term, unless there was an explicit warrant for their arrest—getting into the crosshairs of the Gestapo was certainly not difficult.

Towards the end of the war, there was an increasing turnover amongst the Norwegian helpers. They are named in *Rype*'s rosters, although they might not all have given their real names. Some are just listed by name only, while others are specified as "station complement," that is, they enlisted specifically to help out on the base. On April 30, Harald Larsen, for some unknown reason, is listed as duty to hospital. Vestgöte, Kjell Sørlie, and "Sverre" left for the Woodlark base. That day four Norwegian Resistance fighters joined them, three brothers plus Karle

Berre, who would soon rise to the center of attention (see above). On April 29, the mysterious Gaer left for Woodlark and Agnar Andersen left for Stockholm. After the Woodlark men had left Gjefsjø, Hans Leirmo and Herbert Helgesen traveled down to Snåsa to recruit reinforcements. This was contrary to the operation orders, but the situation was desperate, as it was impossible to secure the base and carry out monitoring and control of nearby areas with only 16 men. This was disheartening, not least since they believed that at least 50 Germans were out looking for them after the Lurudal attack.

In Snåsa, 11 men signed up, among them two former second lieutenants from the prewar Norwegian Army and a doctor. One of the volunteers, Leif Aune, gave an account of their journey to Gjefsjø Farm. They were transported by truck to a location called Bellbumoen around noon, some 10 kilometers as the crow flies, west-by-northwest of Gjefsjø. The vehicles were disabled, and the parts removed were hidden in the forest. Helgesen and Leirmo soon appeared to guide them further into the mountains. Leirmo and Helgesen were the only ones who were armed, and the newcomers were a bit anxious about their chances if they ran into Germans. They started out in the evening and made good use of the terrain, staying down in the valleys with their cover of trees and brush. They skied eastward until they reached the western slopes of Plukkutjønnfjellet and arrived back at Gjefsjø about 22:00 hours on May 3. There, they were issued weapons and given rudimentary instruction in their use. Then followed food, real coffee, and rest in brand-new sleeping bags. Next morning, more equipment was issued—white caps, anoraks, backpacks, and more.

By the beginning of May, Colby considered the mission fulfilled. It might be added that Bolland, in his report dated October 1945, stated that Operation *Rype* was "planned with flexibility to accommodate changes in mission from one of sabotage to others like: arming, organizing and training the Underground in Northern Trøndelag, running an avenue of escape to Sweden of Norwegian nationals in trouble with the Germans … These of course within the limitations imposed by SHAEF and the charters of operation for the OSS."[11] This does sound very much like an embedded contingency plan, perhaps influenced by the initial mission given to Woodlark about training and arming resistance fighters and furthered by Helgesen, who is believed to have been present at least in the later stages of the planning of *Rype*.

In total, there seem to have been 22 volunteers from the surrounding communities stationed at Gjefsjø. Security had been beefed up after the German patrol incident. According to Leif Aune, there were three guard posts, two to the west of the farm and one north of the lake. They pulled two-hour shifts, added to an unknown time to get to and from the posts. The weather was mostly still and the sky clear, so sounds could be heard across long distances. While standing guard, one man reported having heard woodchopping around Livsjøen to the north. A patrol consisting of Farnsworth, two other Americans, and two Norwegians went to investigate. The tension was high among the newcomers, who expected to be shot any second. It was also a strenuous trip, as they had to cross three open creeks. One of the Americans fell, and his skis were taken by the current, so he had to borrow a ski—thus there were two men with only one ski each. They went east and south of the lake, then headed back to Gjefsjø without seeing either people or tracks. However, they came upon three reindeer digging up moss with their hooves, which probably explained the sound heard by the guard—all the effort and alarm had been for nothing.

On May 5, Windh and Vestgöte returned, and 14 other Norwegians arrived. While previously volunteers had come from the Snåsa area, the 14 new men arrived from Verdal. On May 1, the Gestapo had made several raids in Verdal, south of Snåsa, aided by Rinnan and his infamous gang. Eleven MilOrg members escaped and sought out Rype and wanted to join them rather than cross the border. At the same time, they relayed a warning about a Norwegian policeman who had assisted the Gestapo in the "whipping" (torture?) of the Norwegians. This group also expected a weapons transport, and it became paramount to stop it, as there was no longer anyone to receive it except Nazi provocateurs posing as resistance members. That Rype was being sought out by people from that far away should have been considered a security breach, but they did not seem to dwell on that. The chances of somebody being caught and revealing their presence under torture must have been considerable. The refugees had the idea that it was only a matter of days before the war would be over and they did not want to cross into Sweden. Colby was more than willing to let them stay. The new "recruits" were armed and given basic training so that they could be put on security duty around Gjefsjø. With their helpers included, the entire group now consisted of 42 men. On May 6, a landmark was reached, as the Norwegians outnumbered the Americans for the first time—three officers and 17 enlisted men versus three officers and 28 enlisted men. The total number of people on Gjefsjø peaked on May 7, with four more men arriving from Snåsa, among them a man named as Joma, while Lian and Sørlie returned from Stockholm. The next roster is dated May 9. By now the war was over, and 11 of the men who had arrived from Verdal had left again. The following day, more people, this time those who arrived from Snåsa on May 4, also left, thus on May 10, the Americans were again in the majority.

As Operation *Rype* was ongoing or just before, the OSS was reckoned to have had 85 special forces and intelligence operatives in Norway. By comparison, only five were deployed to Denmark. During the anticipated occupation by the Allies following the German surrender, 23 would remain in Norway compared to 10 in Denmark.[12] This could of course be explained by the difficult geography of Norway, but also its strategic position and the assets known to be kept there by the Germans, especially in naval intelligence. The purpose of continued intelligence operations in both countries was to establish contact with Danish, Norwegian, or other intelligence agencies in those countries, because:

> There is presumed to be valuable intelligence in these countries at the time of their liberation which might be of assistance to the United States military Forces, Chiefs or United States Diplomatic Missions, and to OSS.[13]

Although it is not possible to establish if Colby and NORSO acted on this, it should not be excluded. At the time, the threat of a German last stand in Norway seemed very real indeed. Their new commander in the country following General Falkenhorst's resignation, *Generalleutnant* Franz Böhme, as well as *Reichskommissar* Terboven, swore to fight to the bitter end even if Berlin surrendered.[14] The awareness of these statements deeply troubled the leadership of *Rype*.[15] According to Norwegian historian, Tore Pryser, the OSS also feared that the communists would attempt a coup d'état at the moment of a German surrender.[16] However, there is nothing in the material related to *Rype* mentioning this possibility. Either Colby was not entrusted with this information, or neither he nor anybody in his chain of command shared that fear.

As the war drew to a close, it meant the sabotage actions were stepped down since more destruction of infrastructure would probably damage the Norwegians more than the Germans. On May 1, Rype received the order to not attack any "major bridges," and that instead they had to be content with "minor attacks."[17] Rype's orders were now to also prevent the Germans from conducting scorched earth tactics, as had been practiced on the Eastern Front and in the county of Finnmark. On May 3, the following message was received in three parts from London, issued by the Norwegian Armed Forces High Command, but also applicable to Rype:

> Instructional orders from F.O. to H.S. [Hjemmestyrkene—Home Forces] [.] In the present situation as the possibility for a general German capitulation exists [,] it is of decisive importance that absolute calm and discipline is preserved ... Action or aggression by H.S. or others against the German troops [,] German or Norwegian police or Norwegian Nazis has at this moment no military purpose [,] but may only cause the greatest difficulties for an orderly German capitulation [.] It is now more imperative than ever before that an unbreakable discipline is preserved and that officers and "Jegere" [resistance members] keep their heads clear ...[18]
>
> Orders according to the above must be issued forthwith to officers and Jegere [.] Furthermore, [it] must be ascertained that all leaders keep continuous contact with superiors as well as subordinates [.] If the Germans capitulate [,] we endorse standing orders that ... [?] ... [parts of the message obviously not received] shall respect the armistice and take up tasks mentioned for this alternative ...[19]
>
> Any break of the armistice on part of the H.S. might cause inestimable damage [.] If Germans contrary to all reason should continue the opposition in Norway after the war is finished in Germany [,] it is important that the organizations are kept intact and ready to fight so as to be able to support from within the liberation of the country in cooperation with arriving Norwegian and Allied forces.[20]

On May 6, they also received orders to take control of, or destroy, a so-called "Schwellenpflug" (railway plough) located at Grong Station. The device was designed to be pulled by a locomotive to tear up railway sleepers. This was in accordance with the OSS's T-Force program, aimed at preventing German destruction of industrial and technological targets in wake of their withdrawal.[21]

At the same time a pattern from SFHQ in London became clear—when Rype suggested making contact with other Allied sabotage groups, recruiting Norwegians to do resistance work, making contact with the Germans to get them to surrender, or for Rype to take control of an area, they got immediate responses ordering them to keep quiet. Colby must have known the risks this entailed in such a precarious situation when it came to advising about German capitulation. But as the war neared its end, it did not mean that the drama was over.

CHAPTER EIGHTEEN

Peace

From what was heard on the radio from London, there was no doubt that the war was now over, but the Rype group knew little about the situation in Norway. The intelligence basis for *Rype* warned that the if opportunity arose, it was highly likely that the Germans could choose to continue the fight in Norway even after Berlin had surrendered. On May 5, the German supreme commander in Norway, *Generalleutnant* Franz Böhme, made a statement that could be interpreted to mean he was determined to make a last stand, and only a direct order from his superiors in Berlin convinced him to order his men to lay down their arms.[1] NORSO had trained together with Greek counterparts. Now in Greece, a bitter civil war was raging between the communists and government forces supported by the British. France too had been balancing on the edge of open conflict as competing resistance organizations jockeyed for supplies and influence.[2] Could something similar happen in Norway? A postwar survey of the reports received by the Scandinavian desk of the special intelligence branch had a separate category for reports on the attitudes of former resistance groups in Denmark, but not in Norway (though the latter had one for the "growth of communism").[3] Colby especially feared that Quislings would try to hold on to power after the Germans had surrendered. The same threat was also considered by the Norwegian underground.[4] On May 5, Colby suggested in a telegram to London that he and Langeland should contact the local German commander to negotiate his surrender. SFHQ reacted immediately and ordered NORSO to keep calm and do nothing rash.[5] Neither contact with Germans nor Norwegians was desirable, and if they made "unauthorized contact with the enemy or MilOrg groups, it would lead to immediate disciplinary action."[6]

When the courier finally arrived on May 6, he did not have anything from London. They also wanted to establish radio contact directly with Stockholm in order to make the supply chain more effective. Items requested in addition to food were combat boots, uniforms, and a regimental medical kit. They also wanted a permit to cross into Sweden to be able to pick up supplies at Överäng, because there were no Norwegians available with the necessary travel permits. London informed Rype on May 7 about where the Germans had been ordered to gather in their AO; there were camps at Grong, Ekker, Snåsa, Verdal, Steinkjer, Rinnleiret, and Levanger. Rype were ordered to avoid all contact with these and make no attempt at disarming them if they stuck to the surrender terms.[7]

All over the country, Germans were required to pull back their guard posts and gather in such places as were picked out by the Allies until the Norwegian or Allied forces could come to collect their weapons. Rype answered, referring to rumors they had heard from Sweden that they would be requested to enforce security in Snåsa or "other remote communities." Colby suggested this was a misuse of uniformed Allied troops that could be better employed "to a more dramatic value," as well as keep an eye on the "peacefulness of the Germans in the Trondheim area."[8] The positive PR effect on the Norwegians of uniformed Allied troops appearing immediately after the German surrender was not lost on Colby. But again, Rype were firmly rejected by London and asked to keep calm.[9]

A cable from the Joint Chief of Staff to General Eisenhower, dated September 13, 1944, gave a brief but consistent direction for their conduct. In case of an enemy surrender, OSS special operations personnel had orders to contact the HQ of the occupational force and furnish communications with local resistance and civilian leaders. Further, they were to assist in the prevention of civil war, assess the status and secure vital infrastructure and prevent the risk of further damage either through wanton destruction or planned scorched earth tactics. In short, to minimize the various risks associated with the termination of German occupation.[10] It is fair to assume that at least Colby had some insight into these instructions and attempted to act upon them.

In the final weeks of the war, all the information they had on how the war progressed they got from regular radio broadcasts. And though they knew the end was near, they were completely in the dark on the developments in Norway and if the Germans or Norwegian Nazis showed signs of making a last stand. Naturally, they mentally prepared for the worst. They also learned of the surrender of German forces in Norway through the BBC. Then they had to move everything back again to Gjefsjø, and their recently added Norwegian helpers were discharged two days later. There were no further orders that could make them useful—besides, the helpers were eager to get home to their families. One of them was given a parachute—he was to get married that summer, and the fabric of the 'chutes made excellent material for wedding dresses. On May 7, Colby messaged London to inform them that they had crossed over and taken residence in the "Kronahyttan" (cabin) to avoid more trouble with German patrols. By May 8, there was no doubt that, according to BBC broadcasts, the war in Europe was over. Rype too were eager to head down to civilization in order to be included in the celebration of the peace, and Colby was worried that Allied forces who came to Norway were going to take all the credit from those who had worked hard and still found themselves out in the wilderness:

> Give precise orders [.] Can we go to valley [Snåsa?] If so, we must contact German commanders for our security [.] Have we any further mission? Please get us out of the hills [.][11]

But London failed to respond. When Rype sent the same message on the emergency frequencies, they still had no answer. Unanswered messages were not uncommon in the OSS world, as was frequently experienced in France; it stemmed from the simple fact that the desk officers were swamped with communications, some of which seemed ridiculous from their point of view, or they were unable to grasp the context from which they originated.[12] Within Rype there was now also a gnawing fear that German patrols could be near and that they had not been notified about the surrender. So the request was repeated on May 9 but this time it was rejected by London who warned of Lieutenant Colonel Bolland's immediate arrival at Gjefsjø. On May 10, however, after London's request, they reported that the supply situation was deteriorating fast. Until recently there had been more than 40 men, feeding off the dwindling stock of food. According to Colby's report, they were by now living off grut (a kind of oatmeal) from the farm. Fifty years later, Langeland was still full of resentment, speculating that "everyone in London headquarters was out celebrating the victory after having left an office girl in charge."[13]

However, Alfred Andersson's son, who was nine years old in 1945, later claimed there had been lots of food left on the farm. Although testimony from someone who was a young boy at the time must be taken with a pinch of salt, it could also be that the food issue was used as a pretext to get the green light to pull out of Gjefsjø and go down into the Snåsa community. A message from Erichsen to Colby, dated May 2, indicated one possible explanation for the delay, the "peace crisis [had] caused great commotion here as regards to manpower," and this could be assumed to have affected several of the service functions supporting Rype, from FANYs to packers of supplies who were busy servicing units elsewhere. However, supplies were also held up on the Swedish side due the spring thaw.

Colby warned that the prospect of Allied troops arriving in Norway achieving all the "praise and glory" instead of those who had "worked and fought for the liberation," took a heavy toll on the unit's morale:

> The whole world celebrates, Norway madly greets arriving occupying Allied troops(,) while the first Allied uniformed troops in in Southern and Central Norway sit in hiding in the hills on reduced rations without orders or even information with which to plan.[14]

On May 11, they got the long-awaited order from Skabo by radio to head down to Steinkjer and report to the local MilOrg commander, Torberg Johansen. From then on, they would be under the command of Norwegian Army's Colonel Hans Reidar Holtermann in Trondheim.

In 1940 Holtermann had led the legendary defense of Hegra Fortress and was one of Norway's most celebrated commanders. He had escaped to the UK, and had commanded the Norwegian Brigade in Scotland before he returned as head of the district command Trøndelag.

Colby and his men left Gjefsjø just after midnight May 11/12, saying goodbye to the isolated mountain farm that had been their home and safe haven for 1½ months. On May 11, as they were about to depart for Snåsa, the group included seven Norwegians. An additional three Norwegians, however, had to be left on the farm to receive Lieutenant Colonel Gerhard Bolland if he, despite their recommendations, chose to come that way. Major Colby and his men skied to Snåsa, leaving behind excess equipment, perhaps also acting on orders to leave surplus weapons to Woodlark. That they chose to leave for such an arduous trip late in the afternoon, is a testimony to how badly they wanted to leave their mountain hideout.

When the Rype party approached the settlements in Snåsa, they had to abandon their skis as the snow was gone, rivers and creeks were swelling, and the bogs were impossible to traverse; it was undoubtedly the worst time of the year to negotiate Norwegian terrain. They were picked up by car by the Norwegians who had just been discharged at Mollan, a small settlement some 10 kilometers north by northwest from Gjefsjø as the crow flies.

Together with sergeants Kai Johansen and Odd Andersen, Colby contacted the local German commander in Snåsa, who was clearly nervous. The rest of the group waited in the distance while Colby tried to establish if it was safe to bring everyone down from Gjefsjø. They feared the local garrison would be uncooperative, but the German commander assured Colby that his men were going be disciplined and remain calm. In Snåsa, they received a short but overwhelming welcome with the mayor at the head of the crowd, among whom the Americans could see several familiar faces—those of the men who had sought them out and offered their assistance in return for a safe haven from German persecution. Several joined them in their "victory tour," so they amounted to 32 men when they arrived in full uniform at Steinkjer on May 12.

Colby chose the two tallest men of the group to enter Steinkjer first, Sergeant Odd Andersen and Corporal Kai Johannesen. They were two guys who normally were easy going and modest, but for this occasion they had to show extra "military bearing." The local marching band played the Royal Norwegian anthem and the *Star-Spangled Banner*, but Colby could not help but remark later that it sounded as if it had been a while ago since they had practiced. The men were tired and the ceremonial part was over after five minutes. After their arrival in Steinkjer, a formal reception dinner and subsequent festivities were held on Hegge Farm, owned by the resistance fighter Thoralf Lian, who was well-known to the Rype group. In Steinkjer, Colby received a telegram ordering him to report to the district commander in Trondheim. Rype also requested that Bolland brought Jeeps with him from Stockholm, but if he did, he made no mention of it himself. Later pictures show some Rype men in Willys Jeeps in Trondheim, but it remains uncertain how they got there. The men also requested coffee, candy, cigarettes, and American flags—all-important ingredients in a successful victory tour.

Meanwhile, on May 8, Bolland's journey to Norway had started with transport to Metfield Air Base in Suffolk for the first leg by air to Stockholm. Upon being reunited with Rype, he would take command of the unit and direct further operations. At Metfield, he awaited Sergeant Jøa and five other NORSO men who were supposed to have been dropped into Norway on March 24/25. Together, they took off on May 10. He arrived safely in Stockholm and arranged with Erichsen to meet Erik Gaundal. Bolland was alarmed to learn that there were about 60 people at Gjefsjø (at that point the Norwegian helpers had actually been discharged, but that was the latest available intel).[15] The concerns about food supplies were suddenly felt to be urgent. Bolland also got word that Colby planned to relocate his unit somewhere close the road network, probably in the direction of Lierne. Given the spring thaw, transporting supplies overland would be a nightmare. However, Erik Gaundal could also provide the additional information that Colby and his men had moved to a location on the Swedish side of the border. Bolland now put things in motion to get supplies dropped to the group. He had Gaundal phone Björkede and get them to summon Lieutenant Saether so he could call back at 10:00 the next day and give the group's exact location.

The next morning, Björkede returned the call. Colby had received the message but had by then received orders from Skabo to relocate to Steinkjer. Also, they had messaged London and warned that due to the spring thaw, it would take Bolland three days to get from the nearest road connection on the Swedish side, and up to Gjefsjø, and then two more days to get to Snåsa. Colby suggested they met in Hell, that is, the small community just south of Stjørdal where the railway from Sweden connects with the Nordland Railway. Bolland decided to meet up with Colby in Steinkjer instead. Rather than taking the arduous route used by the couriers, Bolland opted for the more convenient means of travel, taking the train which crossed the border at Storlien in the south. Still worried about the supply situation, he secured 225 emergency rations to take with him, and a further 700 rations to be sent to Steinkjer as early as possible. The train with Bolland aboard, as well as Jøa and his men, would leave at 22:00 on May 12. This gave Bolland time to go through the communications between Colby and Erichsen, further talks with Gaundal, as well as securing "comfort articles" such as tobacco for Rype. For the first time, and to his surprise, Bolland also learned of Colby's attempts to open direct communications with Waxwing, contrary to the instructions as Bolland understood them. Although circumstances suggest that contact of some sort was made (such as Bangstad's also having voiced the Lierne Plan), Bolland had no reason to believe that Colby had actually violated his orders. Bolland further obtained "operational funds" of 20,000 Norwegian kroner and 2,000 Swedish kroner from the American Legation in Stockholm. The train left on time and was the first civilian train to cross the Norwegian–Swedish border since VE Day. From the border, they traveled west through the village of Meråker and down the Stjørdal Valley were Værnes Airfield is located. Bolland and his men then reached Trondheim before continuing to Steinkjer.

On May 13 Langeland, now field promoted to second lieutenant by Colby, reported back to London that NORSO had relocated to Steinkjer and that the Germans in the area, some 3,000 strong, had behaved in an exemplary fashion. Also arriving at Steinkjer to join them were Harald Larsen, Agnar Andersen, Robert Andersen, Jon Moan, and Leif Granås. The latter was a cover name for Ludvik Kruksve. And only now did the reports reveal the real names of Helgesen, Moan, Agnar, and Robert Andersen. A day later, the base at Gjefsjø was abandoned by those who had been left there. A messenger who was dispatched from Sweden told them that Bolland, following Rype's advice, had already taken another route to Steinkjer. Rype also had orders to leave surplus weapons for Woodlark, possibly for arming Norwegian Resistance fighters who by then they had probably picked up.

When he arrived at Steinkjer on May 13, Bolland got to debrief the Norwegians, before they were discharged. From them, he got another picture than that of austerity presented in the dispatches from the field to London and Stockholm. Food and tobacco had not been scarce, except perhaps for the last few days when numerous resistance fighters from all around the district stumbled into the mountain farm. Kjell Sørli also remembered the abundance of Camel and Lucky Strike cigarettes. This also contrasted with the regular life of people in occupied Norway.

Bolland was informed that three cows were butchered on the farm, and he immediately took steps to make sure that Alfred Andersson was compensated for the loss of the cows as well as any other damage to his property.[16] The men from Woodlark, supposedly discharged, were also still with the NORSO Group and had probably never been separated from them in the first place. When Bolland arrived, the Rype group numbered 38. There were four American officers and 23 enlisted men, the rest were Norwegian helpers from Woodlark and other resistance fighters. They followed the Americans to Trondheim, where the Norwegian District Command officially approved their incorporation into NORSO on May 16. Two more Norwegians had been released to their homes in Steinkjer, and on May 14, Hans Leirmo and another Norwegian departed. It is not hard to guess that the mountain man accustomed to the solitude of the great expanses felt hemmed in amidst the cheering crowds.

Bolland also learned that Colby had left for Trondheim to meet with Holtermann. Colby returned to Steinkjer on the morning of the 15th and informed Bolland that he and the Norwegian commander had arranged for NORSO to take part in the May 17 parade in Trondheim, Norway's national holiday. On their way to Trondheim, the Americans paraded through the towns of Verdal, Levanger, and Stjørdal. The presence of Allied soldiers, no matter how few, also had a calming effect upon both the population and the 3,000–4,000 German troops still in and around Steinkjer, according to Bolland.

The victory parade was a huge success, both according to Bolland's report and from the many pictures taken. People came out in great numbers to greet their liberators. Local dignitaries met with them, and speeches were made before cheering crowds. Thus, they would be the first Allied soldiers many Norwegians in the region would see, and American uniforms and voices would be forever tied to the memory of how freedom tasted for the first time in five years. This must have been a major public relations coup, by far outweighing the purely operational importance of *Rype* upon the outcome of the war itself. The publicity part of the operation must have been in Colby's mind also before the German surrender. In a message, dated May 2, included the passage "why no publicity yet on our attacks [?]."[17] Being the only American sabotage team in Norway, he felt they could at least have expected a note in *Stars and Stripes*.

Fred Johansen also got the chance to be an angel of salvation after the German surrender. At an unknow location near Trondheim, a mother approached them with her little girl who was very sick. He gave her some penicillin, but the fever would not go down. Fred asked the mother what the girl had been given to drink, and she answered orange juice. In its early days, there must have been a notion that penicillin was neutralized by citric acid, so Fred told her to lay off the juice and in two days the girl was up and playing again.[18]

During the May 15 victory tour, Bolland inspected Værnes airport. His statement that he "discovered that the Værnes airport lay just outside the city,"[19] indicates that this inspection was improvised. The Germans still controlled it, and Bolland drove over all the runways to ensure they were in good condition. There were no signs of sabotage and no mines, although some of the aircraft parked around the base were boobytrapped. He also gathered technical data to assess what types of aircraft could land, opening a vital communications link between Trondheim and the outside world. For the Americans, this would be an important opportunity to get the remaining NORSO men flown in with Holtermann's approval. A German document kept by Lieutenant Roger Hall dated May 25 and titled "Empfangsbescheinigung" (recite), solemnly declared the transfer of one passenger car, one medium truck, and a tractor to the Americans—even in defeat, the Germans lived up to their reputation for a fondness for red tape.[20] Pictures from Roger Hall's collection, however, show a lineup of seven German vehicles with a white star on their sides, indicating that Allied troops were their new masters.

Upon arriving in Trondheim, Bolland must have figured out that it would be necessary to handle public relations in an orderly fashion. Lieutenant Saether was appointed publicity officer and ordered to convey the story of the group to newspapers as well as manage any pictures or newsreel footage to be taken of the group. This function was also mentioned in Saether's letter of recommendation for the Silver

Star. But the handling of public relations did not prove to be entirely hassle-free for Bolland. The general mood during the weeks following immediately after Allied victory and liberation was one of unrestrained celebration, and the eve of the national holiday on May 17 was a further excuse to go all in. On the morning of the big day, one NORSO man and one of the native Norwegians took it too far when they engaged in random shooting with a pistol. Luckily, they did not hit anything worse than a car tire and some other property, but it was enough to produce an awkward situation that had to be diffused. An investigation was launched with the help of the Norwegian courts, taking a sworn testimony both from the NORSO men involved and the owners of the damaged property. The Norwegian was discharged and sent home, while the American, a sergeant, was demoted to private. The incident was hushed up and did not do any permanent damage to the group's reputation.

As with the victory tour, Bolland let Colby lead the unit while he was content to take up a position on the review stand together with Colonel Holtermann and other Allied dignitaries present. The parade is one of the most photographed events in the unit's history. However, there was another parade on June 10, during Crown Prince Olav's visit, and the two events are a bit difficult to tell apart in the photographic material. In what could be assumed to be from the May 17 parade, Colby is marching side by side with Helgesen. Other units taking part were the Swedish-trained Norwegian Police Troops, men from the resistance as well as the Royal Navy. Among Rype, the Norwegians are easy to single out in the pictures as they mostly wore berets or field caps, as well as British battle dress while the Americans wore the overseas garrison cap. The exceptions are Helgesen and Vestgöte who both wore US uniforms with the garrison cap.

On May 24, Rype was ordered to hand all radio equipment over to the local MilOrg commander in Trondheim, and sever direct contact with London, leaving command of *Rype* totally in the hands of the Norwegians. Colonel Holtermann was worried about the security situation in the district, given that most of the Germans were still armed and he had precariously few men by which to disarm them. He had tried to acquire more weapons in Sweden but failed. Bolland offered the assistance of the OSS, and approximately 1,000 US carbines, the reminder of the service's stocks in Britain, were flown in. On June 6, four B-24s landed at Værnes, carrying the carbines in 59 containers and the guns were handed over to the district command. NORSO also helped to solve another of Holtermann's problems. The Germans in the Namsos area were acting up, especially those from the *Kriegsmarine*. The local police chief had requested help, and Holtermann dispatched Colby and the others from NORSO I to Namsos to help sort things out. The men of Rype felt they were sent there to get out of the way of the British who demanded more hotel rooms. Historian Sigvart Tøsse, even suggests that the British wanted the Americans out because Norway was their turf and they did not want to share the glory of having liberated Norway.[21] This probably originated with Langeland's account:

> [Rype] committed the unpardonable mistake of occupying one of the best hotels there. This did not sit well with the British occupying forces which later arrived and who had command of the area. An excuse was quickly found to send the unit to some remote village [Namsos] to control the Germans in that area.[22]

Colby and his men left Trondheim by rail on the evening of May 18, while Bolland established an office in the district command HQ. According to Colby's report, there were about 10,000 Germans in the Namsos area[23] whereas the aforementioned Trapphagen listed the German force in Namsos at 3,810 from the *Kriegsmarine*. The total Rype force arriving at Namsos on May 19 was three officers and 23 enlisted Americans plus one Norwegian officer (Helgesen) and 10 enlisted Norwegians. They were also joined by an American cook, an assistant cook, and a handyman. Colby was authorized to accept the surrender of German personnel in the city and they could inspect facilities but did not have the authority to arrest anyone. NORSO noted that the *Kriegsmarine* was more reluctant to accept defeat than the German Army. It amounted to some minor brawls in the streets, and on one occasion five German ships were cruising around the port while the crews shouted "sieg heil." The morning after, Colby called on the German commanding officer and on coming aboard, his message was simple: the war was over. The group in Namsos also became a channel for communication between the Allied Disarmament Commission and the German commander in the area.

One of the missions performed by Rype in the Namsos area was inspecting German coastal defenses along the Namsen Fjord. According to a report dated May 23, the Germans had already removed the firing mechanisms of the canons and stored them elsewhere. Colby and his men visited the battery at Hoddøya, Stattland, the onshore torpedo battery at Ledangholman and Utvorda. The guns were mostly older French models, and there were also some heavy mortars, stationary flamethrowers, light and medium anti-aircraft guns, radar sites, and radio stations. The Norwegian Home Army reported back to the district command in Trondheim that at least one of the sites was mined, but that the minefields were clearly marked. At Ledangholman, the German guards were visibly drunk, and did not attempt to hide it as a new bottle was being opened during the inspection. From there also, shots had recently been fired against passing vessels, reportedly warning shots to make them keep their distance. The shots were most probably with anti-aircraft guns, whose firing mechanisms were removed at the time of the inspections but were stored on site.[24] So even peacetime missions were not entirely risk free for Rype.

After being notified that the airfield at Værnes was in good shape, Skabo had arranged to have NORSO II flown in. Three Liberators carrying him and the remaining NORSO men took off from Harrington Airfield at 09:00 on May 20, 1945, and stopped at Peterhead in Scotland for refueling. The planes flew in formation, the sea was calm, and the weather was excellent. On May 20, only two of the B-24s landed at Værnes. The Germans at the airfield were only given a few minutes notice of their arrival, probably for security reasons in case any die-hard Nazis amongst them would be tempted to commit an act of sabotage as the planes came in. The group was originally to be commanded by Major Olmsted, however, he was still in France, so command was taken over by Lieutenant Roger Hall. With Hall were:

Technical Sergeant Kyllo
Technician Fifth Grade Sunde
Technician Fifth Grade Olaf Hall
Technician Fifth Grade Syrstad
Technician Fifth Grade Ness
Technician Fifth Grade Bonin
Technician Fifth Grade Hans Flater
Technician Fifth Grade Elmer Kvarsager
Technician Fifth Grade Lars Rottinger
Technician Fifth Grade Lilleby
Technician Fifth Grade J. Anderson
Private First Class Tex Nolan Cooper

The third plane carrying Lieutenant Colonel Skabo and another seven of the men developed engine problems and had to make an emergency landing near Bergen, and Hall was left to deal with a delicate situation by himself. The airfield was still very much under German control, and Colby and his men were already in Namsos. According to Hall's memoirs, first published in 1957, one of the planes "upheld tradition by landing in Sweden," but with no assessment of how much delay it caused.[25] But at least for the first hours in Norway, Hall had only six men under his command, and if the Germans made trouble, he could also call upon the crew of the aircraft. At Værnes, they were met by about a dozen Norwegian Resistance fighters, one of whom spoke fluent German as well as English. However, the Norwegians warned Hall that at least seven German battalions were present at Værnes. Their officers were ordered to report to Hall for their formal surrender. One *Oberst* Stiefel of the SS refused to surrender to an officer below him in rank, but complied under the threat of having his quarters burned down with phosphorous grenades.

Skabo's plane, now stuck in Bergen, had its outboard motor quit on them first, but the pilot decided to take his chances and continue to Værnes. Over Sognefjorden, the inboard engine on the port side lost oil pressure, and the pilot realized they had no chance of reaching Værnes and asked Skabo if he knew of an airfield where they could land, and he said he knew about the airfield at Herdla outside Bergen but had no idea of the length of the runway. The other aircraft in their formation were instructed to continue while Skabo's flight turned about and headed for Bergen. The runway at Herdla turned out to be about 1,000 meters, while a full 1,800 meters was required to be within the safety margins for a B-24 that was fully loaded upon take-off. But the pilot, Lieutenant Pittman made an excellent landing according to Skabo, only damaging the right wheel and the tail skid. However, the two port engines were unserviceable.[26]

There were no Allied personnel yet at Herdla, but the Germans still in place at the airfield proved helpful and put every facility at the disposal of the Americans. They tried to contact Værnes, to inform Bolland and Hall of their status, but could not get through. Skabo did manage to get through to Lieutenant Colonel Robert Chew, representative of the Allied Armistice Commission in Bergen. Chew promised to send a boat to pick them up and take them to Bergen. They spoke at about 16:45, but when by 20:00 no ship had yet arrived, they commandeered a speedboat at Herdla and together with the pilot of the B-24, Skabo set course for Bergen. Approximately 5 miles from Bergen, they met a British minesweeper on its way to Herdla to pick them up. Skabo decided to transfer to the British vessel which took him to Bergen, where he was met by Squadron Leader Saunders of the RAF. Skabo managed to relay a message to the UK through a British destroyer, and then met with Captain Brinsley D. Nicholson, the senior Allied naval officer in Bergen, at the Hotel Terminus. He stated that he did not want any Allied personnel at Herdla for the time being, instead, the crew and NORSO men at the airfield were picked up and taken to Bergen together with equipment and supplies. On May 21, the planes that had reached Værnes departed. One flew directly to England with a sample of German aviation fuel while the other headed for Bergen in an attempt to pick up Skabo and the rest of the men, who were:

Staff Sergeant John Halvorsen
Technician Fifth Grade Erling Olsen
Technician Fourth Grade Einar Christiansen
Corporal Arne Hoff
Corporal Karl Larson
Corporal Salvesen
Technician Fifth Grade T. Johansen

However, realizing how short the runway was, they could not take off again for Værnes with the plane loaded with supplies, equipment, as well as Skabo and the seven men, so the aircraft stranded in Bergen was stripped of navigational instruments and this, plus all loose equipment, was loaded onto one of the Liberators. The flight engineer of the stranded aircraft followed on the second to give a report, and the two aircraft returned to Harrington.[27] Skabo and his men then returned to Bergen with their supplies. Arriving at 18:00, they met with Nichols again who placed a minesweeper at their disposal so they could finally depart for Trondheim. Their departure, however, was delayed by minesweeping of the SS *Bergensfjord* and they could not sail until May 23. The pilot and the crew of the abandoned B-24 at Herdla left for Stavanger and proceeded from there to the UK. The minesweeper left Bergen at 08:00 and arrived in Trondheim the next day at 18:30. Skabo finally met with Lieutenant Saether who had returned to Trondheim, staying at the Britannia Hotel, and learned that the rest of the men were at Værnes as there was no available accommodation in Trondheim. Therefore, they loaded the equipment onto trucks and drove back to Værnes.

At 10:00 on May 25, Skabo was back in Trondheim and met with Bolland, who was staying at the Müller Hotel. After an update on the operations thus far, Skabo realized that continuing the NORSO presence in Namsos was pointless. He wanted to gather the men at Værnes to reorganize. At 14:00, they met with Colonel Holtermann and explained the situation. They agreed that Skabo would proceed to Namsos to investigate the situation. Together with now Captain Saether, Lieutenant Hall (the latter promoted to captain the next day), and an unnamed driver, Skabo left for Namsos that evening. They arrived at 04:00 on May 26, and after just a short rest, Skabo met with Colby. On the agenda was the entire operation.

Skabo found the men in Namsos in good condition and high spirits, but they were obviously bored and frustrated by the limitations on their efforts. They had strict orders not to contact any German camps in the area, which by now seemed well behaved, and the main worry of the local police was that the huge number of former Soviet POWs would act up. The Resistance and Allied groups such as Rype were also instructed to tell former POWs to return to their camp if they were encountered outside them, as this was the only way to keep them fed and safe. Before Skabo could release Colby and his men, he arranged a meeting with the German and the Russian commanders and did some investigations. When he felt quite confident that there was no risk for a fallout between the Soviets and the Germans, he could recommend to Holtermann that there was no reason for NORSO to remain in Namsos.[28] On May 26 or 27, Skabo, Sæther, Helgesen, and Stiansen left Namsos and returned to Trondheim. Skabo's car experienced several breakdowns and did not arrive at Værnes until 17:00. On the morning of May 28, Skabo met with Holtermann and Bolland to discuss the further operations for Rype. Holtermann wanted the Americans to take part in the disarmament of the German troops, pull guard duty in Trondheim, and be a reserve in case of trouble in the district. At this point it was becoming evident that the Americans did not want to prolong their stay and be swept up in the general Allied occupational force. Bolland refrained from letting NORSO take part in disarmament but agreed to the rest and to be placed under the command of Lieutenant Colonel Gjedde, Holtermann's executive officer. He conferred with Holtermann who agreed that NORSO would return to Trondheim, be reunited with NORSO II at Værnes, and placed into Group II, the Norwegian unit of the district command garrisoning the area around Trondheim. Colby and his men left Namsos by boat on May 29 and arrived in Trondheim at

23:00 on June 1. They proceeded to Værnes by truck, and Colby was given orders to reorganize the group into a single unit of three sections. Meanwhile, Skabo himself continued to Oslo together with Captain Saether.

The NORSO Group was also instructed to act as the reserve for the district command. However, Bolland did not intend to get his men entangled in a prolonged mission of guard duty and disarmament of German troops and was eager to have them released and returned to England as soon as possible. NORSO deployed to Trondheim airport, where they provided security in the nearby area. On May 30, Helgesen and Larsen arrived at Værnes. When Helgesen approached Hell Bridge to take over security from the local MilOrg group, he was said to have been well adorned with machine guns and hand grenades. The Norwegian Resistance member who stood there with just a prewar Norwegian Krag bolt-action rifle over his shoulder could not avoid noting drily, "watch out so you don't shoot yourself in the foot."[29] On June 2, the first regular Allied occupation troops of one British battalion arrived. The Norwegian district command was placed under the command of Brigadier Henry Gilbertson Smith, Zone Commander, Trondheim Area, Allied Forces.

NORSO now amounted to eight officers and 54 enlisted men in total. As Allied troops were spread thinly at first, the Germans were required to disarm themselves. The deadline for beginning this process had been set to May 23, and there was much tension in the air. The process proceeded slowly at first with worries that former Soviet POWs would react when their former masters and tormentors were rendered defenseless. Naval personnel proved more reluctant than their army counterparts. About 130,000 Soviets, Poles, and Yugoslav prisoners had been sent to Norway because the domestic workforce proved insufficient for the extensive building schemes of the Germans. If they had decided to seize the opportunity for revenge, there would be little the Norwegians and their allies could do to stop them. There was also a prospect of looting of German military stores, stealing vehicles, weapons, and ammunition, etc., both by the Soviets and the local population. However, to the great relief of the Allies, everyone behaved themselves quite well.

On June 1, two Americans and one Norwegian led by Harald Larsen, returned to Gjefsjø. It is not certain what their mission was, but it is likely that they were to transport the equipment left there when they departed on May 12.

Representation was a substantial part of NORSO's mission after the German surrender, which also included a lot of traveling between Oslo, Trondheim, and Namsos, at least for the officers. On June 9, they lined up at the airstrip outside Hangar Five at Værnes to receive the Norwegian crown prince, who flew in from Oslo on a Lockheed Loadstar. Returning to Trondheim as the prince's bodyguard was Arthur Pevik, a childhood friend of Helgesen and whose brother Johnny had been tortured to death by the Gestapo at Misjonshotellet in 1944. There is a photograph of the crown prince inspecting the unit, consisting both of the original NORSO members as well as the Woodlark fillers, guided by Saether, now wearing his captain's bars.

The next day, Rype would take part in a parade in Trondheim in the crown prince's honor. Meanwhile, Bolland had turned over command of NORSO to Colby and traveled to Oslo to report to the OSS Chief of the Scandinavian Section on the group's activities for the period May 8 through June 6.

Some curious names pop up on the roster. On May 20, "Nordang" is listed as being left in the UK with Olmsted, and "Tallaksen" and "Dymbe" travel to Oslo. The latter two could be the cooks or one of them the handyman sent to Namsos. On May 21, one "Rolf" is with the Værnes group. They also maintain a presence at Værnes with one or more officers, possibly to liaise with the Norwegians for air transport. On May 29, Skabo, Saether, and a Norwegian lieutenant named "Dahl" left for Oslo. Again, Skabo's travels were disrupted by engine trouble, and they had to spend the night at Lillehammer before continuing the next morning. Arriving in Oslo the following afternoon, he sought Major Arne W. Brøgger, Vetlesen's second in command to discuss further operations, without any luck. The SFHQ in Norway was located at Drammensveien 105. The property in the diplomatic neighborhood had been the offices of Nazi Organizations such as Regiment Nordland, Norske Legion, Germanske SS Norge, and SS Storm Oslo. Skabo finally met with Brøgger and Vetlesen on June 3 and 4. He recommended that Bolland be relieved as chief of the NORSO Group, and that Colby would resume command of the field forces. Skabo saw no reason to have two field commanders in Norway, and felt that Colby was entitled to command the men in peacetime since he "had so ably led them in operational period," to which Brøgger and Vetlesen agreed.[30]

On June 10, Colby and Langeland went to Oslo too. The rest of the NORSO Group followed and arrived in the Norwegian capital on June 28. At Skabo's suggestion, a two-week furlough was arranged for those who wished to visit families and relations in Norway. A similar arrangement was made for the men of the 99th Battalion who arrived in Oslo as part of the Allied occupational force. Leif Oistad used the opportunity to visit his parents in Fredrikstad for the first time in five years. The first group departed for the UK on June 18, the remainder on June 28. Farnsworth is listed as departing from Norway to the UK on June 18, and Colby and Bolland on June 19, however, all three were present at a party that MilOrg threw at the Vesteråt Hotel in Trondheim on June 19. The sergeant who was demoted following the May 17 incident was again promoted by Bolland, who had demoted him to private in the first place.[31]

After the war, the OSS presence in Norway was to be reduced to a "small nucleus of experts … who would operate under Embassy sponsorship."[32] On May 12, a group of 14 officers, under the leadership of Major Melvin O. Benson, arrived in Oslo to establish an OSS mission with representatives of all branches except for the SO. This was done under SHAEF authorization and with close cooperation with the head of the FO II (Second Bureau of the Norwegian High Command), Colonel Roscher Lund and his deputy, Major Finn Nagel. In early July, just two months after VE Day, SHAEF dismantled their missions in both Denmark and Norway, presumably because the situation in the country developed in an orderly fashion. The budgets of the OSS were rapidly being scaled down, which led to a drastic cut in its presence, and remaining personnel in Denmark and Norway were transferred to the embassies and the American military mission in Norway. By mid-October 1945, the entire OSS presence was reduced to three personnel attached to the embassy. [33]

After the German surrender, the OSS and the Swedish intelligence bureau, C-byrån, embarked upon a joint operation to secure the cooperation of German intelligence officers who had experience from the Eastern Front. The objective of this enterprise, dubbed Operation *Claw*, was to gain information on the Soviet Red Army, whose doctrines and equipment were mostly unknown to Western intelligence. The operation took place mainly in the southeast of Norway, in the Lillehammer area and without the knowledge of British or even Norwegian counterparts.[34] However, there is no evidence in the available material in the NORSO files that Colby or anybody else in the group was assigned any part in this mission. One possible explanation is that they worked too closely with their Norwegian partners to be able to keep it secret from them or the British, so if any part of Operation *Claw* took place in Trøndelag, it may have been orchestrated by others rather than NORSO. However, Norwegian historian Tore Pryser suggests that Kjell Sørli, acting on behalf of "the Americans," might have staged the mysterious escape of Rinnan in order to extract information from him on local communists. Rinnan was apprehended later and was sentenced to death and executed on February 1, 1947, without revealing anything other than that he was under the vague impression that he was going to be saved at the last minute.[35]

CHAPTER NINETEEN

The Legacy

The OSS was disbanded on October 1, 1945, after having spent around 135 million dollars. According to Alsop and Braden, the money was very well spent.[1] The Research and Analysis Branch was transferred to the State Department. The Secret Intelligence and Counter-Espionage branches were transferred to the Strategic Service Unit (SSU) formed on October 1, 1945, under General John Magruder and answering to the War Department. On January 22, 1946, the SSU was transferred to the Central Intelligence Group, which was supervised by the National Intelligence Authority, a body composed of the Secretary of State, Secretary of War, Secretary of the Navy, and a representative of the president. All these bodies were disbanded with the National Security Act of September 18, 1947, which established the National Security Council and the CIA.

Those who served in central Europe at the time of VE Day were all awarded the Central European Battle Star. As the NORSO personnel were not eligible and there was no prospect of a similar award for Norway, they were signed up for other awards. William Colby and Tom Saether got Silver Stars for their efforts; the rest were awarded Bronze Stars, presented to the men by Major General Donovan himself in a ceremony in Washington, D.C. on September 28. The 2671st Special Reconnaissance Battalion (Provisional), which the OSS OGs were a part of at the end of the war, would also earn a Presidential Unit Citation.

Those NORSO members who were not yet fully fledged American citizens all got their papers in order, except for one. At Gjefsjø, Alfred Anderson and his family returned to their home, but the farmhouse was a mess. Up to 50 men had stepped in and out with dirty boots for two months. They got a small compensation from the US government, but neither asked for nor received anything from the Norwegian government. On April 6, 1948, the US military attaché in Norway, Kai Rasmussen, decorated Kjell Sørli, Jørgen Havig, Hans Leirmo, and Robert Andersen in Oslo. After the war, and for as long as members of Rype remained alive, strong ties remained on both sides of the Atlantic and across it, particularly maintained by numerous reunions and raising of memorials. In 1947, a monument was unveiled at Plukkutjønn, commemorating those who had died in the crash on April 6. The monument consists of a pyramid with a plaque bearing the names of both the NORSO men and the aircrew who died there on April 6, two years before. Both Colby and Donovan were present. The occasion was also covered by the Norwegian Newsreel (Filmavisen). Herbert Helgesen wrote a letter, with the heading "Dear Friends," which he apparently sent to all former Rype members for whom he had an address. In it he had translated a newspaper article on the ceremony from the local newspaper, *Adresseavisen*. The article said he had laid wreaths, but he wanted to point out in the letter that it was on behalf of all surviving members of Operation *Rype*.[2] The field at Walliwall, where the B-24 crashed, was never farmed again out of respect for the fallen. However, in the 1980s Walliwall Farm was torn down to make way for a new road. On the 70th anniversary, a small ceremony was held at the field at Walliwall to commemorate the fallen, attended by the honorary consul to Norway and a representative of the Kirkwall branch of the Royal British Legion. A plaque is also planned to be raised at the site.

The mid-1970s saw a surge in the activity relating to the *Rype* legacy. Many of those who took part were by now middle-aged men with perhaps more time on their hands and the means to travel, and Colby as the natural focus point had been dismissed as CIA director. This all happened to coincide with the 35th anniversary of Operation *Rype*. In the files of the CIA, there is a translation of an article published in the Norwegian paper *Aftenposten* covering the October 1975 reunion in Minneapolis. This was arguably the most elaborate gathering, which was also attended by King Olav V of Norway. A total of 47 survivors attended the event, for which the above-mentioned yearbook was produced.[3] Colby also visited Plukkutjønn Mountain in 1977 with the secretary from the US embassy in Oslo, Eugene Klebenov; Norwegian Defense Minister, Rolf Hansen; District Commander, Major General Arne Heimsjø; and other dignitaries. Others from NORSO known to have been present were Helgesen and Nipe, the latter quite fitting since he had been closest to the crash site in 1945. The initiative for Colby's visit in 1977 was taken by King Olav V and the occasion was renewal of the name plaque on the monument, as the original one had been subjected to mountain weather. Although mid-July, the event took place in a freezing cold wind as a local marching band played the *Star-Spangled Banner* and the Norwegian national anthem. The Norwegian Home Guard offered one of the wives of the 16 veterans present military boots and woolen socks—she had walked the 16 kilometers to the summit in stockings and sandals—but she refused. The visit was covered in several Norwegian newspapers, but not everyone was positive. The local paper *Levangeravisa* was highly critical, quoting Colby's CIA legacy in Vietnam.[4] In 1978, it also became known that Colby had been involved in the build-up of Norwegian stay-behind groups during his assignment to CIA's Stockholm station from 1951–1953. This story resurfaced in 1995, when the Norwegian government investigated unauthorized security and intelligence work during the Cold War.[5] Allegedly this work also included Herbert Helgesen.

For the 70th anniversary in 1995, a monument was raised at Jørstad Bridge, commemorating both Operations *Rype* and *Woodlark*. The unveiling took place on May 8, the official Liberation Day. By then, many of the men had already passed away, and for others it would be the last time they were together. Present were Ludvik Kruksve, Jon Moan, Karle Berre, Kjell Sørli, Harald Larsen, and William Colby. On that occasion, Colby and Sørli also laid flowers on the grave of Hans Leirmo. The German ambassador was invited to the ceremony, something that caused an uproar in the Norwegian press. Former mayor and leader of the committee responsible for the project, Arne Sandness, even received death threats. In the end, Ambassador Helmut Wegner declined the invitation, supposedly after a request from the Norwegian government who even offered to pay for the event if it was postponed to a date other than Liberation Day. In the end, only Germany's Honorary Consul in Trondheim, Erik Solberg, was present to plant the trees of peace, together with County Governor Inger Lise Gjørv, and Harold E. Meinheit from the US embassy in Oslo. According to an anecdote told to the author by Arne Sandness, one of the Norwegian veterans showed up at Værnes Airport hiding a fully loaded Thompson sub-machine gun under his trench coat. When this was discovered by comrades, he said that "we have to protect the chief," meaning Colby. The others promptly commanded him to put the weapon back into the trunk of his car. The publication of Traphagen and Solhjel's book in 2001 also led to an uproar, and the claims that the German patrol were murdered in cold blood spurred a debate in local newspapers with demands of a revision of the text on the memorial, supported by the mayor of Snåsa, Alfred Berget. Neither of the book's authors supported such a revision, and the texts remained unchanged.[6]

Among the other less controversial aspects of *Rype*'s legacy was the reuse of parachutes. As often happened with the silk of the parachutes in World War II, those dropped by mistake into Sweden on March 25 also went into making clothes. In 1999, Ron (formerly Sivert) Windh and Leif Oistad visited Lien, the small Swedish community they had visited 54 years previously because of their mishap. The occasion was the unveiling of a monument to the event, erected by the initiative of the Swedish military officer and freelance military historian Lars Gyllenhaal. Present were head of the local community council in Krokom, Rolf Lilja, commanders of the local Home Guard, Arthur Egervärn and Lars Eliason, and chairman of the local history association, Per Fredrik Eriksson.

When the Norwegian Home Guard established their task forces in 2005, the unit of the Home Guard District 12 chose Rype as its name in a homage to Colby and his crew. The 2015 joint exercise between the Home Guard District 12 and the Minnesota National Guard (NOREX 2015) retraced some of Rype's ski tracks. In addition, a memorial service was held at the Jørstad monument. During the NATO

Exercise Cold Response 2016, commanding officer of Task Force Rype, Major Gard Ommedal, happened upon a young Marine lieutenant who was examining some posters on Operation *Rype* hanging in the halls of the task force HQ at Værnes. Upon addressing the lieutenant, he learned that his name was Arthur Colby, who was none other than William Colby's grandson and happened to be in Norway on the exercise with the 2nd Marine Expeditionary Brigade. The field exercise was winding down, and as a courtesy, the Home Guard took Lieutenant Colby on a skidoo tour in the mountains so he could visit the places where his grandfather spent the final months of the war.

One of the more physical and lasting manifestations of the *Rype* legacy is the restoration of the main building at Gjefsjø Farm in which the NORSO Group were billeted during most of their stay in the Snåsa Mountains. The restoration has been performed by the OSS Gjefsjø Foundation, and the future goal is to establish an adventure center focused on the *Rype* legacy.

Conclusion

> This operation was characterized by most severe climatic and physical obstacles which were overcome by the spirit and determination of the men comprising the unit. The results of this operation consisted in slowing down the German evacuation from Norway, as its military result, and through the chance that these were the only Allied uniformed troops operating in Norway prior to the capitulation, a political result of considerable favorable reaction viz-a-viz the United States upon the people of Norway. This last result was brought about to some extent by the extensive publicity in Norwegian papers given the unit before its departure from Norway.[1]

Operation *Rype* serves as an example to modify the impression that Scandinavia was a purely British theater of operations when it came to special operations. It shows that under special circumstances, such as the pressure from of the Battle of the Bulge and the prospect of fresh German troops from Norway reaching the western ETO, Americans were allowed in. In addition, the war was wearing down Britain's own resources and US contribution must have seemed like a necessary evil. But when the strategic necessity of cooperation on Britain's part resided with the breakdown of the Ardennes Offensive, the support for *Rype* from London grew lukewarm at best. It also shows that while the British could accept American sabotage teams operating on their turf, fraternization with "their" resistance would not be tolerated, probably because they realized that it could increase American prestige and influence in postwar Scandinavia. However, from reference literature, as well as primary sources, it is well known that the interservice rivalry transcended the British–American divide—and the OSS experienced far more serious obstructions from Department of State, the FBI, and army and navy intelligence, than from its British counterpart, the SOE.

Also, it does not seem that Colby's superiors had any problems discussing the Lierne Plan with him, as could be interpreted from Skabo's undated report, probably written sometime in early June 1945. "Certain mistakes" were pointed out to Colby, the Lierne Plan obviously among them, but not so much the plan itself, but that he kept bringing it up. Colby defended his position by expressing that it had been his impression that the signals from *Rype* were received by the Scandinavian Section of the OSS, SO Branch directly, while it was in fact relayed through the joint SFHQ desk. In other words, in plain view of British eyes and ears. Another point is that

Erichsen on his part supported the plan, his input coming from written reports carried across the border with couriers and talking to Colby face to face. Another reason for not seizing and holding territory was the ghosts of Vercors, SHAEF feared that any action seizing and holding territory would inspire the Norwegian Resistance to rise up in an open fight, which the Germans would be most certain to crush with a heavy hand. It could also be feared that large-scale recruitment of resistance members into Rype might also cause things to get out of hand.

Stanley P. Lovell, Director of Research and Development, recalled how the SOE (or "Subversive" Operations Executive as he dubbed them) viewed their American allies as "second class Colonials with provincial, second-class abilities."[2] But *Rype* showed the dynamics of the relationship between the British and American components of Allied World War II special operations. On September 11, 1945, Major General Gubbins wrote a commendation of Major Arne W. Brøgger for a Certificate of Commendation. Brøgger had been Vetlesen's assistant before being assigned to the SFHQ in April 1944. Gubbins lauded his work on the establishment of the OSS bases along the border between Norway and Sweden (the *Sepals* bases), and "due to his visit to Stockholm in March 1945, better cooperation was secured from the OSS Mission [*Westfield*] out there and more satisfactory distribution of stores from the UK was arranged."[3] This suggests that cooperation or obstruction also was a matter of personal chemistry between representatives of British and American special operations officers.

Accidents and weather also led to delays, failed insertions and drops, and finally an end to all flights. Colby and NORSO could argue with a certain justification that the relative failure of their mission was due to procrastination from the British, as well as delay by other circumstances such as weather and technical problems. From the autumn of 1943, the Allied special forces coordination increased with the creation of a joint headquarters. But there was little doubt that the British still perceived Norway as their AO. Balchen, who was much involved in the shuttle flight in Scandinavia, expressed the same thing. But the resentment lay neither with Churchill, Wilson, the operators on the ground, nor instructors at the military schools, but rather in the staffs who ran the logistics and communications. It was perhaps not so strange considering all the resources and prestige the British had invested in the resistance movement and special operations in Norway and in mid-Norway in particular. It must have seemed as if the Americans came in at the last moment to steal the laurels of victory. The relationship between Rype and British forces in Trøndelag after the liberation was certainly not the best.

The reluctance of the British to allow the Americans to get too acquainted with the Norwegian Resistance could of course be one of operational security; the more contact between underground groups, the larger the risk of them being compromised. This would be exaggerated by the danger of somebody being captured by the Germans from one group, and them spilling the beans about the location of bases and the numbers of other groups. However, one cannot help but see the potential of a British long-term political concern beyond the more immediate wartime spheres of operations, that with fraternization between the Americans and the Norwegians, the prestige and influence of the United States would grow in postwar Scandinavia at the cost of the British. What was the Norwegian take on this rivalry? In the first place one might think that American influence would give the exiled Norwegian government "more legs to stand on" as a counterweight to the British dominance, but it does not seem to have been a major consideration. After all, America could offer more resources and still held some kind of magical aura as the focus of many people's dreams of a better future with marvelous tales of great achievements. If they even grasped it, they did not seize the opportunity to capitalize on it and play one ally up against the other for their own gain. Rather, their loyalty to the British seemed to be unquestionable. In general, the image of America as the land of the free was an important asset. Many other nations, such as the French or those of many Asian countries, embraced the Americans as new blood in contrast to the British, with whom they had long-standing grievances as rivals or targets of colonial aspirations. But not so the Norwegians. Even in the postwar world, Norway would remain loyal to the British rather than the Americans when their views differed.[4] Colby never commented in public on the strained relationship with the British, who in turn explained that they would not let "American amateurs upset their difficult relations with the Norwegian Resistance." It has also been suggested that there was some "bad attitude" towards American airmen with the Norwegians after the bombing of the Hydro plant at Rjukan on November 6, 1943, which cost the lives of 20 Norwegian civilians and did not accomplish much.[5] The Norwegian armed forces' high command also began to be less enthusiastic about the railway sabotage as peace grew nearer, and from the beginning of April, signaled that further damage to the civilian infrastructure could hardly be justified by claiming that it brought the end of the war any closer. The Norwegians may also have thought that the more Germans who left by their own devices, the slimmer the chance that the Nazis would make a last stand in Norway and there would be fewer to process as POWs after their capitulation.[6]

One obvious question for posterity is whether the effect of Rype's attacks on the German troop transports justified the sacrifices made. According to the official war report of the OSS, completed in 1949, the two attacks by Rype reduced the transport of the German troops from one battalion a day to two battalions a month.[7] SHAEF came to a similar conclusion in July 1945, that the attacks against the railway in Norway had reduced the German troop transports out of the country from four to one division per month. How they arrived at these numbers remains unclear. A mere decrease in traffic does not reveal anything about the causes of that development. Given the delays in the assessments of both the NSB and German intelligence, it is more realistic to suggest that this reduction was the total result of all the sabotage missions performed against the railway along the whole stretch between Mosjøen and Trondheim by four different groups (Coton, Waxwing, Woodlark, and Rype).

However, given the many factors contributing to the German transport problems, it is difficult to ascertain their effect, let alone that of one single mission. Whether or not the Allied actions against Nordland Railway helped to slow down the withdrawal of German troops is a matter of debate. There were many other bottlenecks, such as the volume of rolling stock, coal supplies, and not least the ship capacity to transport troops and materiel further over the Skagerrak separating Norway and Denmark. The latter was especially crucial after the Swedes shut down the German transports through their territory in November 1943. And Rype's contributions probably came too late to be significant. Yet this all rested on decisions way above Colby and his men and should not detract from the struggles they overcame to achieve their task, even if unbeknownst to them it might already have been redundant. Langeland expressed in his comments that the "potential effectiveness of this unit was never tested," a testimony that the group itself came to question the success of their mission.[8]

In the end, it can also be questioned why *Rype* was set in motion at all, or not stopped at an earlier stage when the first attempts at drops failed in February, or when they only managed to insert half the force and resupply proved immensely difficult. It might be argued that SHAEF and SFHQ must have figured out by then that the war would end soon. However, this reasoning that might seem obvious in hindsight was not so obvious at the time, and for good reason. After the initial optimism during the liberation of France had been quashed by the German offensive in the Ardennes, and the stubborn resistance in Germany, it is understandable that nobody dared to get their hopes up. In the worst case, the situation could have been volatile well into summer when the roads inland in the mountains dried up. From Colby's position, and that of his superiors, a multitude of scenarios had to be considered, such as the war dragging on for several weeks, continued German resistance in Norway after Berlin had surrendered, and that the Norwegian Nazis, with nothing to lose, would seize power. A subordinate political goal for *Rype* was to show solidarity with a small, occupied nation, and it would look bad for posterity if they left the impression that they just sat out the war in the mountains. They may also have hoped that sabotage would have a psychological effect upon the Germans, reducing their will to make a last stand in Norway.[9]

When *Rype* first was scheduled, and 100 highly trained specialist soldiers earmarked for the winter war in Norway were at the ready, one may also assume that the operation was carried through by the force of its own momentum, even if the initial delays arguably left Operation *Rype* redundant—you do not sharpen a knife to simply leave it to rust in a drawer. When *Rype* finally reached Norway, the bar for cancelling was raised even higher. By comparison, an SOE account of operations in Norway stated that:

> Discussions had been going on for some time in regard to the deployment of SAS troops and the OSS Operational Groups, both of which had completed their operations on the Continent. Here again was a case simply of an attempt to find a use in Norway for men who could not be employed elsewhere.[10]

An impression of success could also be produced by the right choice of words. Bolland in his report wrote rather cunningly that "Major Colby was ordered to begin attacking the Nordland Railway which he did during the entire month of April. These attacks included the destruction of the Tangen Bridge and 3 km [*sic*] of rail between Lurudal and Agle Stations." "The entire month of April," might make a reader believe that there were more than these two attacks. He also claimed that together with Woodlark, they "managed to keep the railroad in a state of continual confusion by a staggering and coordination of their attacks through SFHQ in London."[11] These possible exaggerations must also be seen in the context of considering the OSS's struggle for its life and legacy in face of its post war shutdown.

Towards the end of the war, the OSS became more eager to secure a US presence in Norway when the hostilities were terminated:

> To increase the American quota and to confirm the impression among Norwegians of Anglo-American cooperation, the Scandinavian section through the Planning Section addressed a letter to commander-in-chief Force 134, requesting that sections of the SF Detachments be made tri-partite, i.e., American–British–Norwegian.[12]

Operation *Rype* also emphasized specific challenges for special operations in Scandinavia. Snåsa was on the limits of the range of a fully loaded B-24, leaving little margin for error. But operating this far north offered further obstacles in the form of difficult atmospheric conditions. With inexperienced crews and worn-out machines, it seemed like a lost cause to get Rype inserted on schedule and keep them resupplied and reinforced without accidents. No wonder the OSS had Balchen's name on the list—if anyone could have pulled it off, it would have had to be him.

Another issue raised especially by the mis-drop of Leif Oistad's group, was the inherent danger of the diverging interests of NORSO operatives and the aircrew. Everybody's primary concern was, of course, to make the insertion as timely and as on location as possible—but when this failed, there was an inherent conflict of interest. The range of the aircraft with fuel capacity stretched to the limit meant the more the aircrew tried to correct navigational errors, the less were the chances for their own safe return to friendly territory. At some point, it would not be possible to carry both the operatives and equipment back again. Equipment could be dropped, the whole aircraft stripped, but what about the operatives? Whether or not the aircrew dropped Oistad and his men in a cynical move to ensure their own safe return is impossible to judge in hindsight. However, it does raise some ethical dilemmas and questions that would better have been answered before take-off. It would have been a fair deal to drop the operatives close to the border when there was an acute danger of neither being able to execute the infiltration successfully according to plan nor return to British soil. The alternative was after all to risk everybody having to bail out or crash land closer to the coastline with fewer chances for everyone for a safe exit from enemy territory. However, without any agreement or standing orders for this option, Oistad's anger at, as he saw it, being blindsided by the aircrew, is highly understandable.

The Lierne Plan is one of the more curious aspects of the Rype mission, and there is reason to ask whether the young Major Colby realized the sheer scale of his proposal. Its implementation would require major shifts in Allied strategy and policies at the top level, involving government-level agreements between Sweden and SHAEF. Even the *Sepals* bases had required lengthy talks between the Norwegian exiled government and their Swedish counterparts. Once in place, the proposed plan would require setting a large number of men in motion to resupply the enclave, not forgetting risking the lives of Norwegian civilians as well as volunteers in an operation of no comparative strategic significance. But rather than being seen as a testimony of a grandiose mindset in Colby, the idea is rather a testament to the creativity and ability of the OSS to think outside the box that often limits the ingenuity of more traditional military officers. It must be noted, however, that Colby made no move to execute the plan without approval from his superiors as other OSS mavericks might have done.

Biographies

Corporal Sverre Aanonsen

Corporal Sverre Aanonsen was born in Fevik, a village in southern Norway, in 1911. He took part in *Percy Red*, one of the *Jedburgh* operations, jumping into France near the village of Haute Vienne on the night of July 21/August 1. When he was called up, he lived with his brother, Olaf Aanonsen in New York. Sverre Aanonsen's personnel files are missing and no awards can be confirmed.

Technician Third Grade Odd Anderson

Odd Anderson was born in Norway in 1922. He emigrated with his parents to the USA and settled in Chicago. Anderson is one of the few members of Rype who had a college education, albeit only for one year; he was a student at the time of enlistment in October 1942. In August 1943, he joined the OSS. He had a background in the Signal Corps, was noted as a radio operator, and in his personnel files, he is listed as a Technician Third Grade and a squad leader, although he seems to have risen to Staff Sergeant in August 1945. During training in Scotland, he twisted his knee.

His citation for the Bronze Star mentioned:

> his willingness, courage and high ability, he met all circumstances with a high degree of skill and ingenuity. Technician Third Grade Anderson's outstanding conduct and resolute endurance in extreme circumstances reflects great credit upon himself and the armed forces of the United States.[1]

It is also especially commented on in his service records that his achievements were made despite his limited ability to ski, and his unfamiliarity with near-Arctic conditions. He was also mentioned as helping the unit's demolition officer (Farnsworth) in calculating and preparing the demolition charges,[2] and also remaining conscious of his responsibility as one of the first representatives of the United States in Norway.

On his evaluation card, he is listed as "superior" in all categories, and it says he "is a good radio operator, young, intelligent, and has been recommended strongly for Officer Candidate School." He did not want to continue in the Army upon returning to the US but must have changed his mind during his furlough in late August. The reluctance might have been due to:

> [t]he death of this sergeant's only brother at Bastogne caused the collapse of the mother. She is now partially recovered, but her health is dependent to some extent on the presence of the subject soldier. Although he has a perfectly sincere desire to go overseas, and might even welcome the order to go, he feels obligated to seek an assignment in the States for a few weeks or months. He is a strong, well-motivated, unassuming individual with loyalty to his C.O. [commanding officer] and to the organization. He is highly recommended for Far East duty with the necessary reservations noted above.[3]

Anderson continued to serve with the War Department, in the Strategic Services Unit, one of the fragments left from the breakup of the OSS, until March 1946. His service records do however contain some peculiar entries. Anderson is noted for a battle credit for the Rhineland Campaign, which took place February 8–March 27, 1945, when he was preparing for and beginning Operation *Rype,* and for an OSS mission to France on August 7, 1945. What the operation in France consisted of, is not mentioned in his records. The first, and probably also the latter, must be due to a mix up of identities.

After the war Odd Anderson moved to Illinois, graduated from Northwestern University, and had a career at General Dynamics. According to the 1975 yearbook, skiing and mountain climbing were not among his hobbies.

Corporal Knut Andreasen

Knut Andreasen was born on April 8, 1915 in Nøtterø, Vestfold County in Norway. Like so many NORSO men, Andreasen was originally a sailor. When the Germans invaded Norway on April 9, 1940, he was a 2nd mate on the M/T "*Beau.*" On November 2, 1942, he disembarked the M/T "*Noreg*" (Motor Tanker "*Norway*") in New York. His personal files indicate that he enlisted at Fort Myer, Virginia on July 24, 1943. What he did in the interval is not known. Further, his files indicate that he spent three years at high school, which might refer to his education as a navigator back in Norway. Andreasen is also listed as a trained radio operator, which might have been part of his civilian training, but he was never employed as such by the OSS. No mention of awards was made in the available record.

Lieutenant Colonel Gerhard L. Bolland

Gerhard Bolland was born in 1909, and grew up in Madison, Minnesota. He was a West Point graduate, class of '34, with a BSc in Military Engineering. In 1945 Bolland was married but had no children yet. Bolland had been a student at the infantry school January–September 1942, and then held various positions as battalion commander of parachute infantry and as an executive officer in the 507th Parachute Regiment. On D-Day he jumped out of the lead plane of the 82nd Airborne Division.

Bolland entered service with the OSS on September 17, 1944, and was a staff and operations officer before leaving for Norway on May 10, 1945. He was originally intended as the overall commander of Rype of which Colby's group would be one of two but, as events developed, he would take effective command of Rype only after the war ended. Bolland was discharged from the OSS on October 17, 1945.

In his rating he scored "excellent" in all categories, except "Ability to work with others" were he scored "very satisfactory." In the remarks the interviewing officer wrote, "A sound and capable professional officer, somewhat lacking in force."[4] Bolland was by far one of the most professional officers that NORSO encountered. The rather mediocre ratings could reflect the frustrations he must have felt by the time of the interview after being sidetracked by events and being unable to assume de facto command of Rype in the field. His motivation for continued service with the OSS was also rated "below average," possibly a reflection of the same. His personnel files reveal that he signed up for the OSS for the "Norwegian job" only, which might have reflected on his post-operational interview. One may also suspect a clash of cultures between Bolland's background as a regular army officer and the adventurous OSS. Personal differences with some superior officers is also a possible explanation, but it appears that he had a good relationship with both Vetlesen and Skabo, as well as Colby.

After World War II he served in Korea and Japan before retiring from the Army in 1951. He died in 1999.

Major William Colby

The group (NORSO I) that was sent on Operation *Rype* was led by Major William Colby (1920–1996). He was born on April 4, 1920, in St. Paul, Minnesota. His father was originally a teacher but chose a military career a year after Bill's birth. William Colby never regarded himself as a leader, except for when he was serving in the National Guard, which he joined through the Reserve Officer's Training Program at Princeton University where he studied law. Colby was a fierce anti-fascist, probably influenced by being a student in France during the Spanish Civil War (1936–1939). He failed entry to West Point because of poor vision, but that did not stop him from getting into the parachute school at Fort Benning, Georgia. There he met General Donovan for the first time as the latter was looking for recruits who could speak fluent French, a skill Colby had acquired during his studies in France.

After participating in the *Jedburgh* operations in France, he met the Chief of US HQ Scandinavia, Gerry Miller, who gave him the choice to either go to China or become chief of the NORSO Group that would be inserted in Norway. Colby had lived in China while his father was stationed there, but as it would take time before an operation in China could be mounted, he chose Norway. He was not of Norwegian but Irish-English ancestry, however, he had partially grown up in Minnesota, so he was used to being surrounded by Scandinavians. As an afterthought, Miller asked if he could ski, and Colby could answer "Yes" as he had been an active skier during his college days. Helgesen, one of the Norwegian Resistance fighters attached to Rype, described Colby as well-liked by his subordinates, inspiring because he never granted himself any advantages even when entitled to them by his rank.[5] Everyone who served with him in NORSO viewed Colby as a natural-born leader, and Helgesen for one had felt for himself how difficult it is to lead when leadership is disputed. Colby was calm under fire, leading by example, as well as just and energetic. He never had to force anyone to take chances they were not comfortable with, which created a discipline that worked well in the field. This did not prevent him from thinking through all possible consequences of his actions, especially bearing in mind the risks they would imply for Norwegian civilians and ensuring the Germans were never left with any reason to suspect that the local population had anything to do with the attacks he led. According to Kjell Sørli, the Norwegian courier, Colby was the only one among the Americans who did not smoke.

For his wartime effort, Colby was awarded the Silver Star and the Norwegian St. Olav's Medallion. In his recommendation for an unspecified Norwegian award to Colby, Helgesen emphasized that he did not make any distinction between the NORSO men and the Norwegian Resistance fighters attached to the unit.[6]

In 1950, Colby joined the CIA, where he ended his career as chief (1973–1976). His time in the executive chair was, however, turbulent, marked by the Church Committee and Pike Committee hearings in Congress, initiated because many believed that the agency was out of control. He also received personal criticism for his time as the CIA's station chief in South Vietnam (1959–1971) from those who believed that the United States was behind the murder of President Ngo Dinh Diem. Hearings suggested that the CIA's Phoenix program to infiltrate the Vietnamese Communist guerilla movement degenerated into a liquidation campaign against the Saigon regime's opponents.

Colby maintained his friendship with the men of NORSO and he also corresponded with their resistance helpers in Norway. He took part in the unveiling of the memorial on Plukkutjønnfjellet in 1948, and in the 40-year anniversary of the demolition of the Jørstad Bridge in 1995.

Colby died in 1996, when he probably had a heart attack and fell off his boat and drowned. He was found dead in the water after a sailing trip near his home in Maryland. Coroners concluded that he had had an episode and tumbled into the water where he drowned, however, that has not prevented speculation about murder and suicide.

First Sergeant Einar Eliassen

(The handwriting in his personnel files is difficult to decipher at some points).

Einar Eliassen was born in Stavanger, Norway, in 1917. He had been a US citizen since 1930 after having emigrated with his father Anton (born in Bergen), a barber, and his mother Erikka (born in Trondheim). Eliassen had attended Brooklyn Technical High School for six terms, before joining the US Army in June 1935, and had served with the 33rd Infantry at Fort Clayton in the Panama Canal zone and reached the rank of corporal before being honorably discharged in 1937. Eliassen lived at various addresses in Brooklyn, which was famous at the time for its large colony of Norwegians. Eliassen had been married to a Swedish woman, but they divorced in 1942. He worked at shipyards, including the Brooklyn Navy Yard as a ship fitter until he was recalled into the Army on January 30, 1941, as a technical sergeant.

He served with the 99th Battalion from September 1942 to July 22, 1943, before joining the OSS on July 27. He was promoted to First Sergeant in September 1943 and took part in the *Jedburgh* operations in France from August 15, 1944, to September 12, 1944. Colby recommended him for continued service in the Far East after *Rype*, despite his demotion after the incident on May 17, 1945.

In his personnel papers he was described as 175 cm tall with brown hair and hazel eyes. His build was described as "medium." Eliassen's rating listed him as "superior" in leadership, and "excellent" in all other categories. This might seem to contradict the remark below, describing him as a "regular soldier whose knowledge and adherence to regular army principles has enabled him to fulfil the post of First Sergeant." One might suspect that this ambivalence had something to do with his demotion to private on June 4, 1945.

After being discharged from the OSS in August 1945, Eliassen served at Fort Dix in New Jersey.

Eliassen's citation for the Bronze Star read:

> The Bronze Star is awarded to Private Einar A. Eliassen (then First Sergeant), 6871912, Infantry, United States Army, for meritorious service in connection with military operations while serving with the Office of Strategic Services, European Theater of Operations, from 25 March 1945 to 8 May 1945. Private Eliassen, then First Sergeant, ably and successfully fulfilled his responsibilities in his assignment while on a special mission. By endurance and precise and accurate execution of orders in extreme circumstances, he aided materially in the ultimate successful completion of this mission. Private Eliassen's services during that period reflect great credit upon himself and the armed forces of the United States.[7]

It is also worth noting that Colby later proposed Eliassen for promotion, it is not known if he received it before he was discharged.

First Lieutenant Glenn J. Farnsworth

Glenn Farnsworth was born in Chicago in 1921, to Margaret Farnsworth. His personnel files make no mention of his father. Farnsworth moved with his mother to Baltimore, Maryland, which was listed as his home address upon enlisting on February 3, 1941. Before that, he had been in the National Guard. Prior to military service he had worked at the Montgomery Ward Warehouse and Retail Store in Baltimore as a stock clerk. He had listed four years of high school as education, and boxing as among his athletics skills. Farnsworth served with the 3rd Army as an infantry man and with anti-tank units. He attended Officer Candidate School from July 11 to October 5, 1942. He received his demolitions education at the parachute school and spent a few months at the 541st Parachute Infantry Regiment (some papers say 394th Parachute Infantry), activated at Fort Benning on August 12, 1943. There, he was a platoon leader in the headquarters' company.

On December 24, 1943, Farnsworth was transferred to the OSS. When he volunteered for *Jedburgh* operations, he was deemed unsuitable for fieldwork by the British Student Assessment Board at Cranleigh, Surrey. The tests took place over a four-day period to assess the psychological makeup of the agents. He took the decision hard, but it was somehow overruled, and he served as a demolition instructor for the Norwegian and French OGs. Farnsworth was assigned to the OSS Headquarters in the European Theater of Operations, United States Army (ETOUSA) in July 1944. He was parachuted into France on September 4 and was behind enemy lines until September 23.

In October, he was recruited into NORSO by Colby. Farnsworth, who was hospitalized at that time, was wanted because of his demolition skills and as he had been an instructor on the subject at SCOTCO's Battle School. He did not join up with his unit until January 1945. At the time, NORSO were going into the Grampian Mountains of Scotland for ski training, but Farnsworth had strong doubts about his skiing skills. Despite his shortcomings on skis, Farnsworth also acted as a section leader during the attacks performed by Rype.

After *Rype*, he was promoted to the rank of captain on August 29, 1945, and recommended for service in the Far East as a demolition instructor for local guerillas. He expressed desire for continued service with the OSS but was discharged from the OSS on September 11, 1945. Farnsworth was then stationed at Fort Mead until relieved of active duty on October 11.

Colby recommended Farnsworth for the Silver Star, but he was only awarded the Bronze Star. His recommendation contained the following citation:

> ... the Bronze Star Medal was awarded to First Lieutenant Glenn J. Farnsworth for meritorious service in connection with military operations while serving with the Office of Strategic Services, European Theater of Operations, from 25 March 1945 to 8 May 1945. First Lieutenant Farnsworth with a small group volunteered to parachute into the heart of hostile territory and to harass the enemy from within. This mission was a fight against two opponents: hard-hitting, experienced enemy troops and the ferocious Arctic storms. Battling a vanishing enemy in drifting snows not only causes the body to become extremely tired and fatigued, but also produces a terrible sinking sensation in the mind. Although confronted with these almost unsurmountable obstacles, First Lieutenant Farnsworth performed his dangerous mission successfully and added to the glorious traditions of the Army of the United States.[8]

Farnsworth also scored "superior" on all categories of his rating, as well as the assessment of Traits and Abilities, and received the following remark: "A superior field officer, outstanding in his leadership of his men and his instructional capacity.

An expert in demolitions." His motivation, practical intelligence, emotional stability, social relations, and teaching skills were also rated "superior."[9] Farnsworth was even recommended for higher echelon service, and highly recommended for middle echelon, and as an intelligence officer.

After his service, he moved to Williamsburg, Virginia.

Technician Fifth Grade Gravdal Åsmund

Gravdal was born in Tønsberg, in southern Norway, in 1921. He had emigrated with his father to America. His mother and two brothers remained in Norway. Before enlistment, he lived with his father in Brooklyn, New York, and had been a sailor, working oilers and tugboats. He had seldom held a job for more than a year and listed "dissatisfaction" as the reason for leaving, except for the last position when he left to join the Army.

He enlisted with the 99th Infantry Division in September 1942 and was transferred to the OSS in either August or December 1943. Gravdal was actively sought by the OSS. He was a bit of a troublemaker—while with the 99th he served a sentence of 62 days in confinement for an unknown sentence, and he also went AWOL for two days in October 1944. However, there is nothing in any reports suggesting that he did not excel in the field. He received the ETO Service Ribbon and Bronze Star for action in France and Germany and a Bronze Star for Operation *Rype*. His citation mentioned that "outstanding conduct in extreme circumstances reflects great credit upon himself and the armed forces of the United States."[10]

Technician Fifth Grade Eddie M. Hovland

The personnel files of Eddie M. Hovland are missing, and not much is known about him. He was born in Flekkefjord, southern Norway. As part of *Percy Pink*, one of the *Jedburgh* operations, he jumped into the Dordogne Department in France on the night of August 11/12. No known awards due to the missing personnel files.

Technician Fifth Grade Fred Johansen

Fred Johansen's parents were born in Sweden, but Fred was a US citizen by birth and would become Rype's medic. He grew up in Jamestown, New York. Prior to joining the OSS in October 1943 at the age of 19, Johansen served in an unknown capacity at the Fitzsimons General Hospital and in the 99th Medical Company attached to the 99th Battalion. Before that, he had finished high school and worked as a bank teller and clerk.

In an obituary, Leif Oistad remembered Fred Johansen as very cheerful and multi-talented. He used to play the horn with the 99th when the regular bugler called in sick. During training in Scotland, he helped evacuate one of the men who had broken his leg while skiing down a steep slope. On another occasion, he patched up a man who had accidently set off a pencil fuse.

Johansen was rated "excellent" for stability and physical ability, "satisfactory" for motivation and practical intelligence, with only "satisfactory" on leadership and ability to work with others. This rather mediocre evaluation seems a little at odds with him being able to perform the task of medic in dangerous and stressful situations. Sometime during an operation (probably during the Lurudal attack), Johansen ruptured an eardrum which left his recommendation for service in the Far East in doubt.

His aid to Karle Berre, who was wounded on May 2, and taking part in the following evacuation, was especially mentioned in Johansen's recommendation for the Bronze Star. He was also lauded for his ability to impress the Norwegian peoples favorably with the efficiency of the United States Army. He received the Bronze Star for action in both France and Norway.

After the war, Johansen lived in New York State and served some time with the Coast Artillery Corps before he went into the insurance business.[11]

Sergeant Kai Johansen

The personnel file on Kai Johansen has gone missing, according to NARA. From newspaper articles it is known that he originated from Arendal in south Norway and was originally a sailor. The area in which he grew up lies by the sea on Norway's southernmost tip, and it might be assumed that he might not have been among the most proficient skiers of the group.

A report in *Nordisk Tidende*, dated December 31, 1942, reveals that he was 22 then and serving with the 99th at Fort Snelling, and that he had been living in Bay Ridge (Brooklyn?) for several years. No awards are known.

After the war, Kai Johansen moved to Mississippi and piloted a shore vessel supplying the oil industry.

Technical Sergeant Borge Langeland

Borge Langeland was born in Flekkefjord, Norway, in 1914 to Peder Olsen and Elise Eliassen Olsen. Langeland was a resident of Brooklyn, New York, with "single" listed as his marital status in his personnel file. He had been the telegraphist on board a merchant vessel that had just been sunk by a German U-boat when he arrived at Camp Hale. He went on to become the W/T man for Rype. With his skills with the radio, Langeland was not even asked about his proficiency in skiing.

Borge Langeland was not a US citizen when the war broke out. His next of kin was listed a Clara Pettersen residing at the same address, probably his landlady. Langeland was also one of the original members of NORSO, having been transferred on December 20, 1943. The *Request for Security Investigation* papers states that the OSS sought Langeland on his first contact with the service. Langeland also parachuted into France, where he was shot in the leg and wounded. He was promoted to second lieutenant on June 10. In his assessment of Langeland, Colby noted that he scored "superior" on motivation, practical intelligence, emotional stability, and ability to work with others. The officer who interviewed him upon return to the United States, however, rated him "average" on practical intelligence, but did recommend him for service in the Far East. Langeland recived a Purple Heart after being wounded in France on September 13, 1944 (circumstances remain unknown) and a Bronze Star for service in both France and Norway.[12]

After the war, Langeland was a pilot on a boat in the Panama Zone.

Corporal Halvor Nipe

Halvor Nipe's file is missing from the personnel files. From newspaper articles, it is known that he was from Risør in south Norway. The area in which he grew up, lies by the sea on Norway's southernmost tip, so he probably did not have great proficiency as a skier.

After the war, he lived in Connecticut and was described in the 1975 "yearbook" as a "quiet, clean and cautious type of soldier."[13]

Staff Sergeant Arne Listeid

Arne Listeid's file is also missing from the personnel files. A report in *Nordisk Tidende*, dated February 13, 1947, records that he was from Lista in south Norway, and had been awarded the Norwegian War Cross. The area in which he grew up, lies by the sea on Norway's southernmost tip, so as with the others from an area without snowy slopes his skiing skills probably were not the best.

After the war, Listeid moved to Ohio, where he is said to have worked in a steel service in Cleveland, according to the 1975 yearbook.[14] As late as 1997, he was awarded the Norwegian War Medal. Due to the missing personnel file, any US awards remain unknown.

Colonel Harold P. Larson

Harold P. Larson was of Scandinavian descent. He was a native of Madison, Wisconsin, and graduated from the University of Wisconsin with a Bachelor of Science in Pharmacy and held a Master's degree in Hospital Administration from Baylor Universal in Waco, Texas.

At Fort Benning, Georgia, he took the Rifle and Heavy Weapons Course and the Staff Officer's Course. Larson was also educated as a gas officer at the Chemical

Warfare School at Edgewood Arsenal, Maryland and he attended the Command and Staff's College at Fort Leavenworth, Kansas and the Officers Career Course and the medical Field Service School, Fort Sam Huston.

Larson began his military career as a second lieutenant in 1941 and served both in Europe and in the Far East. In the latter capacity, he led the training of Chinese guerillas for which he was awarded the Bronze Star. Larson was one of the few from NORSO that had a long career in the military. It could be said he was the father of the NORSO, having built up the unit from scratch. When Colby succeeded him in December 1944, Larson was transferred to HQ ETOUSA to assess and evaluate targets for possible operations for the NORSO in Norway. He was assessed by the OSS Personnel Board for further duty in April 1945—the interviewer did not deem him suited to lead an operations group and did not recommend further overseas duty. However, Lt. Col. Alfred T. Cox, commander of the Operations Group China, did not agree on that assessment and insisted Larson joined the group and got his way.

After World War II, in 1947 he joined the Medical Corps and held numerous high-ranking posts both stateside and in Europe. In addition to the Bronze Star, he was given several American and foreign awards.[15] He retired as a colonel.

Technician Third Grade Marinus Myrland

Marinus Myrland's file is another of the missing personnel files. From newspaper articles it is known that he was from Harstad, Norway. It's by the coast, but so far north that he may yet have had good opportunities to have learned to ski well at a very young age. From Colby's "*Skis and Daggers*", we know he was a ship's engineer, and his most notable feat of *Rype,* according to some accounts, was confronting the German patrol. As his personal file is missing, the medals he got cannot be confirmed.

After the war, Myrland moved to San Francisco and worked as a printer.

Technical Sergeant Leif Oistad

Leif Oistad was born in Fredrikstad, Norway, on March 12, 1922, to Hans and Clara Oistad. The port town had about 10,000 inhabitants before the war. He spent his early youth skiing, hiking, and sailing. He attended grammar school for seven years and seaman was given as his occupation when joining the OSS.[16] Oistad went to sea at the age of 15, as so many young Norwegian men of his generation did. At the time of the economic depression, there was not much alternative to unemployment. He sailed on Texaco Oil Company tankers and was an able-bodied seaman in the middle of the Atlantic when the Germans invaded his native Norway. Oistad disembarked in the United States sometime in 1942. He had an uncle living in Long Island and two elder sisters living in Canada. He also had two brothers who were listed as serving but there are no details on what this service was, nor for which country.

Oistad enlisted on September 28, 1942, and went into basic training at Fort Lee, Virginia. He was transferred to the 99th Battalion in July 1943. Oistad was assigned to the OSS on December 29, 1943. In his personnel file, the *Request for Security Investigation* document shows that the OSS actively sought him out.

On September 4, he dropped into France and served with the Jedburghs until September 23. Oistad described himself on forms as 175 cm tall, of medium build, with green eyes and grey hair, surprising for somebody that young. He was rated "superior" on physical ability and "excellent" on all other categories. He was noted as: "Young and hot-blooded but works extremely well and calmly."[17] His evaluation for extended service read: "[t]ough, capable, and intelligent. Gives impression of being an excellent field man. No emotional problems, and excellent motivation. Retention recommended." Oistad was also recommended to be sent to China as an instructor of guerilla tactics and to accompany sabotage groups in the field.[18] Oistad must have indicated that he wanted to continue to serve and was recommended for further service in China. On September 19, 1945, he was discharged from the OSS and reassigned to the Army.

His recommendation for the Bronze Star made special mention of leadership and handling the situation after being dropped into Sweden. In addition to Norway, he was also awarded the Bronze Star for his service in France and Germany.

After the war, Oistad lived in Louisiana and piloted an oceanographic research vessel for Shell Oil. He also worked hard to keep the Rype group's legacy alive and brought the veterans of NORSO together on several occasions. He edited newsletters and was present at reunions and unveiling of monuments in the US as well as in Norway and Sweden.

Technician Fifth Grade Alf Paulsen

Alf Paulsen's personnel files are also missing, and not much is known of his life before the war, except that he was native of Stavanger in Norway and later lived in Crosby, North Dakota. When signing up, Alf Paulsen was asked if he would volunteer for hazardous duty. He replied, the whole US Army is hazardous duty.[19] On the night of July 31/August 1, 1944, he jumped into France, in the vicinity of the village Haute Vienne and took part in *Percy Red*, part of the *Jedburgh* operations. Due to the missing personnel files, no awards can be confirmed.

Technician Fifth Grade Matti Raivio

Matti Raivio was born in Ruovesi, southern Finland, on September 25, 1923, and was a Finnish national upon entering service. In addition to grammar school, he attended two years of trade school (night school). He was described as 173 cm tall, of medium build, with blue eyes and light brown hair. Raivio's father, a blacksmith, had fought in the Finnish Civil War, 1917–1918, and had military education from

Germany. After his father was killed in 1927, Raivio and his mother moved to the city of Tampere. Raivio had served in the Finnish military as a ski trooper despite his young age and had reached the rank of corporal and worked a truckdriver between October 18, 1939, and July 25, 1940. This service would have taken place during the Winter War with the Soviet Union, but his records make no mention of him seeing combat.

After the war with Russia, Raivio sailed on the Finnish ship SS *Rosenberg*, which happened to be in Port of Spain in the British territory of Trinidad when United Kingdom declared war on Finland on December 5, 1941. Raivio (and presumably the rest of the crew) was taken as a POW. After almost a year in captivity, he was released and moved to the United States (which was never at war with his native Finland). There he worked at a US Marine hospital and as a truck driver and repairman before enlisting in March 1943. Raivio's home address in the United States was in Brooklyn, New York. He was married to an English woman, residing in Manchester, whom he presumably met when NORSO received their parachute training at Ringway. He served with the 12th Engineer Battalion, based at Fort McClellan, Alabama, from May to September 1943. Raivio transferred to the OSS, after they sought him, on September 14, 1943, and was dropped into France on September 4, 1944. He stayed behind enemy lines until September 24.[20]

In his recommendation for the Bronze Star, a special mention is made of him carrying an extra load as a BAR man, and that he was part of Colby's group attacking near the Plutten Tunnel. In his personnel files there are two rating cards. On one signed by Colby, he scored "superior" on physical ability, otherwise, "very satisfactory" on motivation, practical intelligence, and ability to work with others, and "satisfactory" on stability and leadership. On the other card, where the name of the immediate superior officer is illegible, he also scored "superior" on physical ability and "excellent" on all others except leadership, which was simply marked with "unknown."[21] His discharge did not come through until November 30, 1945. In his papers he is listed as a driver and weapons technician. Because of his late discharge, he did not take part in the September 28 ceremony in Washington D.C., and his Bronze Star award came at an unknown date. His citation is dated January 7, 1946:

> Technician Fifth Grade Matti Raivio, 32905009, Infantry, United States Army, for meritorious service in connection with military service while serving with the Office of Strategic Services, European Theater of Operations, from 25 March to 8 May 1945. Technician Fifth Grade Raivio, as a member of a special operation, met an arduous and difficult situation with outstanding acumen. By his willingness, coolness, courage, and high ability, he contributed, in large measure, to successful completion of this operation. Technician Fifth Grade Raivio's outstanding conduct in extreme circumstances reflects great credit upon himself and the armed forces of the United States.[22]

After the war, Raivio changed his name to Karl Hoffman and moved to California, where he worked as a mechanical engineer.

Technician Fifth Grade Tom Rusdal

Tom Rusdal is yet another NORSO member whose personnel files has gone missing. From newspapers reports, it is known that he was from the coastal town of Flekkefjord, south Norway. This places him in the group of men, who, we might assume, were not born with skis on their feet. As his personnel files are missing, there is no confirmed information of any awards.

After the war, Rusdal moved to Spokane, Washington, and worked in lumbering.

First Lieutenant Tom Saether

Tom Saether was born in Tromsø, in northern Norway, in 1920 where his father Carl was British vice consul, and a broker of coal mined at Svalbard. Carl became a US citizen in 1905 but returned to Norway that year. Both Carl and his wife Gina, a store owner, were born in Trondheim. As a kid, he had both been an active skier and a boy scout back in Tromsø, so he was probably more prepared for the climate and physical strains than much of the rest of the group. Tom Saether was married, living with his wife Dorothy in North Hollywood California. They had a child in 1945. In Saether's personnel files, she is listed as living in Denver, Colorado, prior to Operation *Rype*, and it can be assumed that she moved there to be close to her husband when he was stationed at Camp Hale. Saether's brother, named Carl after their father, served in the Norwegian Navy. Saether listed that he had 2 months of training with the "Norwegian Militia" in 1936—this was probably with Leidangen, a semi-government volunteer organization, as he would have been too young for regular service at that time. He was enrolled at the Moldenæs Business School in Tromsø in 1939, but went to sea instead, first on a Norwegian survey vessel and then as a deckhand on an oil tanker.

He came ashore in the US on April 9, 1940, due to a throat illness, and found work as a shipping clerk. Tom was employed by the Howard Supply Co in Los Angeles, but when the company signed a contract with the government, he was laid off because he was not a US citizen. Saether entered the Army on October 1941 and would join the 99th Battalion. He became a full US citizen in May 1942. Saether rose to the rank of first lieutenant on September 13, 1943, and was transferred to the OSS from July 26 to December 20, 1943. His *Request for Security Investigation* papers state that the OSS sought Saether on his first contact with the service.

His transfer papers described his physique as "rugged." Colby also described him as the best skier in NORSO.[23] He hurt his right foot on September 4, 1944, when parachuting into France, but not badly as he was only treated in the field. In France he also earned a Battle Participation Credit along with all other NORSO personnel taking part in the Jedburgh operations. Saether had damaged his fourth vertebrae during a parachute jump just before being sent into Norway, but he kept the injury secret for fear of being discarded. He was also noted for being fluent in German, another advantage in occupied Norway. In his personnel files, the following remark was made: "An extremely strong officer, of high courage, but needs supervision," the latter probably due to him scoring only "excellent" in the categories of motivation and leadership ("superior" was the next level up, on which he was ticked off in every other quality). In his recommendation for decorations, Tom Saether was listed as an executive officer of Rype and a section commander. [24]

The citation for the Silver Star reads:

> … the Silver Star is awarded to Captain Tom Saether [then First Lieutenant] for gallantry in action as Executive Officer of a section thereof [US Army], from 25 March 1945 to 8 May 1945. Serving in the uniform of the United States Army behind enemy lines, Captain Saether, by his coolness, daring and dauntless courage, led the men under him to the successful completion of an extremely dangerous mission. Despite almost insurmountable obstacles of terrain, weather, and enemy counter action, he led his unit with persistence, bravery, and ability. At great personal risk, he was responsible for the evacuation of a seriously wounded scout and the subsequent saving of his life. Captain Saether's awareness of his responsibilities and the high standard he set, reflect great credit upon himself and the armed forces of the United States.[25]

His calmness and discipline, command of the situation and value to his commanding officer were underlined. Saether was also recommended for a Norwegian award by Helgesen. He described Saether as a born leader who commanded much respect from the men, and who was always calm and carried more than his weight. He was also very popular with the Norwegian Resistance fighters who found him easy going.[26]

After the war, Saether expressed no desire to continue his military service, and was notified of his discharge on August 31, 1945, while still in the UK.

Technician Fifth Grade Oddberg Stiansen

Not much is known about Oddberg Stiansen except that he was born in Mandal in southern Norway in 1917. He is also registered as a war sailor, Stiansen signed up as Motor Man on M/T *G.C. Brøvig* on November 3, 1939. He then sailed with the Panamanian ship *M/T Norvinn* from June 22, 1941 to January 6, 1941. On the night of July 31/August 1, 1944, Stiansen jumped into France, in the vicinity of the village Haute Vienne and took part in *Percy Red,* part of the Jedburgh operations. Due to the missing personnel files, no awards can be confirmed. Stiansen was later registered as living in Toms River, New York. He died in 1991.

Technician Fifth Grade Sivert Windh

Sivert Windh was born on June 4, 1922, and raised in Hässleholm, Skåne, in southern Sweden. In 1939 he emigrated to the United States, where he worked as a restaurant waiter. His mother, Stanne Windh, remained in Sweden, but he had an aunt living in the United States. No father was mentioned in his OSS files. Windh's education was limited to two years of high school, but in addition to Swedish and Norwegian, he had listed German and Spanish as language skills.

He joined the 99th Battalion on September 10, 1942, and served with that unit until November 1944. On January 5, 1945, he joined the OSS and was promoted to technician fifth grade on March 16. In his rating he was listed as "very satisfactory" in leadership—the middle grade. On physical ability, he achieved top score despite having flat feet. In the remaining categories he scored "excellent." The remarks contained only one word—"Contentious." Windh's assessment also noted that he had an above average emotional stability. In all, he was highly recommended as a member of a group, but not for leadership.[27] Windh was a trained machine gunner with the BAR and would frequently carry this weapon during Operation *Rype*.

Windh was one of the more highly decorated men of NORSO due to his combat experience prior to joining Rype. He had been awarded the Purple Heart after being wounded by shrapnel, and won the Combat Infantry Badge and Battle Stars for Normandy, North France, and Rhineland. Windh was also recommended for Far East service. Windh's recommendation for the Bronze Star stated that he "distinguished himself by meritorious service" and "courageous and outstanding conduct in extreme circumstances," as well as made specific mention of his conduct after being parachuted into Sweden.

Glossary

20. Gebirgsarmee	The German Lapland Army
AO	Area of operations
AOK	German Army Command in Norway
BAR	Browning Automatic Rifle
C-byrån	Swedish Intelligence Service
CIA	Central Intelligence Agency
COI	Coordinator of Information (Precursor to the OSS)
COSSAC	Chief of Staff to Supreme Allied Commander
DZ	Drop zone
ETO	European Theater of Operations
ETOUSA	European Theater of Operations, United States Army
FANY	Female Auxiliary Nursing Yeomanry
FO II	Second Bureau of the Norwegian High Command
GBP	Gerhard Bolland's personal papers
GEE navigation system	A British hyperbolic radio navigation system from WWII that worked by measuring time delay between two radio signals. Accurate up to 560 km
Hird, the	The Norwegian Nazi Party's version of the German *Sturm Abteilungen*
Kompani Linge	The Norwegian Independent Company No 1, also called NORIC
MAMSL	Meters above mean sea-level
MI6	*See* SIS
MilOrg	*Militærorganisasjonen*—the military wing of the Norwegian Resistance.
MI IV	Major Axel Baumann, leader of the MilOrg office at the Norwegian Legation in Stockholm
MTB	Motor torpedo boat
NS	*Nasjonal Samling*, the Norwegian Nazi Party
NARA	The U.S. *National Archives and Records Administration*
NORSO	Norwegian Special Operations Group
OG	Operational Group

OP	Observation Post
OSS	Office of Strategic Services. (The intelligence agency of the United States during World War II, formed as an agency of the Joint Chiefs of Staff to coordinate espionage behind enemy lines.)
RKT	Rustkammeret, The Armoury of the Norwegian Armed Forces Museum
ROTC	Reserve Officer's Training Program
Säpo	Swedish Security Service
SCOTCO	Scottish Command
SFHQ	Special Forces Headquarters
SHAEF	Supreme Headquarters Allied Expeditionary Force
SIS	Special Intelligence Service, also known as MI6. British foreign intelligence service
SOE	Special Operations Executive
SSU	Strategic Service Unit
Stortinget	Norwegian Parliament
USTAF	United States Strategic Air Forces
W/T	Wireless/telegraphy
XU	The Norwegian intelligence service

Bibliography

Abrams, Lynn. *Oral History Theory*. London & New York: Routledge, 2016.

Alsop, Stewart, and Thomas Braden. *Sub Rosa, The O.S.S. and American Espionage*. New York: Harcourt, Brace & World, 1964.

Brunsell, Trygve. *Coton, Kompani Linges Gruppe, Et tilbakeblikk*, Småskrift, no. 8. Herøy: Helgeland Historielag, 1989.

Cave Brown, Anthony (ed.). *The Secret War Report of the OSS*. Berkley, CA: Berkley Publishing Corporation, 1976.

Colby, William E. "OSS Operations in Norway: Skis and Daggers," unpublished historical document, https://www.cia.gov/static/e064d0992d04237c4201c23378f6c5c8/Skis-and-Daggers.pdf [Log 29.12.2022]

Colby, William E., and Peter Forbath. *Honorable Men: My Life in the CIA*. New York: Simon & Schuster, 1978.

Færøy, Frode. *Fiende eller forbundsfelle? Den kommunistiske motstandsbevegelsen i Norge*. Oslo: Dreyer Forlag, 2017.

Flyum, Ola. *Sjongløreme: Seierrherrenes spill with Henry Rinnan*. Oslo: Aschehoug, 1997.

Gebhardt, Major James F. *The Petsamo-Kirkenes Operation: Soviet Breakthrough and Pursuit in the Arctic, October 1944*. Leavenworth Papers No 17. Leavenworth, KS: Combat Studies Institute, US Army Command Staff College, 1990.

Heimark, Bruce H. *The OSS Norwegian Special Operations Group in World War II*. Westport: Praeger, 1994.

Henry, Thomas R. "The White War in Norway," *National Geographic* (December 1945), 612–640.

Hewins, Ralph. *Quisling: Prophet without Honor*. New York: The John Day Company, 1966.

Kjeldstadli, Sverre. *Hjemmestyrkene: Hovedtrekk av den militære motstanden under okkupasjonen*, vol. 1. Oslo: Aschehoug, 1959.

Kjeldstadli, Sverre. *Hjemmestyrkene: Hovedtrekk av den militære motstanden under okkupasjonen*, vol. 2. Oslo: Aschehoug, 1959.

Kjenstad, Helge. *Gjevsjøgubben*. Oslo: Grøndahl & Søn Forlag AS, 1983.

Lillegaard, Leif B. *Siste patrulje*. Oslo: Cappelen, 1978.

Liptak, Eugene. *Office of Strategic Services: The World War II Origin of the CIA*. Oxford/New York: Osprey, 2009.

Lulushi, Albert. *Donovan's Devils: OSS Commandoes Behind Enemy Lines—Europe, World War II*. New York: Arcade Publishing, 2016.

Nyquist, Gerd. *The 99th Battalion*. Oslo: Aschehoug, 1981.

Prados, John. *Lost Crusader: The Secret Wars of CIA Director William Colby. The True Story of One of America's Most Controversial Spymasters*. New York: Oxford University Press, 2003.

Pryser, Tore. *USAs hemmelige Agenter: Den amerikanske etterretningstjenesten OSS i Norden under annen verdenskrig*. Oslo: Universitetsforlaget, 2010.

Riste, Olav, *Londonregjeringa*, vol. I and II. Bergen: Samlaget, 1979.

Skjei, Jarle (ed.). *Operasjonene Woodlark og Rype: et 50-årsminne*. Snåsa: Komiteen, 1995.

Skodvin, Magne. *Norden eller NATO*. Oslo: Universitetsforlaget, 1971.
Smith, Richard Harris. *OSS: The Secret History of America's First Central Intelligence Agency*. Los Angeles/London: University of California Press, 1972.
Solhjell, Kåre Olav, and Fredrich Traphagen. *From War to Peace: The Focus of the Snåsa and Nord-Trøndelag*. Eel: Boksmia, 2001.
Stimson, Henry L., and Bundy McGeorge. *On Active Service in Peace and War*. New York: Harper & Brothers, 1948.
Sveri, Elisabeth. *Vindu til fortiden*. Oslo: Kvinners frivillige beredskap, 1998.
Waller, Douglas C. *Wild Bill Donovan: The Spymaster Who Created the OSS and Modern American Espionage*. New York: Simon & Schuster, 2011.
Woods, Randall B. *Shadow Warrior: William Egan Colby and the CIA*. New York: Basic Books, 2014.

Endnotes

Introduction

1. Hall, Roger, *You're Stepping on My Cloak and Dagger* (Annapolis: Naval Institute Press Kindle ed, 2004), loc. 2995.

Chapter 1: Existing Literature and Sources

1. Randal B. Woods, *Shadow Warrior: William Egan Colby and the CIA* (New York: Basic Books, 2013).
2. Smith, Richard Harris, *OSS, The Secret History of America's First Central Intelligence Agency* (Los Angeles/London: University of California Press, 1972; 2005 Kindle edition used in further references).
3. Smith 2005, loc 4695.
4. Lulushi 2016, loc 5499.
5. Eugene Liptak, *Office of Strategic Services 1942: The World War II Origins of the CIA* (New York: Osprey, 2009) (Kindle ed.).
6. Max Hastings, *The Secret War: Spies Ciphers and Guerillas 1939–1945* (London: Harper Collins, 2016).
7. Roger Hall, *You're Stepping on My Cloak and Dagger* (New York: Norton, 1957).
8. Jay Jakub, *Spies and Saboteurs, Anglo-American Collaboration and Rivalry in Human Intelligence Collection and Special Operations, 1940–45* (New York: St. Martin's Press, 1999).
9. Tore Pryser, *USAs hemmelige agenter, Den amerikanske etterretningstjenesten OSS i Norden under annen verdenskrig* (Oslo: Universitetsforlaget, 2010).
10. Herbert Helgesen, "Railway Sabotage," in Fløtnes, Olav & Skirstad, Ole (ed), *Partisaner, Soldater og SD* (Trondheim: A. Holbæk Eriksen & Co A.S. Forlag, 1945), 85.
11. GBP, Gerhard Bolland, *Operation "Rype,"* 1 October 1945, Gerhard Bolland's Personal Papers.

Chapter 2: The Strategic Background

1. Olav Riste, *"London-regjeringa" Norge i krigsalliansen 1940–1945* (Oslo: Samlaget 1979), 130–134.
2. *Op.cit.*
3. Major James F. Gebhardt, *The Petsamo-Kirkenes Operation: Soviet Breakthrough and Pursuit in the Arctic/October 1944*, Leavenworth Papers No 17 (Leavenworth, KS: Combat Studies Institute, US Army Command Staff College), 4.
4. University of Nebraska, HQ & HQ Detachment Office of Strategic Services European Theater of Operations, US Army APO 418 (Main), William Colby to Commanding General, Office of Strategic Services, Washington D.C. *Report on Operation Rype of NORSO Group*, June 30, 1945.

5. University of Nebraska Collection, OSS Maj. Harold P. Larson to Unger Vetlesen, *Transmittal of Appreciation*/311G (date unreadable).
6. *Norsk Tidend*, July 19, 1944, 8.
7. Anthony Cave Brown (ed.), *The Secret War Report of the OSS* (Berkley Ca.: Berkley Publishing Corporation, 1976), 314.
8. National Archives (UK) HS 7-175—Appendix "G" to the *SOE Norwegian Section History 1940–1945, Norway, Action Against German Controlled Norwegian State Railways.*
9. National Archives (UK) WO219-612 SHAEF SOE—OSS ACTIVITIES IN NW EUROPE Aug 44–Jan 45, From SHAEF Main Signed Eisenhower to SCOTCO (Scottish Command) G (OPS) (No title).
10. National Archives (UK)—HS 7-174, *SOE Norwegian Section History 1940–1945.*
11. University of Nebraska Collection, OSS Maj. Harold P. Larson to Unger Vetlesen, *Transmittal of Appreciation*/311G (date unreadable).
12. Frode Færøy, *Fiende eller forbundsfelle, Den kommunistiske motstandsbevegelsen i Norge* (Oslo: Dreyer Forlag, 2017).

Chapter 3: The OSS

1. Henry L. Stimson and Bundy McGeorge, *On Active Service in Peace and War* (New York: Harper & Brothers, 1948), 188.
2. Liptak 2009, loc 33.
3. Jakub 1999, 1.
4. Alsop & Braden 2016, loc 147.
5. Smith 2005, loc 452.
6. Alsop & Braden 2016, loc 1631.
7. Liptak 2009, loc 276.
8. Smith 2005, loc 297–304, 324.
9. *Op.cit.*
10. Liptak 2009, loc 29.
11. *Op.cit.,* loc 33.
12. *Op.cit.,* loc 44.
13. Alsop & Braden 2016, loc 200.
14. Liptak 2009, loc 44.
15. *Op.cit.,* loc 100.
16. Smith 2005, loc 614.
17. Hall 2004, loc 2934.
18. Smith 2005, loc 2448.
19. Alsop & Braden 2016, loc 224.
20. Smith 2005, loc 2394.
21. Alsop & Braden 2016, loc 423.
22. NARA Microfiche, Roll 6, Vols 1–3 (part 1) SO War Diary, 14.
23. NARA, *War Report, Office of Strategic Services, vol 2 Operations in the Field,* History Project, Strategic Service Unit, Office of the Assistant Secretary of War, War Department, Washington, D.C. 1949, 4.
24. Smith 2005, loc 2712.
25. *Op.cit.,* loc 2717.
26. Cave-Brown 1976, 311–312; OSS 1949, 135.
27. NARA Microfiche, Roll 5, Target 3, V08B2, 316.

28. NARA Microfiche, Roll 6, Vols 1–3 (part 1) SO War Diary, XIIII.
29. Pryser 2010, 101–103.
30. NARA Microfiche, Roll 6, Vols 1–3 (part 1) SO War Diary, XIIV.
31. Gerhard Bolland, Operation "*Rype*," 1 October 1945, Gerhard Bolland's Personal Papers (GBP).
32. OSS 1949, 4.
33. Pryser 2010, 101.
34. NARA, Larson, Harold P. OSS 0-408800.
35. NARA Microfiche R10T09 Vol 1 Book II *Commanding Officer Strategic Services Officer*, 122.
36. Smith 2005, loc 681.
37. Douglas Waller, *Wild Bill Donovan, The Spymaster Who Created the OSS and Modern American Espionage* (New York: Simon & Schuster, 2011).
38. Smith 2005, loc 1785
39. Pryser 2010, 91–94.

Chapter 4: Norwegian Special Operations Group (NORSO)

1. Smith 2005, loc 569.
2. RG 208 United News Roll 17. Franklin D. Roosevelt Presidental Library and Museum.
3. NARA, War Diary SO Branch, OSS London, Vol. 4-A Operational Groups, 10.
4. Colby wrote he bought this book in London when he arrived there in 1943 (Colby & Forbath 1978, 37).
5. NARA, 320.2/23 (Inf) (R)—Groups Headquarters Army Ground Forces Army War College, Washington DC to Commanding General, Second Army, 99th Infantry Battalion (separate), July 10, 1942.
6. NARA MID 322.171 Norway, Military Attaché Colonel Oscar Klingenberg to The Foreign Liaison Officer, War Department, Camp Ripley, Little Falls, Minnesota, September 17, 1942.
7. RKT, Arne Sandness Private Archives Leif Oistad to "Richard," July 1998.
8. NARA MID 343, Hayes A. Koroner, Brigadier General, Chief, Military Intelligence Service, *Memorandum for the Adjutant General, Norwegian Battalion of the United States Army*, July 29, 1942.
9. #2917 109 to Heppner, Telegram Office of Strategic Services Official Dispatch, March 8, 1945.
10. *Jumping into Occupied Europe*, Dixie, August 24, 1969, 14.

Chapter 5: German Forces in the Area of Operation—Grong to Snåsa

1. University of Nebraska Collection, HQ & HQ Detachment Office of Strategic Services European Theater of Operations, US Army APO 413, *Field Order No. 1*, SO Scandinavian Section January 29, 1945.
2. Interview with Arne Sandness.
3. *Norsk Tidend*, July 19, 1944, 8.
4. University of Nebraska Collection, OSS Maj. Harold P. Larson to Unger Vetlesen, *Transmittal of Appreciation*, (date unreadable).
5. RKT, Arne Sandness Private Archives, Trapphagen og Solhjell Friedrich Traphagen to Arne Sandness 13/7 2004.
6. *Op.cit.*

Chapter 6: Operation *Carpetbagger*

1. William Colby, *OSS Operations in Norway: Skis and Daggers* (Kindle edition: CIA Studies in Intelligence, 2013).
2. National Archives (UK), HS 7-175, *Appendix "K"* to the *SOE Norwegian Section History 1940–1945, Air Transport Operations, The Problems of Air Supply to Norway.*
3. University of Nebraska Collection, Office of Strategic Services, ETO USA to Major General F. Anderson, Director of Operations USSTAF *Requirements for Air Drops—Scandinavia*, 18 October 1944.
4. National Archives (UK), HS 7-175, *Appendix "K"* to the *SOE Norwegian Section History 1940–1945, Air Transport Operations, The Problems of Air Supply to Norway.*
5. University of Nebraska Collection, Office of Strategic Services, ETOUSA, to Major General F. Anderson, Director of Operations, U.S.S.T.A.F., *Requirements for Air Drops—Scandinavia*, 18 October 1944.
6. National Archives (UK), HS 7-175, *Appendix "K"* to the *SOE Norwegian Section History 1940–1945, Air Transport Operations, The Problems of Air Supply to Norway.*
7. Based on calculations, using the online services of the Norwegian Mapping and Cadastre Authority: https://www.kartverket.no/til-lands/kart/turkart/magnetisk-misvisning#:~:text=Vinkelen%20mellom%20geografisk%20nord%20og,%C3%B8stlig%20misvisning%20i%20%C3%98st%2DFinnmark. Log 07.01.2023.
8. Balchen 1946, 15.
9. Smith 2005, loc 2390.
10. *Op.cit.*, loc 2390.
11. NARA, Roll5 Target 7V12B1B1 SI (Tom Esminger), 64.
12. *Op.cit.*, 65.
13. *Op.cit.*, 67.

Chapter 7: SOE Operations Against the Nordland Railway

1. Olav Riste, *Londonregjeringa*, vol. II (Bergen: Samlaget, 1979), 21–63.
2. RKT, Herbert Helgesen, Report on Operation *Woodlark*—13/9 1944–7/5 1945 & Operation *Rype*, October 10, 1945, 13.
3. *Agnar Andersen, -høyt dekorert krigshelt* (Journal Article, undated and from unknown Norwegian publication).
4. RKT, Herbert Helgesen, Report on Operation *Woodlark*—13/9 1944–7/5 1945 & Operation *Rype*, October 10, 1945.
5. Norwegian Resistance Museum SOE Collection, To D/S from 8627. N641, October 13, 1944, *Woodlark*.
6. Norwegian Resistance Museum SOE Collection Remarks on Pte Hans Hoel's report of November 10th 1944 by Odd Sørli.
7. *Op.cit.*
8. RKT, Herbert Helgesen, *Operasjon Woodlark—13/9.1944–7/5.1945.*
9. University of Nebraska OSS Collection, Operation *Rype*, Office of Strategic Services, European Theater of Operations, United States Army, *Certificate*, June 18, 1945.
10. RKT, Herbert Helgesen, Report on Operation *Woodlark*—13/9 1944–7/5 1945 & Operation *Rype*, October 10, 1945.
11. RKT, Sections of the Norwegian State Railways, Nordland and the Meråker Railway, Copy No 7. *Inter-Service Topographical Department* was a joint British Army-Royal Navy service.

12. RKT, Erik Gjems-Onstads Private Archives.
13. Trygve Brunsell, *Coton, Kompani Linges Gruppe, Et tilbakeblikk*, Helgeland Historielag Småskrift nr. 8, 1989.
14. An extensive account is given in: Ola Hjulstad, *Krigens dagbok 1940–1945* (Steinkjer: Røyrvik og Namskogan kommuner, 1985).
15. University of Nebraska OSS Collection, Major Nordlie FO IV to General Hansteen, *Concerning use of parachute troops to hinder the enemy's overland evacuation of troops from Northern Norway*, London, January 15, 1945.
16. Pa 760 NS Partiarkiv, Nasional Samling. Hirden. Gruppe Ill. Møteprotokoll, 10, Norwegian National Archives.
17. Langeland, Msg. Nr. 7., received March 30, 1945.
18. RKT, NSB's Krigshistorie\Sabotasjeaksjoner 1944–1945.
19. Erling Vogstad, *Deutsche Soldatenfriedhof 1939–1945, Trondheim Havstein, Havstein Krigskirkegård* (FMU: Rustkammeret, 1992).
20. Report by E. G. Onstad, made in Stockholm on April 9, 1945.

Chapter 8: Planning of Operation *Rype*

1. NARA, R10T09 Vol 1 Book II *Commanding Officer Strategic Services Officer* (Tom Esminger) NARA, 51.
2. Arnfinn Haga, *Klart til storm: med de norske commandos i annen verdenskrig* (Oslo: Cappelen 1984, 47–69.
3. NARA Microfilm Publications, Roll 6, Target 2, Vol. 2, Special Operations Branch: Planning, 33.
4. NARA Microfilm Publications, Roll 6, Vols 1–3 (part 1) SO War Diary, XIIV.
5. NARA Microfilm Publications, Roll 9, Target 1, Vol. 4-A JANUARY–JUNE 1944, OPERATIONAL GROUPS, 8–10.
6. NARA Microfilm Publications, Roll 9, Target 1, Vol. 4-A JANUARY–JUNE 1944, OPERATIONAL GROUPS, 12–13.
7. GBP, Gerhard Bolland, Operation "*Rype*," 1 October 1945.
8. *Op.cit.*
9. University of Nebraska HQ & HQ Detachment Office of Strategic Services European Theater of Operations, US Army APO 418 (Main), William Colby to Commanding General, Office of Strategic Services, Washington D.C. *Report on Operation Rype of NORSO Group*, June 30, 1945.
10. Hall 2004, loc 3024.
11. HQ & HQ Detachment Office of Strategic Services European Theater of Operations, US Army APO 418 (Main), William Colby to Commanding General, Office of Strategic Services, Washington D.C. *Report on Operation Rype of NORSO Group*, June 30, 1945.
12. Hall 2004, loc 3021.
13. OSS 1949, 159.
14. I.S.T.D./B/259A. 1s2 Norwegian Railways Photographs, Inter-Service Topographical Department, May 1944
15. University of Nebraska Collection, OSS Maj. Harold P. Larson to Unger Vetlesen, *Transmittal of Appreciation*/311G (date unreadable).
16. Field Order No. 2.
17. I.S.T.D./B/259A. 1s2 Norwegian Railways Photographs, Inter-Service Topographical Department, May 1944, 31–32.
18. Field Order No. 2.
19. Gerhard Bolland, Operation "*Rype*," 1 October 1945, GBP.

20. *War Report, Office of Strategic Services Vol 2, Operations in the Field* (Washington D.C.: History Project, Strategic Services Unit, Office of the Assistant Secretary of War, War Department 1949), 4.
21. OSS War Report 1949, 138.
22. RT1oT08 Vol 1 Book II Commanding Officer Strategic Services Officer, 95.
23. Vol. 8. To 15 June 1945 Reports division Roll 5, Target 2V08B2 (Tom Esminger), 368.
24. University of Nebraska OSS Collection, Major Nordlie FO IV to General Hansteen, *Concerning use of parachute troops to hinder the enemy's overland evacuation of troops from Northern Norway*, London, January 15, 1945, 312A.
25. *Op.cit.*
26. University of Nebraska OSS Collection, Untitled, date not legible, 312 G.
27. University of Nebraska OSS Collection, Untitled and undated, 312 C.
28. University of Nebraska OSS Collection, Untitled, date not legible, 312 G.
29. University of Nebraska OSS Collection, Major Nordlie FO IV to General Hansteen, *Concerning use of parachute troops to hinder the enemy's overland evacuation of troops from Northern Norway*, London January 15, 1945, 312A.
30. University of Nebraska OSS Collection, Major Nordlie FO IV to General Hansteen, *Concerning use of parachute troops to hinder the enemy's overland evacuation of troops from Northern Norway*, London January 15, 1945, 312A.
31. University of Nebraska Collection, OSS Maj. Harold P. Larson to Unger Vetlesen, *Transmittal of Appreciation*/311G (date unreadable).
32. University of Nebraska OSS Collection, Major Nordlie FO IV to General Hansteen, *Concerning use of parachute troops to hinder the enemy's overland evacuation of troops from Northern Norway*, London January 15, 1945, 312A.
33. HJM SOE Collection / Supplementary report Re Road and Railway Sabotage, Hans Hoel (Herbert Helgesen), typed December 20, 1944.
34. GBP, Gerhard Bolland, Operation "*Rype*," 1 October 1945, GBP.
35. University of Nebraska OSS Collection, Skabo (?) to Colby thru Vaudeville, *Westfield* Mission, April 25, 1945.
36. University of Nebraska OSS Collection, OSS Maj. Harold P. Larson to Unger Vetlesen, *Transmittal of Appreciation*/311G (date unreadable).
37. University of Nebraska OSS Collection, HQ & HQ Detachment Office of Strategic Services European Theater of Operations, US Army APO 413, *Field Order No. 1*, SO Scandinavian Section January 29, 1945.
38. University of Nebraska Collection, OSS Maj. Harold P. Larson to Unger Vetlesen, *Transmittal of Appreciation*/311G (date unreadable).
39. Norsk Hjemmefrontsmuseum SOE Collection / Supplementary report *Re Road and Railway Sabotage*, Hans Hoel (Herbert Helgesen), typed December 20, 1944.
40. University of Nebraska OSS Collection, HQ & HQ Detachment Office of Strategic Services European Theater of Operations, US Army APO 413, *Field Order No. 1*, SO Scandinavian Section January 29, 1945.
41. University of Nebraska OSS Collection, HQ & HQ Detachment Office of Strategic Services, European Theater of Operations United States Army (Main) 220.G APO 413 Sather Tom OSS O-1305655 1, June 28, 1945.
42. Langeland 1975, 2.
43. National Archives (UK) HS 7-175, *Appendix "G"* to the *SOE Norwegian Section History 1940–1945, Norway, Action Against German Controlled Norwegian State Railways.*
44. University of Nebraska OSS Collection, *Additional Targets for First NORSO Group and Targets for Second NORSO Group.* Lt. Col. Hans Skabo to Lt. Col Charles E. Brebner, G-2 SO Branch. London, February 2, 1945.

45. National Archives (UK), HS 7-175*Appendix "K"* to the *SOE Norwegian Section History 1940–1945, Air Transport Operations, The Problems of Air Supply to Norway.*
46. University of Nebraska OSS Collection, HQ & HQ Detachment Office of Strategic Services European Theater of Operations, US Army APO 413, *Field Order No. 1*, SO Scandinavian Section January 29, 1945.
47. *Op.cit.*
48. University of Nebraska OSS Collection, Skabo to Vaudeville, January 30, 1945, *Operation Rype*, 312B.
49. *Op.cit.*
50. RKT, Herbert Helgesen, *Operasjon Woodlark—13/9.1944–7/5.1945.*
51. *Op.cit.*
52. University of Nebraska OSS Collection, Progress Report, April 5, 1945.
53. University of Nebraska OSS Collection, *Norwegian Railway Operations, Technical Planning Meeting held at 88 Chilteren Court on 2nd of February 1945.*
54. RKT, Herbert Helgesen, *Operasjon Woodlark—13/9.1944–7/5.1945.*
55. *Op.cit.*
56. University of Nebraska OSS Collection, Skabo to Lt. Col Charles E. Brebner, Exec Off, SO Branch, *Subject: Additional targets for First NORSO Group and Targets for Second NORSO Group*, February 3, 1945.
57. University of Nebraska OSS Collection, HQ & HQ Detachment Office of Strategic Services European Theater of Operations, US Army APO 418 (Main), William Colby to Commanding General, Office of Strategic Services, Washington D.C. *Report on Operation Rype of NORSO Group*, June 30, 1945.
58. Smith 2005, loc 2569.
59. Msg. No. 33, received April 28, 1945.
60. Hall 2004, loc. 3012.
61. National Archives (UK) HS7-174 *SOE Norwegian Section History.*

Chapter 9: Deployment Phase and Supply

1. University of Nebraska OSS Collection, Skabo to Brögger, *Operation Rype*, February 3, 1945, 312G.
2. University of Nebraska OSS Collection, Field Order No. 1.
3. University of Nebraska OSS Collection, Vaudeville to Skabo, *Operation Rype*, 05.02.1945.
4. University of Nebraska OSS Collection, 311G, 8.
5. Stein Ræder, *Kjell Sørli, Motstandsmann I Kompani Linge under den annen verdenskrig*, based on interviews with Kjell Sørlie (Unpubl.)
6. University of Nebraska OSS Collection, 311G, 8.
7. RKT, Herbert Helgesen, *Operasjon Woodlark—13/9.1944–7/5.1945, Operasjon Rype.*
8. HJM SOE Collection / Report No SN/30 Report by Kjell Sørli on a trip to Gauptjønna on February 2, 1945, made in Stockholm on February 19, 1945, typed March 24, 1945; see also Stein Ræder, *Kjell Sørli, Motstandsmann I Kompani Linge under den annen verdenskrig* (Unpubl.).
9. RKT, Herbert Helgesen, *Operasjon Woodlark—13/9.1944–7/5.1945, Operasjon Rype.*
10. *Op.cit.*
11. Helge Kjenstad, *Gjevsjøgubben* (Oslo: Grøndahl & Søn Forlag AS 1983, 117–136.
12. University of Nebraska OSS Collection, SFHQ to Chief, Scandinavian Section, SO Branch OSS, Appendix No III to Field Order No. 2, *Report on dispatch of NORSO Group on Operational Missions* London April 10, 1945.
13. Borge Langeland, *"rype" Norwegian Special Operations Group, O.S.S.* 1975, 2.

14. University of Nebraska OSS Collection, HQ & HQ Detachment Office of Strategic Services European Theater of Operations, US Army APO 418 (Main), William Colby to Commanding General, Office of Strategic Services, Washington D.C. *Report on Operation Rype of NORSO Group*, June 30, 1945.
15. *Op.cit.*
16. *Op.cit.*
17. NARA, Personal file, Farnsworth, Glenn J. OSS O-1299525.
18. National Archive (UK), HS9-215-1, Brogger, A.W. (Certificate of Recommendation), Major Gubbins, 13 September 1945.
19. Langeland 1975.
20. University of Nebraska OSS Collection, SFHQ to Chief, Scandinavian Section, SO Branch OSS, Appendix No III to Field Order No. 2, *Report on dispatch of NORSO Group on Operational Missions* London April 10, 1945.
21. William Colby, *OSS Operations in Norway*, CIA (undated manuscript).
22. Gerhard Bolland, *Operation "Rype,"* 1 October 1945, GBP.
23. Msg. Nr. 30, sent April 21, 1945.
24. Elisabeth Sveri, *Vindu til fortiden* (Oslo: Kvinners frivillige beredskap 1998).
25. RKT, Herbert Helgesen, *Operasjon Woodlark—13/9.1944–7/5.1945, Operasjon Rype.*
26. Langeland 1975, 3.
27. National Archives (UK) HS 7-175, *Appendix "K"* to the *SOE Norwegian Section History 1940–1945, Air Transport Operations, The Problems of Air Supply to Norway.*
28. University of Nebraska OSS Collection, Progress Report, April 5.
29. Helgesen 1945, 86.
30. University of Nebraska OSS Collection, DS/US from Vaudeville, March 28, 1945, 313B.
31. University of Nebraska OSS Collection, Operation *Rype* NORSO Group, Scandinavian Section SO Branch, OSS Detachment APO 413 United States Army, Colby to Skabo, *Progress Report*, April 1, 1945.
32. University of Nebraska OSS Collection, Progress report April 1, 1945—the document of the official report is hardly readable at this point.
33. HJM SOE Collection, Hans Hoel to MI IV (the Norwegian High Command Office in Stockholm), April 19, 1945.
34. RKT, Herbert Helgesen, *Operasjon Woodlark—13/9.1944–7/5.1945, Operasjon Rype.*
35. University of Nebraska OSS Collection, Progress Report, April 1, 1945.
36. *Op.cit.*
37. Langeland 1975, 10.
38. Msg. Nr. 1, sent March 26, 1945.
39. University of Nebraska OSS Collection, Field Order No. 2.
40. Msg. Nr. 37, sent April 30, 1945.
41. Msg. Nr. 2, sent March 27, 1945.
42. University of Nebraska OSS Collection, Erichsen to Colby, May 3, 1945.
43. University of Nebraska OSS Collection, Progress Report, April 1, 1945.
44. University of Nebraska OSS Collection, Progress Report, April 5, 1945.
45. *Op.cit.*
46. University of Nebraska OSS Collection, SFHQ to Chief, Scandinavian Section, SO Branch OSS, Appendix No III to Field Order No. 2, *Report on dispatch of NORSO Group on Operational Missions,* London, April 10, 1945.
47. Thomas L. Esminger, *Spies, Supplies and Moonlit Skies*, Vol. 1. Revised edition (Xlibris, 2009).

48. University of Nebraska OSS Collection, SFHQ to Chief, Scandinavian Section, SO Branch OSS, Appendix No III to Field Order No. 2, *Report on dispatch of NORSO Group on Operational Missions,* London, April 10, 1945.
49. University of Nebraska OSS Collection, OSS ETOUSA, Lester Armour to Major General F. Anderson, Director of Operations, USSTAF, *Requirements for Air Drops—Scandinavia,* October 18, 1944.

Chapter 10: Swedish Escapades

1. University of Nebraska OSS Collection, SFHQ to Chief, Scandinavian Section, SO Branch OSS, Appendix No III to Field Order No. 2, *Report on dispatch of NORSO Group on Operational Missions,* London, April 10, 1945.
2. *"Rype" Norwegian Special Operations Group O.S.S.,* October 10–12, 1975.
3. *Sändingar som hamnade på fel plats,* Östersundsposten, March 26, 1945.
4. *Sabotörerna hadde kulsprutor skjutklara. Landsfiskal anhöll dem, hel billast sprängämnen,* Monday, March 26, 1945.
5. Skuncke 1953, 130–141.
6. Skuncke 1953, 134.
7. University of Nebraska OSS Collection, HQ & HQ Detachment Office of Strategic Services European Theater of Operations, US Army APO 413, *Field Order No. 1,* SO Scandinavian Section January 29, 1945.
8. Skuncke 1953, 136.
9. University of Nebraska OSS Collection, HQ & HQ Detachment Office of Strategic Services European Theater of Operations, US Army APO 413, *Field Order No. 1,* SO Scandinavian Section January 29, 1945.
10. Skuncke 1953, 139.
11. *Op.cit.*
12. Lulushi 2016, loc 102.
13. RKT, Arne Sandness Private Archives, "Kjære venn!" Personal letter from Leif Oistad to Arne Sandness, signed "Leif and Darleen".
14. Rype Norwegian Special Operations Group OSS 1975.
15. Heimark 1990, 154.
16. Langeland 1975, 9.
17. *Kärt återseende i Lien,* Östersundsposten, Monday, June 7, 1999.
18. *"Rype" Norwegian Special Operations Group O.S.S.* October 10–12, 1975.
19. Langeland 1975, 9.
20. University of Nebraska OSS Collection, HQ & HQ Detachment Office of Strategic Services European Theater of Operations, US Army APO 413, *Field Order No. 1,* SO Scandinavian Section January 29, 1945.
21. University of Nebraska OSS Collection, Vaudeville to London, March 28, 1945.
22. OSS War Report 1949, 138.
23. Msg. Nr. 5, received March 29, 1945.
24. University of Nebraska OSS Collection, Apollo to Skabo, March 28, 1945, 313A.
25. University of Nebraska OSS Collection, Colby to Skabo, *Details,* April 19, 1945, 313E.
26. Pryser 2010, 121.
27. University of Nebraska OSS Collection, Appendix No. VIII Operation *Rype* Morning Report.

28. HJM SOE Collection, Hans Hoel to MI IV (the Norwegian High Command Office in Stockholm), April 19, 1945.
29. NARA, Windh, Sivert (Ron) OSS 32441496.

Chapter 11: The Walliwall Tragedy

1. Msg. Nr. 2, sent March 27, 1945.
2. Msg. Nr. 3, received March 27, 1945.
3. Msg. Nr. 6, received March 30, 1945.
4. Lagemeldung 30.3.45.
5. University of Nebraska OSS Collection, SFHQ to Chief, Scandinavian Section, SO Branch OSS, Appendix No III to Field Order No. 2, *Report on dispatch of NORSO Group on Operational Missions,* London, April 10, 1945.
6. Msg. Nr. 7, sent March 31, 1945.
7. Langeland 1975, 15.
8. Langeland 1975, 4.
9. See Lindgjerdet 2016, 54; Tøsse 1983, in Skjei (ed) 2006, 45.
10. Herbert Helgesen, *Operasjon Woodlark—13/9.1944–7/5.1945*, Rustkammerets dokumentarkiv.
11. *Karle reddet liv*, Adresseavisen May 13, 1989.
12. David W. Earl, *Almost Home, The Story of the B-24 Crash at Walliwall, Orkney—31 March 1945* (Staylbridge: Hanover Publications, 2011/2013).

Chapter 12: Attack on the Tangen Bridge

1. Msg. Nr. 10, received April 1, 1945.
2. Msg. Nr. 15, sent April 4, 1945.
3. University of Nebraska OSS Collection, Report from Gunnar Steen and Alf Bromstad, reconnaissance October 10–17, 1944, incased in Nebraska OSS Collection 312C.
4. Accounts differ on who did the reconnaissance, some say Harald Larsen did it (e.g. Langeland 1975, 17), others that it was done by Hans Leirmo (eg. Progress report, April 5, 1945).
5. University of Nebraska OSS Collection, Progress report, April 1, 1945.
6. Helgesen 1945, 91.
7. University of Nebraska OSS Collection, Progress Report, April 5, 1945.
8. Reidar Kvaal, untitled document, December 10, 1989.
9. University of Nebraska OSS Collection, Progress Report, April 5, 1945.
10. Progress Report, April 5, 1945.
11. *Op.cit.*
12. HQ & HQ Detachment, Office of Strategic Services, European Theater of Operations, United States Army (Main) APO 413, *Recommendation for Award of the Silver Star*, June 26, 1945, Personal File, Farnsworth, Glenn J. OSS O-1299525.
13. Msg. Nr. 23, April 8, 1945.
14. Msg. Nr. 19, April 8, 1945.
15. University of Nebraska OSS Collection, DS/US from Vaudeville, April 9, 1945, 313C.
16. Progress Report, April 5, 1945.
17. Sigvart Tøsse, *Del III, Operasjon Rype*, in Skjei et al 1995, 46.
18. 1945-06-18—Certificate Robert Andersen.
19. Colby & Forbath 1978, 47.

20. Herbert Helgesen, *Operasjon Woodlark—13/9.1944–7/5.1945*, Rustkammerets dokumentarkiv.
21. *Op.cit.*
22. Progress Report, April 18, 1945.
23. Langeland 1975, 18; he also suggests that the bridge was guarded.
24. Progress Report, April 18, 1945.
25. Herbert Helgesen, *Operasjon Woodlark—13/9.1944–7/5.1945*, Rustkammerets dokumentarkiv.
26. Skjei & Sandness 1995, 44.
27. Langeland 1975, 18.
28. Skjei 1995, 54.
29. Gerhard Bolland, Operation "*Rype*," 1 October 1945, GBP.
30. Skjei 1995, 54.
31. Progress Report, April 18, 1945.
32. Alsop & Braden 2016, loc 1843; 2608.
33. HQ & HQ Detachment Office of Strategic Services European Theater of Operations, US Army APO 413, to Commanding General, European Theater of Operations, United States Army, APO 887, *Recommendation for Award of Silver Star*, June 28, 1945.
34. Progress Report, April 18, 1945.
35. Progress Report, April 18, 1945.
36. Chas. C. Knights, *What the H.G. Needs to Know About Explosives* (London: Bernard's (Publishers) LTD, The Grampians, (date unknown)), 24.
37. Ludvik Kruksve, interviewed in the Documentary, *Operation Woodlark*, produced by Ingvar Tømmerås, Trondheim, 1995.
38. *Jumping into Occupied Europe*, Dixie, August 24, 1969.
39. Herbert Helgesen, *Operasjon Woodlark—13/9.1944–7/5.1945*, Rustkammerets dokumentarkiv.
40. Langeland 1975, 22.
41. Herbert Helgesen, *Operasjon Woodlark—13/9.1944–7/5.1945*, Rustkammerets dokumentarkiv.
42. Borge Langeland, *"Rype" Norwegian Special Operations Group O.S.S*, 22.
43. HQ & HQ Detachment Office of Strategic Services European Theater of Operations, US Army APO 418 (Main), William Colby to Commanding General, Office of Strategic Services, Washington D.C. *Report on Operation Rype of NORSO Group*, June 30, 1945.
44. Progress Report, April 18, 1945.
45. Helgesen 1945, 85–86.
46. Langeland 1975, 19.
47. Skjei & Sandness 1995, 55.
48. University of Nebraska OSS Collection, Colby to Skabo, *Details*, April 19, 1945, 313E.
49. *Op.cit.*
50. University of Nebraska Collection, Skabo (?) to Colby thru Vaudeville, *Westfield* Mission, April 25, 1945.

Chapter 13: Plukkutjønn Crash

1. Msg. Nr. 19, sent April 4, 1945.
2. University of Nebraska Collection, Skabo (?) to Colby thru Vaudeville, *Westfield* Mission, April 25, 1945.
3. Msg. Nr. 19, sent April 5, 1945.
4. *Han minnes flyhavariet en kald mars-natt i 1945*, Arbeideravisa, July 11, 1977.
5. Msg. Nr. 22, sent April 7, 1947.

6. University of Nebraska OSS Collection Special Forces Headquarters to Chief SO Branch, OSS, *Infiltration of NORSO Group to target*, April 16, 1945, 313D.
7. Gerhard Bolland, Operation "*Rype*," 1 October 1945, GBP.
8. S.O.—Branch OSS (Main) Skabo to Vetlesen, *Report* (not dated).
9. Iverson, Bernard N. 36289300.

Chapter 14: The Lierne Plan and Supply Issues

1. Msg. Nr. 24, received April 24, 1945.
2. University of Nebraska Collection, Erichsen to Colby, May 3, 1945 313I.
3. Msg. Nr. 30, sent April 21, 1945; Msg. Nr. 35, sent April 28, 1945; Msg. Nr. 37, sent April 30, 1945.
4. University of Nebraska Collection, Skabo (?) to Colby thru Vaudeville, *Westfield* Mission, April 25, 1945. The document is hardly readable in this paragraph.
5. Progress Report, April 5, 1945.
6. Progress Report, April 5, 1945; Msg. Nr. 35, sent April 28, 1945.
7. University of Nebraska OSS Collection DS/US from Vaudeville, April 9, 1945, 313C; Progress Report April 5, 1945.
8. University of Nebraska OSS Collection DS/US from Vaudeville, April 9, 1945, 313C.
9. Msg. Nr. 2, sent March 27, 1945.
10. Lieutenant Colonel Bolland's private archive, *NORSO Group OSS Det. SO Branch*, unknown date and origin.
11. University of Nebraska OSS Collection, Colby to Skabo, *Details*, April 19, 1945, 313E.
12. University of Nebraska OSS Collection, Colby to Skabo, *Details*, April 19, 1945, 313E.
13. Progress Report, April 5.
14. Msg. Nr. 25, sent April 18, 1945.
15. Progress Report, April 1.
16. Progress Report, April 1, 1945.
17. Progress Report, April 5, 1945.
18. Msg. Nr. 30, sent April 21, 1945.
19. Msg. Nr. 2, sent March 27, 1945.
20. Gerhard Bolland, Operation "*Rype*," 1 October 1945, GBP.
21. Msg. Nr. 30, sent April 21, 1945.
22. Msg. Nr. 33, recieved April 28, 1945.
23. Msg. Nr. 38. sent May 2, 1945.
24. *Op.cit.*
25. University of Nebraska OSS Collection, *Vaudeville to Colby*, Stockholm, May 3, 313I.
26. *Op.cit.*
27. University of Nebraska OSS Collection, Skabo Appendix to FO II, para III.X., Ma.
28. Field Order No. 2.
29. Msg. Nr. 24, received April 20, 1945.
30. HQ & HQ Detachment Office of Strategic Services European Theater of Operations, US Army APO 418 (Main), William Colby to Commanding General, Office of Strategic Services, Washington D.C. *Report on Operation Rype of NORSO Group*, June 30, 1945.
31. University of Nebraska Collection, George Brewer to Skabo, SN/US and Miller, April 27, 1945.
32. Smith 2005, loc 366.
33. Alsop & Braden 2016, loc 1654.
34. Alsop & Braden 2016, loc 1697; 1818.

35. Smith 2005, loc 378.
36. Roger Hall, *You're Stepping on My Cloak and Dagger* (Annapolis: Naval Institute Press, 2004) (Kindle ed.), 48.
37. Msg. Nr. 28, April 28, 1945.
38. University of Nebraska Collection, Skabo to Colby, thru VAUDEVILLE, *Westfield* Mission, April 25, 1945.
39. Msg. Nr. 37, sent April 30, 1945.

Chapter 15: Attack Against the Lurudal–Agle Railway

1. Herbert Helgesen, *Operasjon Woodlark,—13/9.1944–7/5.1945*, Rustkammerets dokumentarkiv.
2. University of Nebraska OSS Collection, DS/US from Vaudeville, April 9, 1945, 313C.
3. Langeland 1975, 20.
4. Herbert Helgesen, *Operasjon Woodlark,—13/9.1944–7/5.1945*, Rustkammerets dokumentarkiv.
5. Helgesen 1945, 85.
6. Herbert Helgesen, *Operasjon Woodlark,—13/9.1944–7/5.1945*, Rustkammerets dokumentarkiv.
7. Helgesen 1945, 85.
8. Helgesen 1945, 86.
9. OSS 1949, 138.
10. Langeland 1975, 21.
11. Knights 48–49.
12. Helgesen 1945, 92.
13. Operational Report April 27, 1945.
14. Herbert Helgesen, *Operasjon Woodlark,—13/9.1944–7/5.1945*, Rustkammerets dokumentarkiv.
15. *Op.cit.*
16. Langeland 1975, 22.
17. Helgesen 1945, 94.
18. Msg. Nr. 32, sent April 26, 1945.
19. Operational Report, April 27, 1945.
20. Eliassen, Einar A. OSS 6871912.
21. University of Nebraska Collection, Erichsen to Colby, May 3, 1945 313I.
22. Langeland 1975, 19.

Chapter 16: The German Patrol Incident

1. Herbert Helgesen, Report on Operation *Woodlark*—13/9 1944–7/5 1945 & Operation *Rype*, October 10, 1945, Rustkammerets dokumentarkiv.
2. HQ & HQ Detachment Office of Strategic Services European Theater of Operations, US Army APO 418 (Main), William Colby to Commanding General, Office of Strategic Services, Washington D.C. *Report on Operation Rype of NORSO Group*, June 30, 1945.
3. Msg. Nr. 39, sent May 3, 1945.
4. University of Nebraska Collection, HQ & HQ Detachment Office of Strategic Services European Theater of Operations, US Army APO 418 (Main), William Colby to Commanding General, Office of Strategic Services, Washington D.C. *Report on Operation Rype of NORSO Group*, June 30, 1945, 314B. Msg. Nr. 40, sent May 4, 1945.
5. Herbert Helgesen, *Operasjon Woodlark,—13/9.1944–7/5.1945*, Rustkammerets dokumentarkiv.

6. University of Nebraska Collection, HQ & HQ Detachment Office of Strategic Services European Theater of Operations, US Army APO 418 (Main), William Colby to Commanding General, Office of Strategic Services, Washington D.C. *Report on Operation Rype of NORSO Group*, June 30, 1945, 314B. Msg. Nr. 40, sent May 4, 1945.
7. *Karle reddet liv*, Adresseavisen May 13, 1989.
8. *Op.cit.*
9. HQ & HQ Detachment Office of Strategic Services, European Theater of Operations United States Army (Main) 220.G APO 413 Sather Tom OSS O-1305655 1, June 28, 1945.
10. *Deutscher Soldatenfriedhof 1939–1945, Trondheim/Havstein*, Havstein krigskirkegård (Havstein War Cemetary). Prepared by Forsvarets museum, Rustkammeret 1992.
11. *Karle reddet liv*, Adresseavisen May 13, 1989.
12. Leif B. Lillegaard, *Siste patrulje* (Oslo: Gyldendal, 1978), 7.
13. Ola Flyum, *Sjongløerene, Seierherrenes spill med Henry Rinnan* (Oslo/Gjøvik: Aschehoug, 1997), 33.
14. *Krigens første offer*, Trønderavisa, September 29, 2001; Pryser 2010, 123.
15. *Deutscher Soldatenfriedhof 1939–1945, Trondheim/Havstein*, Havstein krigskirkegård (Havstein War Cemetary). Prepared by Forsvarets museum, Rustkammeret 1992.
16. Langeland 1975, 26.
17. Solhjell & Traphagen 2001, 185–187, trans. by aut.
18. Lynn Abrams, *Oral History Theory* (London & New York: Routledge, 2016), 85.
19. *Amerikanere vanæret tyske lik—i Norge,* Dagbladet, January 14, 2012.
20. University of Nebraska Collection, S.O.—Branch OSS (Main) Skabo to Vetlesen, *Report* (not dated).
21. University of Nebraska Collection, HQ & HQ Detachment Office of Strategic Services European Theater of Operations, US Army APO 418 (Main), William Colby to Commanding General, Office of Strategic Services, Washington D.C. *Report on Operation Rype of NORSO Group*, June 30, 1945. 314B.
22. Msg. Nr. 40, sent May 4, 1945.
23. Msg. Nr. 43, sent May 6, 1945.

Chapter 17: Endgame

1. Report No 7/611, Report by Pte Hans Hoel (Herbert Helgesen) Enclosure No. 29 in letter No. 69-L, Stockholm October 1944 (HJM SOE Collection).
2. HQ & HQ Detachment Office of Strategic Services European Theater of Operations, US Army APO 418 (Main), William Colby to Commanding General, Office of Strategic Services, Washington D.C. *Report on Operation Rype of NORSO Group*, June 30, 1945.
3. Msg. Nr. 257, to: 8654, *Woodlark*, London, April 25, 1945.
4. Msg. Nr. 25, dated April 25, received April 26, 1945.
5. University of Nebraska Collection, Skabo to Colby thru Vaudeville, *Westfield* Mission, April 25, 1945. 313F.
6. *Op.cit.*
7. *Op.cit.*
8. Msg. Nr. 33, received April 28, 1945; University of Nebraska Collection, Erichsen to Colby, May 3, 1945, 313I.
9. University of Nebraska Collection, George Brewer to Skabo, SN/US and Miller, April 27, 1945.
10. Msg. Nr. 27, dated April 25, received April 26, 1945.
11. Bolland 1945.
12. NARA, Roll 10, Target 8 Vol. 1, Book II, *Commanding Officer Strategic Services Officer*, 56.

13. NARA, Roll 10, Target 9 Vol. 3, *Commanding Officer: Basic Documents*, 89.
14. Hewins 1966, 338.
15. Gerhard Bolland, Operation "*Rype*," 1 October 1945, GBP.
16. Tore Pryser, *USAs hemmelige Agenter, Den amerikanske etterretningstjenesten OSS i Norden under annen verdenskrig* (Oslo: Universitetsforlaget, 2010).
17. Msg. Nr. 30, received May 1, 1945.
18. Msg. Nr. 31, received May 3, 1945.
19. Msg. Nr. 32, received May 3, 1945.
20. Msg. Nr. 33, received May 3, 1945.
21. R10T09 Vol 1 Book II *Commanding Officer Strategic Services Officer* (Tom Esminger) NARA Microfilm, 53.

Chapter 18: Peace

1. Ralph Hewins, *Quisling, Prophet Without Honour* (New York: The John Day Company, 1966), 347–348.
2. Smith 2005, loc. 2464.
3. NARA, Roll 10, Target 8 Vol. 1, Book II, *Commanding Officer Strategic Services Officer.*
4. Kjeldstadli 2011, 314–315.
5. Msg. Nr. 45, sent May 5, 1945; Msg. Nr. 45, received May 5, 1945.
6. Msg. Nr. 35, received May 5, 1945.
7. Msg. Nr. 38, received May 7, 1945.
8. Msg. Nr. 48, sent May 7, 1945.
9. Msg. Nr. 38, received May 7, 1945.
10. NARA Microfilm, Roll 6, Vols 1–3 (part 2), 90–92.
11. Msg. Nr. 49, sent May 8, 1945.
12. Alsop & Braden 2016, loc 1709; Smith 2005, loc 2578.
13. Langeland 1975, 32.
14. Msg. Nr. 53, sent May 11, 1945.
15. University of Nebraska Collection, Bolland to Chief Scandinavian Section (Vetlsesen), *Chronological Report of NORSO Group Operations from 8 May to 6 June 1945 in Trøndelag, Norway*, June 13, 1945.
16. *Op.cit.*
17. Msg. Nr. 38, sent May 2, 1945.
18. Obituary, Fred Johansen, unknown date and place.
19. *Operation "Rype" Oslo: October 1, 1945. The Bolland Papers*, in custody of his son, Matthew Bolland.
20. Fliegerhorstkommandantur A (o) 105/III Værnes Kraftfahrgerätverwaltung, *Empfangsbescheinigung*, Værnes May 25, 1945, Roger Hall's Collection
21. Skjei & Sandness 1995, 48.
22. Langeland 1975, 35.
23. University of Nebraska Collection, HQ & HQ Detachment Office of Strategic Services European Theater of Operations, US Army APO 418 (Main), William Colby to Commanding General, Office of Strategic Services, Washington D.C. *Report on Operation Rype of NORSO Group*, June 30, 1945.
24. RKT/Boks 13/Mappe 66 Fra H.S. i Namsos til Avsnitskommandoen, Steinkjer. Namsos 23. mai 1945." Avsnitskommandoen, Steinkjer. Namsos 23. mai 1945.
25. Hall 2004, loc 3202.

26. University of Nebraska Collection, S.O.—Branch OSS (Main) Skabo to Vetlesen, *Report.* The report is not dated, but obviously written on a Norwegian typewriter with the letters "æ," "ø" and "å." 314C.
27. S.O.—Branch OSS (Main) Skabo to Vetlesen, *Report* (not dated).
28. *Op.cit.*
29. According to family legend.
30. S.O.—Branch OSS (Main) Skabo to Vetlesen, *Report* (not dated).
31. HQ & HQ Detachment, Office of Strategic Services, European Theater of Operations, United Army (Main), 200.6, to Commanding General, European Theater of Operations, United States Army, APO 887, *Recommendation for Award of Bronze Star Medal,* APO 413, June 26, 1945.
32. NARA Microfilms, R10T09 Vol 1 Book II *Commanding Officer Strategic Services Officer* (Tom Esminger) NARA, 104.
33. NARA Microfilms, Roll 5 Target1V07-SI War Diary, 81.
34. Pryser 2010, 141–148.
35. *Op.cit.,* 168.

Chapter 19: The Legacy

1. Alsop & Braden 2016, loc 3158.
2. Herbert Helgesen (Personal Letter), Trondheim, April 1957.
3. Translation from Aftenposten October 13, 1975, *CIA Director Reminiscences about Wartime Norway,* Minneapolis, October 12, 1975.
4. *CIA-Colby spiste lunch i Levanger—og hylles!* Levangeravisa, July 12, 1977.
5. Dokument nr. 15 (1995–1996) Rapport til Stortinget fra kommisjonen som ble nedsatt av Stortinget for å granske påstander om ulovlig overvåking av norske borgere (Lund-rapporten).
6. *-Ligg unna minnetavla,* Trønderavisa, October 4, 2001.

Conclusion

1. HQ & HQ Detachment Office of Strategic Services European Theater of Operations, US Army APO 418 (Main), William Colby to Commanding General, Office of Strategic Services, Washington D.C. *Report on Operation Rype of NORSO Group,* June 30, 1945.
2. Stanley P. Lovell to Roger Hall, (Personal letter), June 6, 1960.
3. HS)-215-1 Brogger A.W.
4. Skodvin 1971, 44.
5. Cave Brown 1976, 314.
6. Norsk Hjemmefrontsmuseum SOE Collection/Boks 15 FO IV SXO Sabotasje/Notater til FO, 8. April 1945 fra FO II.
7. OSS War Report 1949, 138.
8. Langeland 1975, 35.
9. Tøsse, in: Skjei & Sandness 1995, 50.
10. *SOE Norwegian Section History 1940–1945,* HS7-174.
11. Gerhard Bolland, Operation "Rype," 1 October 1945, GBP.
12. War Diary, Special Operations Branch, Office of Strategic Services, Rolls 1–3 (part 3), 31.

Biographies

1. NARA Box 304, Arnesen, Odd. OSS 36610621.
2. NARA Box 304, HQ & HQ Detachment Office of Strategic Services, European Theater of Operations United States Army (Main), to Commanding General, European Theater of Operations, United States Army, APO 887, *Recommendation for Award of Bronze Star*, Odd Anderson.
3. NARA Box 304, Arnesen, Odd. OSS 36610621.
4. NARA, Bolland, Gerhard L. OSS 019565.
5. FMU The Armory Archival Collection, Herbert Helgesen, Report on Operation *Woodlark*—13/9 1944–7/5 1945 & Operation *Rype*, October 10, 1945.
6. FMU The Armory Archival Collection, Herbert Helgesen, Report on Operation *Woodlark*—13/9 1944–7/5 1945 & Operation *Rype*, October 10, 1945.
7. NARA, Eliassen, Einar A. OSS 6871912.
8. NARA, Farnsworth, Glenn J. OSS O-1299525.
9. NARA, *Theater Service Record*, July 8, 1945, Personal file, Farnsworth, Glenn J. OSS O-1299525.
10. NARA, Gravdal, Asmund OSS 32498841.
11. NARA, Johansen, Fred OSS 32832814.
12. NARA, Langeland, Borge OSS 32876387.
13. *"Rype" Norwegian Special Operations Group O.S.S.* October 10–12, 1975.
14. *"Rype" Norwegian Special Operations Group O.S.S.* October 10, 11, 12–1975.
15. Leif Oistad, *Taps, Harold Larson, Former President and First Commanding Officer of NORSO.*
16. NARA, Oistad, Leif OSS 32502646 Personal History Statement.
17. NARA, Oistad, Leif OSS 32502646 1, Theater of Service Record; NARA, Leif Oistad, *Rating*, June 22, 1945.
18. NARA, Oistad, Leif OSS 32502646 1, Area F, Interviewer's Report.
19. Heimark 2994, 10.
20. NARA, Raivio, Matti OSS 32905009, HQ & HQ Detachment, Office of Strategic Services, European Theater of Operations, United States Army (Main) APO 413, *Recommendation for Award of Bronze Star Medal*, June 28, 1945.
21. NARA, Personal Files, Raivio, Matti, OSS 32905009.
22. *Op.cit.*
23. Hall 2004, loc. 3065.
24. NARA, Personal Files, Sather Tom, OSS O-1305655 (Discharge papers).
25. *Op.cit.*
26. RKT, Herbert Helgesen, *Report on Operation* Woodlark—*13/9 1944–7/5 1945 & Operation Rype*, October 10, 1945.
27. NARA, Windh, Sivert (Ron) OSS 32441496.

Index